THE LEGAL TEAM OF THE FUTURE

THE LEGAL TEAM OF THE FUTURE

Law+ Skills

Adam Curphey

LONDON PUBLISHING PARTNERSHIP

Published by London Publishing Partnership
www.londonpublishingpartnership.co.uk

ISBN: 978-1-913019-64-8 (pbk)
ISBN: 978-1-913019-65-5 (ePDF)
ISBN: 978-1-913019-66-2 (ePUB)

A catalogue record for this book is available
from the British Library

Typeset in Adobe Garamond Pro by
T&T Productions Ltd, London
www.tandtproductions.com

Printed and bound in Great Britain
by Hobbs the Printers Ltd

www.carbonbalancedprint.com
CBP2250

Contents

Preface

The legal services profession is changing. That statement was true even before a global pandemic, and it is all the more true now. A volatile economic landscape, the encroaching deregulation of legal services, new competition for traditional law firms, the evolution of technology and increasingly diverse educational paths to learning law have changed the expectations that clients have of their legal services providers – whether those providers are 'external' law firms or 'internal' in-house teams.

Knowing the law is considered by clients to be an absolute minimum – the 'table stakes' or bare essentials for being in the game, if you will. The demands on law firms and legal departments to be efficient and transparent are increasing, and all while they are facing competition from new entrants to the market. Technology continues to advance and open up new opportunities, legal education around the world is changing as new innovative courses are created, and more and more is being asked of the 'lawyer of the future'. But it is not enough to simply talk about the lawyer of the future. For too long we have piled additional skills expectations on individual lawyers while ignoring learnings – and specialists – from other professions. That is not fair on anyone, least of all our clients. The future of law is collaborative and multidisciplinary.

This book presents a 'Law+' model for the legal profession. The model comprises sixteen skills across four quadrants: Law+People, Law+Business, Law+Change and Law+Technology. We need to stop talking about the lawyer of the future and start talking about the legal team of the future. We need to start talking about Law+.

You will be introduced to a new world of legal services in which multidisciplinary teams work together to solve legal problems for clients – a world in which we do not have to expect the individual 'lawyer of the future' to solve every problem. No individual should be responsible for all of the Law+ skills; instead, a legal team should possess all of them collectively, whether the individuals who make up that team are lawyers, hybrid legal professionals or professionals from other sectors.

This book is for you whether you want to build your own skills, at any stage of your career, and whether you currently work in the legal profession or not; whether you teach skills to future lawyers; or whether you are responsible for managing or training teams. There are three parts to this book, covering the 'why', the 'what' and the 'how' of Law+ skills. You can read from start to finish or you can jump around to different sections that interest you – it is your choice. Before getting started though, it is worth knowing a bit about my background and how I ended up devising a new skills model for the legal profession. My greatest hope is that when you finish reading you start thinking about law a little differently. Who knows? You might even have fun.

MY BACKGROUND

This book has a different perspective from others in this field, with a focus on the practice of law from a global business perspective rather than an examination of legal skills through the lens of the court system or access to practice issues. The examples and principles upon which this book sits are based not just on research and external observation, but also on my own career as someone who currently works in legal innovation and has a career history spanning both education and practice.

My background is rare for the world of law. Over my time in the legal profession I have covered the fields of law, education, technology, innovation and business. My first role in the legal world was at White & Case LLP, as an associate in the capital markets team. While working there, an increasing amount of my time revolved around training new joiners in the practice of law and the technical proficiency they would need to be a capital markets lawyer. That training role grew until I made the decision to join London-based BPP University Law School as a lecturer. There I taught future lawyers on the professional training course that was at the time mandatory for qualification as a lawyer in England and Wales. Teaching and learning became important additions to my toolkit of skills, and during my tenure at the law school I was part of the team that observed and trained new and existing lecturers. All of the lecturers were qualified lawyers, so despite no longer being at a law firm, I was still working with people who thought of themselves first and foremost as lawyers. As a professional training school, the law school itself had exclusive training relationships with around sixty law firms; it therefore needed to be able to tailor its offerings for the world of work.

Over time, the concept of innovation started to become more important to law firms. With that rise in importance came the expectation that legal education would change to accommodate the new skills required to innovate. As someone interested in questioning established norms and in finding new solutions to problems, it became my role to work with law firms to understand what skills were missing. Numerous meetings with lawyers, innovation leads, ALSPs and legal tech companies followed. During these meetings a clear picture started to emerge – one that seemed a little different from the focus of legal innovation education to that point. What future lawyers needed was not just technology skills but a toolkit of skills encompassing the business needs of clients in order to offer contextualized legal advice.

Based on this research I led a team in drafting a legal technology innovation and design module. This was when the Law+ concept first started bubbling away at the back of my mind. Over time my role shifted away from teaching and mainly into innovation, and it was at this point that I made the choice to go back into practice, working at both Reed Smith LLP and Mayer Brown LLP, where I could start putting into practice some of the things I had been discussing and teaching. In legal innovation it is my job to engage with lawyers and clients to find new ways of solving problems, whether that is through the creation of new technology tools, through process mapping and analysis, through the application of problem-solving methodologies such as design thinking, or through designing new ways of practising law and delivering legal services.

Outside of work I volunteer in several groups dedicated to the future of legal services.

I am a member of the O Shaped Lawyer Steering Board, where I am focused on the future of legal education and training to encapsulate human-centric skills.

I served as part of the Lawtech UK initiative, which has brought together a team of industry experts and leading figures from the government and the judiciary with the aim of fostering 'an environment in which new technology can thrive'.[1] Six taskforces were set up as part of this government-backed initiative, including ones dedicated to jurisdiction, regulation and education. I became a member of the education taskforce, headed up by Dr Anna Donovan. We were charged with finding ways to inculcate technology knowledge and skills in lawyers while also instiling legal knowledge and skills into technologists. The taskforce received government funding to create a free learning platform on which to host training in the relevant knowledge and skills (these are discussed later in part III of the book).

I am also an external consultant to King's College London on their professional legal practice modules, including in the areas of legal innovation and technology.

The final point worth noting in relation to my own credentials is that immediately prior to joining Reed Smith I completed a master's degree in education and technology at the UCL Institute of Education. This gave me a new perspective on innovation in the legal profession. We are often told that law is special and that disciplines and schools of thought from other professions cannot be directly applied to legal services. It is not design; it is *legal* design. It is not project management; it is *legal* project management. I have encountered a lot of people who are interested in and supportive of innovation and change in my time, but unfortunately they tend to argue that those methods and techniques are not applicable to their practice area.

Basically, some like the *idea* of innovation but not if it is happening to them. Although I always suspected that law being special was to some extent a myth, it took a degree that had nothing to do with law to show me how true that was.

Take design thinking as an example. It formed a key part of my studies in education and technology, where I learned about the concepts in a generic fashion, divorced even from education or technology. My capstone project involved conceiving and designing a prototype of something that could enhance education along one of several themes. After selecting the theme of 'improving literacy among children', I worked in a collaborative team to interview stakeholders and potential end users, understand their issues and challenges, decide on a single achievable challenge to solve, brainstorm ideas that would respond to that challenge, receive feedback on those ideas and then create a proof of concept that could be tested with the end users to see if it achieved its aim. The end result was an app that could be used to record time that children spent reading, with the ability to enter a narrative about progress and a dashboard showing progression based on the books read and the time spent reading.*

The point is that the design thinking method used to create the solution was exactly the same one that I use when producing client-facing or internal solutions within law firms, only there it is under the guise of 'legal design'. I interview the lawyers and clients involved to understand their requirements, understand the challenge we are trying to solve, check my understanding with the stakeholders, brainstorm ideas, design a proof of concept that can be iterated upon, and then demo it to the lawyers and clients. The only difference is that in my role within law firms, I would then go on to be part of the team that built the final solution rather than stopping at a proof of concept.

The similarities between education and the legal profession do not end there. Take as an example the concept of the 'teacher of the future'. The education sector is concerned with the new skills required to be a teacher now and in the future, the extent to which technology is disrupting the traditional role of a teacher or lecturer,

---

* Essentially, I created the billable hour for children.

whether administrative elements of the teacher's role can and should be automated, how design thinking and being more human-centric can help in providing more tailored educational services, and the extent to which learnings from other professions such as manufacturing can be applied to the education sector in order to make progress. All of these are issues within the world of law that will be tackled in this book, but to take a simple example to highlight the parallels let us look at the barriers to the adoption of technology.

A study by educational theorist Peg Ertmer[2] identified barriers to the adoption of technology in schools. These included a lack of time and prioritization for technology, the absence of necessary support structures for implementation, individual teachers' knowledge about technology, bad experiences with technology and a resultant lack of trust in it to function as expected, and teachers' inability to use given technologies due to inadequate training. In the legal world, a 2021 study on the barriers to legal technology adoption[3] interviewed lawyers of varying levels of seniority and found that the barriers included limited prioritization of technology, a lack of knowledge about technology and its benefits, inadequate training and a lack of trust that the technology will work as promised. The professions may differ, but the issues are the same. While there is nuance in what the experienced lawyer does when specifically advising their client or business, the processes and functions around that advice are in many ways no different to any other professional service. We in the legal profession should not only learn from other professions but actively collaborate with them to improve overall delivery.

Acknowledgements

B ooks are a bit of a lie. They are one of the last bastions of enter-
tainment where a single name is attached to delivery – shared
only, perhaps, with solo singer-songwriters, and even then the music
industry is much more in the public sphere, and people generally
know that there is a group of people responsible for the final product.
With books, though, we know less about the process. Indeed, we
often romanticize the act of writing itself. I can assure you that I
wrote none of this book in a lonely building on a misty moor. There
were no stacks of paper held down by a novelty paperweight. There
was certainly no click-clack of an aged typewriter. And I definitely
did not write this book alone. As a boy from the Isle of Man, it blows
my mind that this book is even a reality, and there are so many thank
yous to make to all those who let me stand on their shoulders.

I must start by thanking my wife. She has put up with me dron-
ing on about the book a *lot*. I have tried out many different bits of
the book on her, despite her having absolutely no legal training. She
has also had to deal with me trying to fit in writing and proofreading
while I should probably have been doing other things. Sorry, Sinead,
but know that I could not have done this without you. I should also
thank my children: my son for asking how the book is going and
seeming like he cares about the answer despite being under ten, and
my daughter who prides herself on being the reason her father works
in 'new law', as she calls it.

Massive thanks go to Richard Baggaley and Sam Clark of LPP,
my publisher, not only for giving me the opportunity to write this
book but for being genuinely nice people and for all their support
throughout the editing process. In the same vein, thank you to

Chris Howard for pointing Richard and Sam in my direction and for reviewing the copy.

There are a whole bunch of other people who merit thanks, and I will inevitably forget someone. Thank you to my reviewers and proofreaders: Lucy Dillon, Catriona Wolfenden, Jordan Galvin and Michaela Hanzelova. You all gave a different perspective on the content and each and every one of your comments made this book better.

Those who gave me permission to use their case studies (and who often improved my drafting) also deserve a special mention. They include Nigel Spencer, Joanne Humber, Dan Linna, Electra Japonas, Andrew Jenkinson and Sadie Baron, as well as Alyson Carrel and Cat Moon. I also thank my little brain trust of people on WhatsApp/ Signal who have helped me bounce ideas around, so thanks to Tom Pieroni for academic insight, Ishan Kolhatkar for attacking foot-notes, Sam Malhotra for giving her business management insight, and Anna Busch for design notes and cover inspiration. I would also like to thank Stephen Allen for introducing me to the concept of innovators as 'spanners'. Others who contributed to this book by giving advice or guidance include Danielle Chirdon, who gave me an insight into US law courses, and Chloe Kennedy, who did the same for Scottish ones. From an employment perspective, it would be remiss of me not to thank Jo-Anne Pugh for recognizing and supporting my interest in innovation; Lucy Dillon for hiring me in my first professional innovation role; and Dan Kayne and the O Shaped group – particularly Catherine Baker, Carrie Fletcher, Natalie Salunke, Clara Garfield, Greg Bott, Sophie Gould, Catie Sheret, John Skelton and Neil Campbell – for being such a support-ive group of awesome people.

PART I

THE WHY

WHY DOES THE LEGAL PROFESSION NEED NEW SKILLS?

The legal services profession is standing at a precipice. Ever since the global financial crisis of 2007–8, legal departments have come under increasing pressure to justify their costs and the value that they bring to their businesses. Reports from consultants such as Deloitte and KPMG show that CEOs and senior leaders want their general counsel to be leaders within the business, understanding technology, maintaining communication and balancing legal risk with business opportunity while also being proactive strategic decision makers.[1,2]

This has led, in turn, to increased scrutiny of businesses' external legal advisors, with monitoring of not only spend and output but also what legal advisors can provide beyond traditional legal advice. External advisor panels have also diversified and shrunk to reflect this new focus.

Meanwhile, deregulation of legal services across the globe means that the external legal advisors that make up those panels need not all be law firms. Instead, they could be one of a range of 'alternative legal service providers' (ALSPs), which might comprise legal engineers; technology companies; the legal arms of other advisors, such as the Big Four accountancy firms (PwC, Deloitte, Ernst & Young (EY) and KPMG); or any one of a number of other new models for legal services delivery. There is suddenly a pressing need for legal services providers to clearly differentiate themselves from one another. Just delivering the law is not enough.

While working with BPP University Law School I was part of a group conducting a series of interviews with law firms, in-house teams, and business services professionals within the legal profession, discussing what the future of law might look like and what the profession needed from its future lawyers in terms of skills. What the various stakeholders wanted were lawyers who could

- identify client or customer problems;
- understand the tools and methods at their disposal;
- collaborate with others to come up with creative solutions; and
- communicate with specialists from other professions, such as people working in innovation and technology, to develop and deploy those solutions.

The overarching requirements when it came to future legal skills were not, as you might think, for 'lawyers who code' or for lawyers who had intimate knowledge of artificial intelligence or blockchain, but for lawyers who have a toolkit of foundational skills in a range of areas that could be used to comprehend the problems that clients are trying to solve and work with others to solve them in the context of a client's business.

The response has been the emergence of new roles and new models within the legal profession. Roles such as legal engineers, data scientists and analysts, legal designers, pricing specialists, legal project managers, legal technologists, innovation managers, product managers and legal technology associates are now available to those who are interested. These roles exist globally, to varying degrees, in many law firms and ALSPs – including the likes of Simmons & Simmons/Simmons Wavelength, Mishcon de Reya, Mayer Brown, Ashurst, Deloitte Legal, DWF Mindcrest/DWF Ventures, Weightmans, Dentons, Reed Smith – as well as in legal consultancies like Dot and in the legal departments of major accountancy firms such as Deloitte. And that is nowhere near a complete list. In addition to new roles, individual lawyers and law firms have have experimented with their delivery models by

- establishing consulting functions (e.g. Addleshaw Goddard with AG Consulting, DWF with DWF Connected Services) that can assist external and internal clients with these new skills;
- spinning off subsidiaries (such as Reed Smith's Gravity Stack technology subsidiary) or managed services functions that employ those with alternative skills (sometimes referred to as 'captive ALSPs'); and
- launching initiatives such as technology incubators (e.g. Allen & Overy's Fuse and Slaughter and May's Collaborate) and new departments such as data science (e.g. Mishcon de Reya's MDRxTech) and legal innovation/strategy teams (e.g. Mayer Brown's Legal Innovation and Strategy team).

In fact, you would be hard pressed these days to find a top law firm in any country that was not offering at least one of these positions or experimenting with an alternative model for delivery. In addition to the proliferation of these new roles, existing roles in knowledge management, library, client value, IT and business development teams are evolving in how they support the delivery of legal services, and they are combining with innovation teams and expanding the remit and make-up of the team by adding those who possess skills that are not traditionally associated with the legal sector, such as process engineering and software development. Indeed, my first innovation role within a law firm was in the knowledge department rather than in any specific innovation team.

Similar changes are occurring in legal education. There are new university courses that offer alternative skills, such as combining law students with computer science students at universities like Northwestern Pritzker School of Law. There are also new courses in professional training, such as the University of Law's postgraduate diploma, postgraduate certificate and master's of science in legal technology, and the College of Legal Practice's master's-level business projects.

However, despite these new roles and models, and the history of requests from clients for advice that goes beyond just the law, the profession still faces the problem that clients are not seeing the skills that they want in their advisors – a problem that was confirmed as recently as February 2020 in a survey of general counsel.[3]

What should have been the beginning of a revolution in legal services delivery instead became a minor evolution that is failing to meet expectations. So why have these changes not been enough for clients? The simple reason is that the skills required to effectively instigate the needed revolution have not been fully introduced to the profession.

The changes that I have outlined above are still at the outer edges of the practice of law. They are essentially experiments. While new university and law school courses are catering to those seeking alternative skills, the learning and development of qualified practising lawyers does not yet reliably include the same types of offering. Among the new roles and models that do exist, they are either junior in nature, senior but with less reward attached than a lawyer of a similar seniority, or they are staffed by current or ex-lawyers rather than by professionals from sectors that specialize in those skills.

Seeking to overcome these challenges have been those who are working towards recognizing and rewarding new skills and competencies by creating and sharing new models for future lawyers. Among those models are the T Shaped lawyer, the O Shaped Lawyer and the Delta Competency Model for lawyers. While each has its merits and is to be lauded and supported, I believe we have not yet gone far enough in recognizing that the delivery of legal services does not need *a lawyer* of the future but *a legal team* of the future. I am also of the opinion that the full range of skills needed to deliver the level of legal services that clients expect requires collaboration between lawyers, legal 'hybrid' roles populated by lawyers specializing in new skills, and professionals from other sectors. Lawyers should be free to advise clients on the law without feeling the pressure of having to possess all of the skills of a 'lawyer of the future'. They should also not only be permitted to specialize in skills beyond law if they so wish, they should be rewarded for doing so.

It is for this reason that I have designed the Law+ model, covering sixteen essential skills split among four quadrants: Law+People, Law+Business, Law+Change and Law+Technology. This book will use real-world experience and examples to introduce you to the Law+ skills, the reasons that they are essential to practice, and guidance on how to introduce and build these skills – not only as an individual but also in universities, law schools, law firms and in-house teams.

CHAPTER 1

The Law+ model

AN ALPHABET OF LAWYERS

To understand how the provision of legal services has evolved, we must look to the past.

As the framework of laws, rules and regulations in which businesses operate became more complex in the 1990s, the role of the lawyer became increasingly specialized. Moving away from being generalist advisors of the law, lawyers started to become experts in their fields, increasingly seeking deep and technical expertise in a chosen area of law. This was valued by clients, and such specialization was how law firms differentiated themselves from their competitors. These deep technical expert lawyers are known as 'I Shaped' lawyers. As time went on, all law firms sought this level of specialization, and from the late 1990s onwards such technical expertise became less of a selling point for clients: they simply expected it from any law firm that they instructed.

Three decades ago, then, clients were already looking for more from their legal advisors than just legal knowledge. This in turn gave birth to the 'T Shaped' lawyer, introduced and popularized by organizations such as IDEO and McKinsey. The T Shaped lawyer has the same solid central pillar of knowledge as the I Shaped lawyer but adds on a new element of cross-disciplinary knowledge across the top bar of the T. What these cross-disciplinary skills are changes according to who is using or adapting the T Shaped lawyer model, and in some cases the featured cross-disciplinary skills can be so numerous that the T starts to look a little top heavy, but they generally include qualities such as creativity, communication, collaboration, project management, empathy, leadership and familiarity with technology.

Despite the prevalence of the T Shaped lawyer model, almost two decades later movements sprang up on both sides of the Atlantic that sought to better encapsulate the skills required by the modern lawyer in new models. In the United States, the concept of the Delta Competency Model was born. First conceived as part of a workshop to redesign the T Shaped lawyer during a ReInvent Law conference in New York, the Delta Competency Model was developed and expanded upon by a working group at a 2018 conference of lawyers, innovators and legal academics including Alyson Carrel (Northwestern), Natalie Runyon (Thomson Reuters), Jordan Galvin (Perkins Coie), Shellie Reid (Michigan State) and Jesse Bowman (Northwestern Law). This model took the cross-disciplinary skills of the T Shaped lawyer and the legal knowledge of the I Shaped lawyer and added a third element: 'personal effectiveness'. In its latest iteration, the Delta Competency Model has the following three elements (arranged to look like the Greek letter Delta: Δ).

The People: understanding and relating to clients, colleagues and ourselves.
The Process: delivering legal services efficiently and effectively.
The Practice: knowing, researching and clearly communicating the law.

The Delta Competency Model is designed as a more holistic set of competencies for a twenty-first-century legal professional, and it continues to evolve over time, with version 4.0 having been launched in 2020 by Cat Moon (Vanderbilt Law) and Alyson Carrel (Northwestern Law).

In the United Kingdom, meanwhile, Dan Kayne (who at the time was general counsel for Network Rail) noticed that the private practice lawyers he hired and with whom he interacted were not showing the more holistic skills he expected of a modern legal professional. In the first iteration of the 'O Shaped Lawyer' model, Dan proposed the following five 'Os' that legal professionals should possess.

Optimism: cultivating a positive mindset so that lawyers are not seen as business blockers.

Ownership: taking more accountability for outcomes.

Openness: possessing a growth mindset, so that lawyers are less defensive and more open to new ideas.

Opportunism: moving away from solely focusing on risk avoidance in legal advice, which is often at the expense of a business opportunity.

Originality: being more creative and innovative in their approach to problem solving.

With these five qualities in mind he built a small group of general counsel, lawyers and legal educators (of which I was one) into an O Shaped Steering Board to test his theory. In conjunction with the legal data research company Pirical (then named Aspirant), the Steering Board conducted a series of interviews with eighteen general counsel from a range of FTSE 350 companies spanning a variety of sectors. What they found – and have continued to find during their sustained outreach activities with the in-house, law firm and law school communities – is that clients need their legal advisors to be more adaptable and resilient, to build better relationships by understanding their clients and their business, and to create value through legal initiatives by identifying new opportunities and solving problems.

Armed with these findings, two workstreams were launched: one to focus on legal education and the other on legal practice. In the legal education space, this meant reaching out to law schools and universities to ensure that O Shaped skills were included in curricula. This engagement was based on an O Shaped competency framework that I was privileged enough to draft with a team comprising Catie Sheret (Cambridge University Press), Meera Ferguson (the Adecco Group), Carrie Fletcher (Leadership Development & Strategy consultant and research fellow at London Business School) and Natalie Salunke (Zilch). In the legal practice space, pilots were launched for new ways of working with clients that focused on the O Shaped skills, and language was introduced for tender requests to ensure that law firms instilled the necessary skills in their legal professionals.

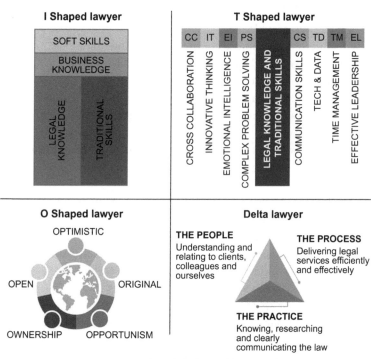

Figure 1. The alphabet of lawyers.[1]

These are not the only models of the skills and competencies of future lawyers, of course. One more targeted skills framework is that from the Legal Technology Core Competencies Certification Coalition (LTC4), which provides a foundational level of core competencies for legal professionals in using technology. And then there are the individual competency frameworks devised by universities and law schools. There is also no shortage of articles, white papers and conferences on the skills of future lawyers, which often offer their own structures and models for categorizing those skills. I have written or spoken at many of these, but over time I started to notice a pattern. The issue is that the focus of each of these models and frameworks is on the '*lawyer* of the future' instead of the '*legal team* of the future'.

THE LAW+ MODEL: AN OVERVIEW

My Law+ model is the result of almost two decades of working in the legal profession, across law, innovation and education. I have been part of many of the movements seeking to disrupt the legal industry and still work in 'the trenches' of the profession today. The model is intended to map both the lawyer and the legal team of the future, outlining the skills required of a collaborative group of legal advisors. Law+ comprises sixteen skills split among four quadrants – Law+People, Law+Business, Law+Change and Law+Technology – organized as below.

Quadrant	Area	Skill
Law+People	Internal self	Adaptability
		Awareness
	External self	Collaboration
		Communication
Law+Business	Domain	Model
		Market
	Direction	Strategy
		Synergy
Law+Change	Process	Mapping
		Management
	Problem solving	Creativity
		Comprehension
Law+Technology	Coretech	Day-to-day tech
		Data
	Lawtech	Delivery
		Discovery

Each skill contains four levels of potential mastery: entry level, established, experienced and expert. When combined, these four quadrants cover the matrix of skills required to deliver legal services in an evolving profession, both now and in the future.

The Law+ model is designed to be used by legal teams in three potential ways.

For leaders. As a leader, you can use the skills to build an effective team when faced with a legal challenge from a client within a business context. The model will also help with recruitment of talent into your team by helping you spot gaps in your current service delivery model.

For trainers and educators. Law+ provides a starting point for a competency framework that guides the progression of lawyers and business services professionals in the legal profession all the way from university or their first days through to the highest levels of seniority.

For individuals. Just as leaders are able to use Law+ to identify any skills gaps in a team, you as an individual can use the model to conduct a review of your own skillset, no matter the stage of your career, and to plot where you might grow your own skills in the manner most complementary to the intended future of your career.

There is an important point to note in relation to Law+ that differentiates it from other models of skills for the future of the legal profession: no individual is expected to master every skill. It is pretty much impossible to do so, and it should not be something you are striving for. Ideally, each person in a team will possess the various skills to varying degrees, and it is only when the skills of each of the team members are combined that we should expect mastery across the quadrants. Even then, the team must be built to respond to the problem at hand. For example, sometimes there will be no need for technology to deliver a legal solution if advice is being sought. The legal team of the future comprises multidisciplinary professionals who can bridge the gaps between each other's skills to collaborate on the provision of client services.

The eagle-eyed among you may have noticed that the skills outlined above contain alliteration and rhyming where possible. There is a good reason for this: displaying the skills in this way means that they are more likely to be remembered and retained.[2] I have always been in favour of taking the complex and making it easier to digest. For instance, when I taught a class on registration of security for loans, I used to read an extract from a story to my law students every year. This was not a legal book by any means – in fact, it was a romantic comedy – but the entire premise of the book was that a lawyer had failed to properly register a security interest, meaning that the lender had nothing they could sell to recoup their investment and that the lawyer was consequently at risk of losing her job. Registering security is a task that is really important for junior lawyers, and telling them about it in this way ensured they had a laugh and that they never forgot.[3] It is the one thing that is always brought up when I encounter old students, more than any other method I used to instil knowledge.

THE LEGAL TEAM OF THE FUTURE

The lawyer of the future means different things to different people. For the O Shaped Lawyer group, it means human-centric and emotionally intelligent lawyers. For those who specialize in legal technology, the lawyer of the future might be a lawyer who is a master of computer coding, while for the STEM Future Lawyers network,[4] it is lawyers with a background in science, technology, engineering and mathematics (STEM). None of these viewpoints is necessarily wrong, and elements of each of these visions of the lawyer of the future are contained in the Law+ model. The issue is that each and every one of them focuses on the future of law solely through lawyers. Having worked across legal education and practice, I have witnessed, facilitated and been part of discussions, groups and even entire conferences dedicated to the 'lawyer of the future'. But this is a phrase that has increasingly grated as time has gone on, and in this book I am requesting – bluntly – that people stop using it.

I predict that the future of the profession is legal teams of multidisciplinary individuals. Teams that comprise pure law, legal hybrid roles (such as legal designers and legal engineers) and specialists from other professional services (e.g. project managers and software developers). The notion of the solo lawyer of the future cannot and should not continue, and there are at least three reasons why it should not.

(i) It puts too much pressure on individuals

The legal services profession is one in which accomplished individuals are expected to perform at the top of their game in high-pressure environments, often involving late nights and complex and intense work. These environments are not conducive to good mental health. Numerous studies have shown that there are high levels of stress and poor mental health at all levels of practice. In 2019 the 'Resilience and wellbeing survey' report from the Junior Lawyers Division of England and Wales found that 48% of junior lawyer respondents experienced mental ill-health and that 6% had suicidal thoughts. In 2020 the *American Lawyer* magazine's '2020 mental health and substance abuse survey' found that 31.2% of respondents felt depressed and 64% felt they suffered from anxiety.

However, we still spend an awful lot of time focusing on *additional* skills that lawyers should possess, with the expectation being that individuals will easily acquire the actual legal knowledge and skills required. The question I have been asked more than any other during my career, though, is how students can learn all of these skills while they are also learning the law. Are we telling those that specialize in an area of highly technical law that what they know is not enough? Are we saying to law students that they need to undertake multiple additional topics and short courses on top of their complex and expensive law degree? Even if you accept, as I do, that the lawyer of the future needs to have skills beyond legal knowledge, the issue is the sheer number of skills we are advising this fictional lawyer to have.

If you are reading this book and you are worried that you have to possess all the skills that are in here, let me reassure you that you do not. Not at all. The law is a varied profession, and it needs many types of people. We still need technical legal specialists, but to stay relevant to our clients in a rapidly changing profession we also need those with skills from other professions and those who can combine those skills in a coherent manner to deliver legal advice. In short, we need cognitive diversity.

(ii) Diverse teams function better

I am a firm believer in bringing more diverse voices into the law, and there are solid business reasons for creating a diverse team. An individual can certainly provide a good service, but studies have shown that diverse teams deliver those services not only better than teams made up of homogenous groups, but also faster.[5] Companies in the top quartile for gender, racial and ethnic diversity have better financial returns, and more diverse companies consistently outperform those that are less diverse – something demonstrated by ten years' worth of studies from McKinsey.[6]

Having diversity of thought, background, experience and identity leads to a broader understanding of problems and a better range of solutions, with more scope for innovation in problem solving.[7] This is already being acknowledged when people discuss wanting 'rounded lawyers' that combine specialized legal knowledge with learning from another discipline. Why not include in your team 'rounded software developers' or 'rounded project managers' who combine specialized knowledge from other disciplines with learning from law?

(iii) It diminishes the role of those within the profession who are not lawyers

Not only does the phrase 'lawyer of the future' affect lawyers negatively, but it also ignores the huge number of people within law firms who are not lawyers. While these people are variously called professional support, business services or allied professionals, another term that is often used is 'non-lawyers'. That alone can be enough to give pause to those lawyers who might be seeking to stop practising in order to diversify in another area, and it might stop those from other professions joining the law. Why join a business that immediately sees you as a second-class citizen? And it is not only the terminology that is an issue.

Those accepting a business services or 'hybrid' legal role can expect less seniority and pay than those who practise law. In the United Kingdom, those in lawyer roles are almost six times more likely than those in business services roles to be earning more than £100,000. In the United States, lawyers are five times more likely than their business services colleagues to be earning the equivalent of £100,000.[8] In addition, the partnership model of traditional law firms does not allow a path for someone who does not practise law to become an owner of the firm. The legal profession is failing to entice those from other professions where they can earn more, and it is not encouraging those who are currently lawyers but want to diversify to stay within the profession. The issue is that the profession needs these people.

Why? Let me give you a real-world example in which a client was being sued for intentionally sending data out of a particular jurisdiction. This was deemed a breach of contract with another party (no names are used here because of client confidentiality). As these things go, lawyers were instructed and, as part of its discovery process, the law firm paid an external data company to extract all the data from the client in order to see where the data in question was being sent. Unfortunately for the client, it *had* been sending data out of that jurisdiction. It was not looking great for the client until the law firm enlisted the help of a business consultant and a team of data scientists and analysts. Between them, the 'non-lawyers' worked with the lawyers and figured out that the client, unlike the law firm, could not afford – and was not expected to engage with – an external data company to do a largescale audit of where all of its data was being sent. All else being equal, it was discovered that although the client *was* sending that data to another jurisdiction, there was no way that the client could have known that it was doing so and therefore it was not *intentionally* sending the data. This finding saved the client a substantial amount of money, as the penalty for unintentionally transmitting the data was much lower than the penalty for intentional transmission. None of this was possible until those who understood data and its business context were added to the team.

Lawyers alone are no longer enough for the legal profession, and this is actually a great thing for lawyers, business services professionals, and clients because it means that lawyers get to focus on giving advice, the professionals get to deliver a great service and build a relationship, and the client gets their advice in a more effective manner. Clients are expecting their legal advice to be delivered in the context of their business needs, and for their legal departments to be a core part of the strategic direction of the business. With that in mind, we cannot effectively future-proof the legal profession by focusing only on law or even just by picking a single discipline to combine with law. Instead, we need to consider a full-scale multidisciplinary approach to the provision of legal services – one that factors in not only legal knowledge but also the Law+ skills outlined in the table on page 9.

WHERE IS THE LAW?

The observant among you will have spotted that the Law+ model does not contain any reference to pure legal knowledge and skills. This is not to downplay the importance of any given lawyer's legal knowledge. Far from it. Legal knowledge is the very essence of what we do, and it is why clients seek advice from their law firms and legal departments – it is called the *legal* profession, after all. But referring back to the study I conducted that assessed the skills required of future practitioners, it is worth noting that in none of those interviews was 'legal knowledge' cited as one of the features of a future lawyer. When questioned about this, those interviewed replied that legal knowledge is 'just expected'. Clients assume that their lawyers possess legal knowledge; it is not treated as a differentiator between law firms or lawyers – it is the expected bare minimum.

If we are asking how to evolve the profession, then, we should be looking not at how much more law we can learn but instead at what more can be done to bring the profession up to the level expected by our clients. People do not come to lawyers because they want to understand the law. People come to lawyers because they want help with solving a problem. The law is only part of the equation. It does not – and should not – exist in a silo divorced from the realities of the commercial landscape that clients inhabit.

It helps to think of the role of a lawyer as being similar to that of a pilot of an aircraft. I think we can all agree that we would not expect the pilot to be the person who built and serviced the aircraft and also the one who serves us our in-flight meal. Indeed, it would be a pretty unsettling flight if that were the case. We expect our pilots to concentrate on flying the aircraft and making sure we reach our destination. In the legal profession, however, there is a historic expectation that the lawyer does it all. I have met and worked with plenty of people within the legal sector who believe that this is the way that things are and should be, but contrary to their beliefs, not only is this not how law *should be* delivered, it is also rarely how law *actually is* delivered today. The work of a lawyer is supported by others in their team, by appropriate technology systems, and by established processes, precedents and practices. These are the co-pilots, mechanics and on-board computers of the legal world, and they are becoming increasingly important as more is expected from legal teams. Gartner predicts that by 2024, in-house legal teams will replace 20% of their 'generalist' lawyers with staff from other professions, thereby allowing those teams to do more with their resources. The percentage of legal departments that have a legal operations manager who is responsible for business services professionals grew from 34% in 2018 to 58% in 2020, with the figure growing even more markedly among 'Fortune 500' companies.[9]

Of course, not all of those who practise law will want to specialize deeply in technical black-letter legal advice. For those lawyers who wish to diversify into Law+ skills, there is something we can learn from the way that the profession is already modelled.

Prior to practice, law schools instil a foundation in legal knowledge in future lawyers. This foundation is then built upon when lawyers qualify and choose a practice area in which to specialize. In a law firm, for example, an individual may join a corporate finance team and start by working on the financing of businesses via shares and debt before later specializing in just debt and then perhaps eventually becoming an expert specifically in private debt issues. In an in-house team, the specialization may instead fall into the business or industry group in which the business operates rather than in a particular area of law, as here there is often less of a requirement to be a technical legal specialist. The point I am making here is that we all can and do happily accept that lawyers do not need to know *all* of the law. A lawyer picks an area and then relies on others to fill the gaps should the matter at hand span numerous practices. At present, though, we do not apply that same thinking to the additional skills we want to see from those working in legal services. There is no clear path where somebody can say, 'I really enjoy tech but I am massively disorganized so there is no point teaching me project management', or for those who say, 'I completely understand the business of my clients but am a bit of a dinosaur in the tech department', and there should be – to ignore this is to ignore how people are.

There is an apt quote from Terry Pratchett that sums up much of the approach to the development of innovation skills in the legal profession:

> He did not look around, and watch and learn, and then say, 'This is how people are, how do we deal with it?' No, he sat and thought: 'This is how the people ought to be, how do we change them?'[10]

The 'he' in the above quote is a somewhat villainous police officer who, in the protagonist's opinion, fundamentally misunderstands the nature of policing. But it could equally apply to the legal profession as a whole when we consistently provide huge shopping lists of skills, expecting lawyers to possess them all. We should stop forcing all lawyers to be all things to all people, instead recognizing that different people are good at different things and that specialization in a Law+ skill is as valuable as being a legal specialist. Those who are not great at technology might be absolutely fantastic at interacting with clients and in understanding their positions; they may be able to analyse business accounts with an expertise approaching (or even surpassing) that of an accountant. These are valuable skills, and to downplay them just because they are not the flavour of the month is to do these people a disservice. Just as lawyers are permitted to specialize in an area (or areas) of law, they should be given the freedom to specialize in Law+People, Law+Business, Law+Change or Law+Technology skills that are complementary to their legal knowledge and skills.

To go back to our pilot example, we do not expect the pilot to be able to fly the plane and also be able to fix the engine should it break down. We do expect them to know about the plane, to understand the terminology the mechanics use, and to work with the mechanics in the event of a fault to help them understand where the origin of the fault lies. It is also likely that some pilots will have additional qualifications in mechanical engineering and therefore could actually fix the engine if required. But at the end of the day, all the passengers need is for the plane to fly them to their destination. They do not care who does what. Provided there is a team of people who work together to fulfil their needs, they are happy. In the same way, we do not expect the lawyer of the future to specialize in every practice area, even when in-house teams require a flexible lawyer who can turn their hand to a few different areas of law. What we do expect is that they will have a basic grounding in each practice area and that they will cooperate with others who are specialists in those areas. The same applies to skills: those who work in future legal services should possess that same ability to understand the broad range of Law+ skills and to work with specialists in those skills as required.

It can be intimidating to be weaker at a skill than someone else, especially for lawyers, who are often held up as people at the top of their intellectual game. But the fundamentals of Law+ mean that you do not have to be all things to all people – you just have to understand yourself and know when to work with others. You cannot improve all your weaknesses but you can excel at your strengths and surround yourself with other people who understand other areas. Lawyers rely on lawyers from other practice areas without necessarily fully understanding their legal specialism, and we need to extend this concept to include those with skills in other Law+ quadrants.

Think of Law+ like tax. I have met many a lawyer who will openly admit to not fully comprehending all the complexities of taxation, and when such issues are raised by clients, they will confidently explain that they will need to involve specialist tax lawyers. We need to become just as comfortable doing the same for Law+People, Law+Business, Law+Change and Law+Technology.

WHERE IS THE KNOWLEDGE?

The focus of this book is on skills, but that is not to say that knowledge is irrelevant. Knowledge is important. This is undeniable, and it is certainly true in law, when understanding the relationships between case law and legislation can sometimes feel like trying to navigate some indecipherable arcane text. University and law school provide a grounding in legal knowledge, and good lawyers will continue to keep that knowledge up to date throughout their careers. However, skills are the fundamental basis upon which knowledge is built. The specific laws that are learned at university or law school will change over time. Even in newer 'innovative' courses that teach students how to use a particular technology, there is no guarantee that the technology used will still be in existence by the time a student enters practice, or that the firm or business you work in will use that technology.

To take an example from my own history, the legislation governing UK company law was changing when I was at law school: from the Companies Act 1985 to the Companies Act 2006. It was a wide-ranging and holistic change of the legal landscape for companies. Did that mean that the business law legal training of everyone who studied prior to the implementation of the 2006 Act was useless? Of course not. That would be ridiculous. What, then, were the lecturers aiming to instil in me and my fellow students? It could not be just the facts. Instead, what we should have learned was the skill of being able to distil information and cogently and coherently outline the law within the context requested by our future clients. Doing that requires skills as well as knowledge. Knowledge needs updating. Skills are the toolkit by which we access and curate our knowledge. Keeping knowledge up to date requires an ability to conduct research; it requires reflection, to appreciate that your knowledge is out of date; and it requires a desire to engage with continuous lifelong learning and the adaptability to learn and apply that new knowledge to your work. The focus of Law+ is therefore on skills that can continue to be applied to any knowledge landscape.

SNAPSHOT OR EVOLUTION

The Law+ model is a lifelong learning model. An individual's proficiency in each quadrant will – and should – change during their working life. It cannot be stressed too strongly that those working in the legal profession need to continue to learn and grow throughout their careers. There are people who currently see themselves as only lawyers but who will in the future diversify their skill set into one of the Law+ skills quadrants. There will be those who stop practising altogether in order to focus on a quadrant. There will be people who are already experts in one of the quadrants who decide to join the legal profession and go on to qualify as lawyers themselves. This is all *fantastic* as it drives diversity and expands the range of options for solving client problems, but it is not necessarily how all those in practice – or about to enter it – think of their careers.

Law students have a lot to juggle during their education. Students at law school are often not simply studying to pass exams but are also trying to get a legal job at the same time, sometimes while working another part-time job to fund their studies. This can take up pretty much all of a student's free time and their mental space. The problem with this is that I have encountered too many people who were so focused on getting a *job* that they had given no thought to their *career*. Through no fault of their own, these future lawyers were like the excited engaged couple who spend a huge amount of time and money planning their wedding and never take the time to think of the marriage that lies beyond that. That sort of short-termism does not make for a healthy relationship. In much the same way, those who do not consider their ongoing career are entering a profession that will become very different from the state at which they enter it. If they have not considered which of the Law+ quadrants appeals to them, then they might find themselves thrust in a direction that does not suit them. Alternatively, they might find themselves feeling stifled when they later realize that they want to progress in a quadrant but have laid no groundwork in that area. Or perhaps, after a significant period of their career, they will find that they are being overtaken in seniority by those who have taken the time to plot out their next steps. Likewise, those currently in practice may believe that they can 'ride out' the changes to the profession, but establishing even entry-level proficiency in all of the Law+ skills is necessary in order to lead the future of legal practice. I have met plenty of lawyers who were just waiting on retirement and who therefore attempted to avoid legal technology and innovation, but there is no more waiting: that technology and innovation are already here.

The traditional path to promotion – where lawyers are either expected to reach for partnership in a law firm, go in-house or leave the law firm altogether – is increasingly only one option among many, and as more law firms diversify their workforces, those who try to ride out change are going to find themselves pushed out by it.

CHAPTER 2

Change in the legal profession

THE AS-IS: HOW THE PROFESSION IS CURRENTLY STRUCTURED

To understand Law+ and its application to the legal profession, it is important to understand the way in which law firms and their clients currently interact. In the world of business improvement, the current state is known as the 'as-is'. In order to move to the 'to-be', you first have to map out how things are currently done so that you can find ways in which the system can be improved. In the case of the legal profession, this means looking at the structures of both law firms and in-house teams and at how they interact with each other.

The law firm structure

The traditional law firm structure is referred to as the 'pyramid'. This basically means that there are fewer lawyers at each more senior level of the hierarchy than in the level below. The usual promotion path for a lawyer is to start as a junior associate and work towards being a senior associate, with the intention of one day being a partner in the firm. Indeed, most law firms have a 'partnership track' that can be anything from a very specific one-year application process to a years-long preparation for transferral into the partnership. As well as usually being highly talented legal advisors, those who make partner tend to be 'rainmakers', i.e. they bring in business and make significant profits for the firm. The idea behind the pyramid is that partners bring in work; that work is staffed and managed by senior associates; and those senior associates then delegate the various tasks to more junior professionals. At each stage the work becomes less technical and the cost to the client decreases. While this is not the only model, it remains the most common across the legal profession.

Within the firm itself, most law firms are divided up into 'practices' or 'industries' or both. When divided along practices, the lawyers belonging to each practice are responsible for different areas of law, e.g. corporate law or litigation, and within those broad umbrellas there may be more specialized teams who work in mergers and acquisitions, say, or employment litigation. A division between industries, on the other hand, involves dividing lawyers across the types of sector in which their clients work, e.g. energy, financial services, transportation or life sciences.

In addition to the lawyers, law firms will usually have teams of 'business services' or 'support services' professionals. Unlike the lawyers, who are categorized as 'fee earners', these business services staff do not usually charge clients for their work on an hourly basis, although some (such as consultants and project managers) may do so. Business services includes everything from back-office teams who handle facilities and administration to the external marketing and business development teams, and even client-facing teams such as innovation or consulting arms. My own roles in innovation have been both internal and client-facing.

The in-house team structure

While law firms service multiple clients across a variety of sectors, in-house legal department teams are the lawyers for a single business or organization. The clients of an in-house team are the businesses of which they are a part, and when referring to clients in this book I am usually using the term to describe both 'clients' of firms and 'clients' of legal departments. For some in-house lawyers, this will mean having a single 'client' as they work for a single business, but for others who work for larger organizations that own multiple businesses, it may mean having almost the same variety of clients as some law firms. While there is a greater flexibility of structures among in-house teams compared with law firms, most in-house teams are structured in either a 'centralized' or 'embedded' model. In a centralized team (which is the most common in-house structure) the legal department is its own business unit, while in an embedded team lawyers are distributed around the business, within other departments or functions. In both cases, the lawyers of an in-house team usually report to a general counsel, although in some organizations they may report directly to the Chief Operating Officer or Chief Financial Officer.

The promotion path for in-house teams is not as defined as it is for a law firm lawyer. Progression depends on the skills that you possess and the business case you build to grow your team or push for promotion. Your seniority and length of service feed into your promotion path, and reaching general counsel level may require you to change organization numerous times.

Despite these differences, there are a lot of similarities between in-house and law firm lawyers. While you might expect it to be easier for in-house lawyers to find work – embedded within their client as they are – the legal department of an organization often still has to 'sell' the value of its capabilities and source work from other teams, much like private practice lawyers have to do with their own clients, meaning business development is important. Most in-house lawyers also started their professional lives in private practice at a law firm.

Interaction between law firms and in-house teams

The primary form of interaction between law firms and their clients is on a lawyer-to-lawyer basis. While many legal problems can be dealt with by an in-house team, where a business is confronted by a legal issue that requires specialist knowledge, that issue is usually referred to – or originates from – the general counsel, who in turn instructs the law firm via their relationship partner. During this process, most of the communication will be between more junior lawyers from both the law firm and the in-house team, and where there is another party involved the clients will communicate with each other through the law firms.

This form of interaction is understandable in a culture in which a large part of the success of a partner is down to their rainmaking ability. This places pressure on partners to foster and maintain personal relationships with their clients so that they continue to be the primary source of income for that client, and it can mean that a partner views a client as 'theirs' rather than as belonging to the firm, especially when their chances of moving jobs (if they want to) are increased by the extra potential client revenue they can bring to any new firm.*

While this picture does not apply to every partner, by any means, it does mean that a sizeable number of lawyers are not actively look-ing for opportunities to work in multidisciplinary teams across their firm, perhaps concerned that they will 'lose' their clients to the wider firm, meaning that any value the partner had from 'owning' a client relationship may be diminished if they want to move to another firm in the future or prove their worth at their current one. In some cases, the only situations in which a partner is likely to reach out to business services teams for support is (i) where a client specifically asks for an alternative delivery method, (ii) when a fee structure is in place that means return is not directly tied to hours worked, or (iii) where the partner is at risk of losing their mandate or engagement.

This lawyer-centricity means that business services professionals do not often get the opportunity to interact with clients or to be part of that relationship, even where their roles are 'client-facing' – as I know only too well. During my career there has often been a long process of gaining the trust of a partner before speaking to their clients. This is understandable, but it means having to sell any new ways of delivering legal services to the partners before getting anywhere near clients, introducing a whole new barrier. Issues may include that the partner (i) does not know the wider business issues of the client, connected as they are only to the legal team; (ii) does not fully understand the technology or methodologies being pre-sented to them and so does not feel confident in passing these on to the client; or (iii) is simply too busy to consider other ways of working. I am positive that some solutions that would be of great benefit to businesses are being missed because lawyers only talk to lawyers.

---

* In some instances this can lead to a situation that feels a little like the seagulls from *Finding Nemo* shouting 'Mine! Mine! Mine!' at each other.

THE TO-BE: HOW THE PROFESSION COULD BE STRUCTURED

The five E's of change

Although there are unique outliers who have structured their legal teams differently, the large majority of organizations continue to function as they have done for many years. It is a structure that has worked well for decades, with profits continuing to rise even during a pandemic.[1] As Richard Susskind has said: 'It's hard to convince a room full of millionaires that they've got their business model wrong.'[2] If law firms are doing so well, then why bother changing?

The short answer is that the profession is facing a perfect storm of (pleasingly alliterative) conditions that are combining to drive that change forward: namely, factors relating to economics, evolution, education, expectation and ease. The importance of these factors was only boosted by the requirement to work from home during a global pandemic, which meant finding new ways to deliver legal services across borders, but much of the change had already started in one way or another. It is important to examine these factors to understand how the world in which we practise law today is not the same world as even a decade ago, and to see how the Law+ toolkit is needed to respond to such changes and to stay relevant in this new world.

Economic factors

Since 2008, legal departments have been under increased pressure over the amount they spend.[3] The resultant push for fixed-fee and capped-fee arrangements and increased transparency from those legal departments has meant law firms turning to new methods of time- and costs-saving in order to increase efficiency. This has included the use of outsourcing for elements of the delivery of legal advice, creating departments and teams entirely dedicated to process mapping and management (such as Pinsent Masons Vario and Reed Smith's Global Solutions Leeds), and the adoption of new technologies that can automate common processes. Even in situations where matters are still billed by the hour, clients are more frequently comparing their external counsel against each other in terms of spend and work product and being more rigorous in reviewing and contesting elements of the bill, commonly excluding work that takes longer than they believe it should or that should be automated. Those firms that show innovative thinking in finding those efficiency gains are also more likely to find themselves with an increased wallet share of the client's legal work.[4]

While law firms managed to perform well during the pandemic, this does not necessarily mean that their clients did too. Price pressures, which were already an issue prior to the pandemic, are likely to be felt even more intensely now, especially after those clients have experienced some of the new ways of working that the pandemic forced upon us: electronic signings, the ubiquity and ease of online video meetings, and the rise of new forms of digital collaboration such as Microsoft Teams, for example. Why should a client pay for a lawyer to fly around the world to attend a signing when it can be done electronically? When I was in practice, I once flew to India with a senior associate just to attend a signing. The law firm on the other side of the deal flew in, did the signing and left again within a couple of hours. I cannot imagine the same situation would be acceptable to a client today.

While clients are pushing back on fees, looking for alternative fee arrangements and carefully reviewing time recording narratives and what they are willing to pay for, there is at the same time a global war for talent that is constantly pushing salaries to new heights. This short-term investment is not being matched in planning for the future.

In the United Kingdom, for instance, businesses spend an average of around 5% of their revenue on research and development (R&D). A survey conducted by Lawtech UK, however, revealed that few legal businesses devote even 1% of their spend to R&D.[5] Using the United Kingdom as an example is important because the legal profession in the country is under comparatively more pressure to change due to the deregulated legal market in which law firms find themselves, something the rest of the world is increasingly moving towards. Considering that R&D is what keeps businesses competitive as their markets evolve, this should be a concern to the traditional players in the legal profession, who are at risk of being supplanted by those who are investing in the future. There are many examples of companies such as Blockbuster and Kodak who failed to spot the movement of the market and lost out to new entrants (like streaming services) or new technology (like digital photography – a technology that Kodak in fact invented and failed to take advantage of).

The argument for change is all around us, with in-house teams not only shrinking and diversifying their external legal panels, but also purchasing efficiency technologies themselves.[6] A recent report from the Association of Corporate Counsel (ACC) – a global bar association aligned with the interests of in-house counsel – showed that the top five technologies that in-house teams are investing in by allocated spend are contract management, compliance, legal research services, intellectual property management, and matter management, with almost one-in-four departments spending money on contract management tech.[7]

While these issues are more common in England and Wales than they are in the United States and other jurisdictions, the current situation in England and Wales is like a crystal ball into the future for America, which is starting to see the trends of deregulation in more states. This is, in turn, giving rise to new ways of delivering legal services.

Evolution

As you will see if you look at the world around you, technology is constantly improving. There is always a new version of a phone or a laptop or a television available – one that has features that once upon a time would have seemed like magic. And as it is in our personal lives, so it is for businesses. This progress has introduced new technologies such as artificial intelligence and robotic automation of manual processes to the legal profession, but it has also introduced new legal quandaries that need to be solved, with technology-related legal risks ranked as one of the top five risks that CEOs believe their general counsel need to prioritize.[8] Staying on top of these developments can no longer be seen as a 'nice to have' when they are impacting the legal advice that is being delivered and how business is being done. Prior to the pandemic, many CEOs and CFOs expected to see investment in technologies that created 'demonstrable business value by delivering growth and innovation',[9] and during the pandemic technology became more important than ever. Can any of us imagine working at home without the various virtual environments and digital collaboration technologies that we now possess? As the priorities of businesses shift, so must those of the organizations that provide services to those businesses, such as the legal and accounting professions.

The rapid evolution of businesses can lead to panic, with individuals worried they are going to be replaced by machines. It is worth pointing out here that while the World Economic Forum recognizes that workers 'will need to learn new skills' to continue to progress in their career, their prediction is that automation will *change* half of all jobs but only *eliminate* around 5% of them.[10]

It must be noted that the evolution of technology is not going to be enough on its own to spur innovation. Indeed, I have seen instances of 'innovation by press release' first hand, where law firms or tech providers will announce new tools and capabilities that, on deeper inspection, either do not exist or do not work as advertised. This is why evolution is only one factor driving forward legal services; an appreciation of technology may be good, but understanding how that technology is affecting businesses and their legal problems is essential if legal services providers are to give the best level of service.

Expectations

Budgetary concerns and the evolution of technology have combined to give different expectations across the profession. Law firm clients are seeing effective uses of technology within their own businesses and among new market entrants to the legal sector, and they are consequently expecting to see the same across all of their providers. Those working in law or about to join the profession are learning about and experiencing new methodologies that can be applied to practice, with new joiners bringing with them an expectation that others will use technology as they do. Almost every request for proposals (RFP) that an in-house team puts together for external advisors is likely to ask that external advisor to prove how they are offering innovative services, cutting costs and effectively using technology, and law firms need to be prepared for questions along these lines. Arguably the best question I have ever seen in such an RFP is to detail how the firm is being innovative *without* using technology.

This expectation that law firms should be providing innovative services does not always equate to an understanding of just what it is they should offer. It is a cliche in innovation to suggest that if Henry Ford had asked his customers what they had wanted when he was developing the automobile, they would have answered 'a faster horse', but law firm clients in many cases do not want to wait around to be asked what it is they want; they need external advisors and in-house teams who can use innovative thinking to find new legal solutions before they even know there is a problem.

Education

While I will talk in much more detail about how legal training and education can evolve in order to provide a solid basis in Law+ skills in chapter 10, legal teams who are expected to possess Law+ skills often push the responsibility for instilling those skills onto universities and law schools. In response, those educational establishments offer an ever-increasing package of alternative legal skills and knowledge, ranging from courses in business and/or technology to sandwich courses and innovation labs. The issue with this is that the law firms are not necessarily always following suit in providing a platform for new joiners to further develop those skills, and this is causing mounting pressure on legal teams to provide a development path that utilizes the new skills with which lawyers are entering the profession. In addition, those courses we *do* hear about are often expensive and time consuming to offer, and they are therefore usually available to only a small number of students. The disservice this does to future joiners is that they are constantly hearing about how important new skills are without being given enough opportunities to actually learn them. In a competitive job market, creating appropriate progression paths that match the skills that future joiners have been taught is essential.

Ease

The pandemic starkly highlighted the importance of work–life balance. In their resilience and well-being surveys, the Junior Lawyer

Division of the Law Society of England and Wales has consistently found a desire from junior lawyers to have a better work–life balance in the legal profession. Innovative solutions that may have once fallen on deaf ears as they reduced hours – and therefore fees – are finding purchase among those who wish to complete the same amount of work in a shorter time, and who want it to be recognized that they have a life outside of the profession. Although this 'E' of change is referred to as 'ease', it is not that these lawyers are looking for an easy ride: it is that they recognize that business must be balanced with purpose and mental health in order to avoid people burning out and to ensure that the people within a given organization remain motivated and do their best work. I am not sure I can say, with hand on heart, that I was performing at the top of my game when I was writing prospectuses at two o'clock on a Sunday morning.

Is it too late?

It can often feel like it is too late to change. Rarely does a week pass by without another law firm winning an award for innovation or a new start-up or acquisition appearing in the legal technology space. It can all be pretty overwhelming. But while it is never too late to implement change, it must be remembered that change takes time. For example, you will not be able to buy a piece of technology tomorrow and have it up-and-running in a week – not without going through the appropriate risk and IT processes, communicating the existence of the technology, and upskilling your lawyers and business services professionals to use it. If you are committed to working in new ways, then you need to build solid foundations. This can seem boring, but it is essential. There is a good reason for the movement among legal innovators and technologists to 'bring back boring' in law.

APPLYING LAW+ TO THE PROFESSION

The left-hand side of figure 2 shows the current state of the legal profession. You can see that the majority of the interaction (shown by the black arrows) takes place behind a wall of lawyers (also represented in black). There may be the occasional interaction with business services (represented by the grey dotted line) at some firms, but even when there is, the interaction rarely goes beyond the legal team of the client, whether or not they are the end user of any solution. The skill sets of those on the left are represented by homogeneous blocks of a single colour, displaying the siloed arrangement of teams and professionals to which many legal teams fall prey.

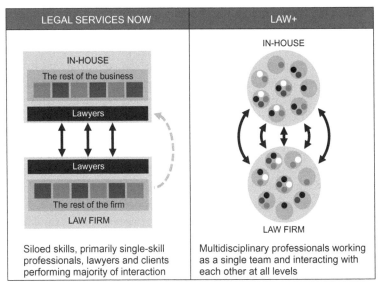

Figure 2. Interaction between law firms and in-house teams.

The right-hand side of the figure, however, shows the Law+ view of how legal services could – and should – be delivered, with individuals represented by circles containing varying degrees of multidisciplinary skills working together at all levels of the hierarchy. There are still those who possess specialist skill sets, of course, as we will always need people who are experts in their fields, but there are multiple interactions at all levels. There remain more black dots (representing legal skills) than there are any of the others – just as the black area is larger than any other on the left of the figure – but then we are in the legal profession.

Getting to the Law+ delivery model is essential, and I think the best way to illustrate why this is so is with a tale I heard first hand.

When I was starting out in practice, as part of the training contract I was offered the opportunity to tour the London Stock Exchange. The tour ended with a senior member of the organization talking us through the history of the exchange and the changes he had seen over his many years working there. The biggest change he described related to the workforce. In years gone by, shares were actually traded on the 'trading floor'. This was a big room where, basically, people shouted loudly while holding slips of paper that represented shares in a company. If you wanted to buy and sell shares, you did so by physically exchanging these bits of paper. Quite often, the person from whom you bought shares was either someone that you knew, someone with whom you had previously socially interacted, or someone with whom you had had a previous good experience. This was usually the case regardless of who had the best price. Those with the best social skills were therefore the kind of people who got hired and who succeeded.

As the processing power of computers increased, and as algorithms were designed to analyse and predict the movements of the markets, those buying shares were able to look for the best deals on a second-by-second basis – and often even faster. Clients on whose behalf you were buying shares had access to up-to-date information about the stock market and price fluctuations, and they expected the best price for their shares. This move to data and analytics caused a shift in the composition of the workforce because social skills now needed to be supplemented and augmented by those with technological proficiency and an understanding of data.

The law is seeing a similar shift now. With in-house counsel under pressure to prove themselves more than a cost centre by analysing spend, businesses require a better rationale for choosing a panel law firm than 'I know this person and have worked with them before'. Businesses expect solid reasons for the inclusion of every member of a panel, something that has improved the diversity of providers; if there are multiple firms on a panel, then the legal department that set the panel up is expected to have a good reason for this. As clients become more sophisticated, they are holding law firms to account based on defined metrics – whether they relate to diversity and equality, innovation, client satisfaction, or environmental, social and governance-related (ESG-related) analytics. An example of this is that there are organizations who have such sophisticated billing requirements that if their law firm does not offer them a secondment or an innovation project in a particular financial year, this leads to a reduction in the overall fees that the firm can charge.

For lawyers, this is an expectation that cannot be managed alone. The relationship partner needs the support of the firm and its multi-disciplinary individuals to identify, measure and meet these metrics. Legal problems are never just legal problems; clients are not asking about the application of a law to their situation out of idle curiosity. There is a business reason, and where interaction takes place solely through lawyers, those lawyers are taking on the role of being the 'translators' of that business need. The issue is that the lawyers may not have the relevant Law+ skills to undertake this translation. Just as we would not feel confident enlisting a conversational speaker of a language to translate a business contract, so must we be careful that the team delivering legal advice contains sufficient familiarity with the 'language' of skills associated with people, business, change and technology.

Involving wider legal teams beyond just lawyers on either side of the client–adviser relationship can provide new perspectives on legal issues. Rather than lawyers talking to lawyers, we can have software developers talking to software developers and project managers talking to project managers, meaning that the non-legal facets of a legal problem can be solved by specialists in their field without having to rely on a lawyer as a translator. We are not always solving the whole problem by focusing on the law.

I was once involved in a project for a client who wanted us to automate some common contracts that were used by the business. The lawyers focused on making sure that the contracts were legally correct and on identifying the areas that could be automated, and the technology team put the contracts into the document automation software so that it could be used. When I spoke to the client, however, I discovered that the issue was not only related to automation: the issue was that the legal team did not have a central place to share information about their documents and how such documents should be drafted. Because the automation was a standard response offered by the law firm as part of its toolkit of innovation, that is the direction that was chosen, but my additional investigation revealed that the in-house team really needed a way to communicate digitally. A short time later we set up a demo Microsoft Teams environment for the client that allowed them not only to store their documents in a single place but also to comment and tag people relating to the documents. It was a simple solution, but it was what they needed and they were very grateful for our help. By combining legal skills with other skill sets, we increased our knowledge of the problems and helped the client in a way they did not initially expect.

Case study. The latticed professional

In response to the rapid evolution of the business model for professional services firms, Oxford Saïd Business School and Meridian West came together to publish a series of research papers aimed at senior leaders in professional firms. The series – 'Creating competitive advantage: strategic learning and development in professional services' – was authored by Dr Nigel Spencer and Stephen Newton and, among other things, it sought to address the kinds of strategic issue that were likely to be on the agenda of professional services firms, including the skills that professionals will need in the future, how learning and development teams can assist with this, and how professional firms can establish new career pathways for their professionals.

In the third paper in the series, Spencer and Newton discuss early career pathways and introduce the concept of 'lattice pathways' for progression in firms. These pathways posit a career journey for professionals that gives greater flexibility and a mindset of ongoing learning. In the example given, a student, 'Alex', goes from studying STEM subjects in school to a degree apprenticeship in a firm, before qualifying and spending three years specializing in law until her specialism, experience and interest in data and analytics takes her into the data analytics team. Over time, Alex gains management experience while leading the technical data analysts and works closely with the firm's 'Client Solutions Centre', where she learns that she is drawn towards facilitating client discussions around broad industry challenges. This path leads her into the 'Markets and Industry Strategy' advisory team, where she uses her data analytics experience to advise industries on using cleaner forms of energy.

Alex's career lattice
A possible future career journey for professionals

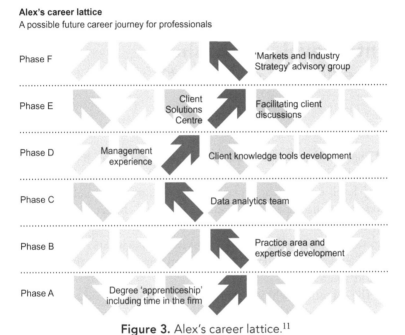

Phase F		'Markets and Industry Strategy' advisory group
Phase E	Client Solutions Centre	Facilitating client discussions
Phase D	Management experience	Client knowledge tools development
Phase C		Data analytics team
Phase B		Practice area and expertise development
Phase A	Degree 'apprenticeship' including time in the firm	

Figure 3. Alex's career lattice.[11]

The paper goes on to advise firms to enable more of these flexible 'latticed' pathways, where people can choose to experiment with different roles, and to engage in open and clear discussions about careers and the available pathways for individuals to progress. Learn more at www.sbs.oxford.edu/strategiclearning.

CHAPTER 3

Entry level, established, experienced or expert?

The Law+ model provides four levels of expertise that the individuals who make up a legal team of the future might possess: entry level, established, experienced and expert. As a collaborative model that encompasses the people, business, change and technology skills that are needed in addition to the specific legal knowledge and skills that a legal team must possess, no one is expected to reach the expert level in all four quadrants, and nor do I think that anyone should aim to.

The intention behind mapping the skills of individuals in this way is to not to show where an individual is lacking, but to see the *composite* of that individual's skills when combined with those of the other members of their team.

On the left-hand side of figure 4 below we can see three radar graphs representing the Law+ skills of three individuals. Reading from top to bottom we might expect these individuals to be (i) a legal technology consultant, (ii) a business analyst and (iii) a process engineer. On their own, none of them probably fulfils the requirements for solving a complex legal problem for a corporate client. When they are combined into a single team on the right-hand side of the figure, however, we see a much more holistic spread of skills.

Once the individuals who possess those skill sets are combined, then the skills of the team are built up. Not every matter will require a team that is expert in all four quadrants; it may be that a particular matter requires expert-level participants in just two quadrants, or

36

even just established individuals in three quadrants. The make-up of any legal team should also ensure that there are open lines of communication between the multidisciplinary professionals.

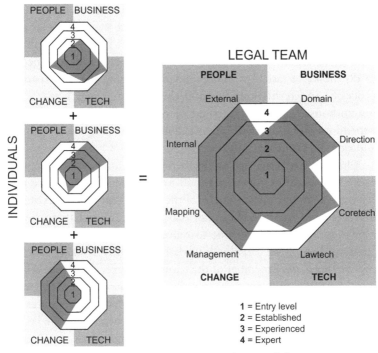

Figure 4. Radial mapping of Law+ skills.

There is more to combining Law+ skills than just bringing together a team of five specialists who know nothing but their own area. Putting a lawyer, a software developer, an anthropologist, a financial analyst and a process engineer together in a room is not going to get you very far – unless, perhaps, you are looking for the introduction to a joke. You need individuals who understand the various quadrants sufficiently to allow information and communication to flow. A good example is when lawyers need to communicate their requirements for the development of software to the IT team. Each side often makes assumptions that the other does not. I have all too often seen lawyers writing instructions for the IT team that require some knowledge of law that they do not possess, or the IT team using an acronym or asking for information in a format the lawyers cannot understand.

How to find the people who comprise the right mix is a factor that needs careful consideration. Some law firms have taken advantage of 'experience search' software and methodologies that can locate the appropriate lawyers who possess the right specialism for a given legal matter. Others have used specific teams of people to do the same task. I would envisage leveraging the same people, processes and technology to build the right mix in a Law+ team. For in-house teams, the method of picking the right people will depend on the individual organization – and may possibly require additional recruitment.

One thing to note with the Law+ model is that it will be rare that every member of a Law+ team will be a lawyer. The presence of a lawyer is already an implied part of the model, just like the existence of legal knowledge and skills is an assumed minimum bar for clients. However, if we take the time to reflect and put aside any preconceptions, I think we can all admit that it is highly unlikely that any client cares if *every* member of the team is a lawyer. What they want is for their legal problem to be solved. They want to work with a team that is able to give them the right legal advice within the context of their business – not just an advisor who tells them what the law is. There is no caveat that states that every member of the team must also be a lawyer and only a lawyer. This is already the case in certain sectors such as conveyancing and eDiscovery, where elements of the delivery of advice are provided by professionals other than lawyers. But this multidisciplinary mixing needs to go much wider, in partnering lawyers with those who have completely different skill sets to enhance the overall delivery.

ENTRY LEVEL

If a team or individual possesses an entry-level skill, that means that they have a foundation level of knowledge in the given quadrant and are able to understand the basics. At this stage no practical application has occurred, beyond perhaps a short training series or similar covering the essentials. The key facets of this level are that the team or individual should

- possess a broad understanding of the area in question;
- understand the basic language and terminology of the specialism; and
- be able to explain the key components of the area to someone else.

As much as I have talked about the possibility of individuals specializing in different quadrants of the Law+ model, I believe that having entry-level competence in every one of the quadrants is *essential* for all of those in the legal profession. Everyone in a legal team should have entry-level skills in Law+People, Law+Business, Law+Change and Law+Technology.

Even those lawyers who specialize deeply in one area of the law should be able to understand the terminology of each of the quadrants – if not for the sake of their own work, then for the ability to understand the world their clients inhabit. Possessing entry-level proficiency in all of the quadrants means being able to understand and communicate with those who are experienced or expert in those quadrants. This means being able to spot where a client's problem might go beyond the legal advice and knowing when to involve other specialists to solve it, whether you are a lawyer in a law firm or one in an in-house team. Business is done through the prism of all the quadrants, so those who are advising on business should be looking through the same prism.

ESTABLISHED LEVEL

The established level is really the first level at which people can begin to differentiate themselves from others, and where teams can start looking at building a range of specializations. Having established proficiency means that someone has a level of *applied* knowledge and practical application in an area. While this applied knowledge may be restricted to testing or simulated environments, rather than someone having been a frontline specialist, it goes beyond the entry level of simply completing some initial training sessions.

In addition to the skills of the entry level, those in the established level should

- possess more detailed knowledge of the quadrant and use that knowledge to enhance the delivery of legal services;
- make recommendations at the intersection of law and their quadrant as to an appropriate solution for a given problem; and
- be able to work with lawyers and those at the experienced and expert levels of the quadrant in order to facilitate solutions and review the solutions against the context and requirements provided.

The types of individuals inhabiting this role include lawyers who have taken an educational specialism in a quadrant, such as a master's-level course or beyond, or those who work in other quadrants that have actively engaged with additional professional training in order to upskill in a new quadrant, such as a project manager who completes a psychology degree to help them communicate better.

An individual may possess the established level in a number of quadrants. For example, a professional support or knowledge management lawyer may have law as their primary specialism but may also have taken a specific interest in Law+Technology and Law+Change. They can then work with lawyers on developing innovative ways of delivering legal services with knowledge of what is possible in the tech space, or on how to turn a legal problem into a process, for example.

While somebody at the established level would not be expected to take the lead on the work related to a particular quadrant, they are 'spanners'. This is not the insult it might appear – this is a term that refers to those who span the gap between law and the quadrants. In a world where each quadrant has its own language, those at the established level are like translators. While they are not necessarily native speakers themselves, they can help to ensure that the requirements of the lawyers are understood by the experienced- and expert-level professionals, and that the communications from the experienced- and expert-level professionals are properly understood by the lawyers.

It would be perfectly possible for someone to reach the established level in every quadrant (understanding that there would probably be a reduced specialization in legal practice itself as a result). The medical equivalent of this would be the GP: a general practitioner who is able to make a diagnosis and then refer their patient onto the appropriate team of specialists.

EXPERIENCED LEVEL

People with an experienced proficiency possess an advanced level of applied knowledge and practical application. This means that not only do they possess the language and an understanding of the quadrant, but they can also be left to work within that quadrant with minimal supervision. A simple example of someone who fits this description is a legal technologist who is qualified as a lawyer but also as a software engineer, or a legal engineer who can break down and improve processes.

In addition to the above levels, those at the experienced level should

- possess in-depth knowledge of the quadrant and use that knowledge to enhance the delivery of legal services;
- be able to work in the area by themselves on tasks with minimal supervision;
- devise and design solutions, understanding where experts are needed and what tasks they need to do; and
- be able to manage projects involving their quadrants effectively.

The experienced level is where we start getting into the realm of dual-specialism individuals. In reality, I would not expect many practising lawyers to progress beyond this level in any quadrant, although there will of course be a small number, such as those qualified lawyers who have chosen to leave practice and pursue another career within the profession. It is highly unlikely that anyone would be able to hit the experienced level in all of the quadrants.

It is at the experienced proficiency level that, for the first time in the Law+ model, we encounter those who will work in teams while possessing little to no legal knowledge. Examples include those in innovation and technology roles, or in business development or learning and development, who may never have obtained a practising certificate but are essential for the delivery of legal services. I would also include at this level business and data analysts who work in the legal sphere without having undertaken legal training.

This is a field in which legal still needs to make significant strides. Although there is increasing recognition that multidisciplinary teams are needed, there is a difference between hiring lawyers or ex-lawyers who have acquired new skills and recruiting those who have only ever worked in different fields. It is here that the structure of law firms works against promoting Law+ skills: where the ownership is comprised solely of lawyers and where all of the reward schemes are primarily built around how lawyers work, it is difficult to entice someone from another field. A forward-thinking in-house legal team, however, may better appreciate and attract talent from outside the profession, having the advantage of structures and reward schemes that are attuned to how a business operates. There is an increased chance of collaboration between legal and business services teams in-house, where legal departments may have the opportunity to integrate and work with specialists from around the business where these talents may already exist.

EXPERT LEVEL

The expert level is reserved for those who are outstanding in their field. Experts possess specialist applied knowledge, have extensive experience in the area, and are able to teach others those skills. In many competence frameworks, the final stage of mastery is being able to share your knowledge with others, and so it is here. It would be incredibly rare to find anyone who was an expert in multiple Law+ quadrants.

More specifically, in addition to the above skill levels, experts should

- possess mastery of the quadrant and use that mastery to enhance the delivery of legal services;

- be able to serve as single points of expertise in their area;
- be capable of teaching others their skills and knowledge;
- have the ability to devise, design and fully implement solutions within their area; and
- work effectively with those from other areas.

The expert level will usually be reserved for those who do not have any background in law but who are just as important as the lawyers in a legal team. Somebody who had become an expert in a Law+ quadrant while still practising as a lawyer and giving advice would be exceptional indeed.

Experts should still possess at least entry-level legal skills in other quadrants – and in law itself – to enable them to work in the legal sphere and to understand what is being asked of them, but it is also likely that there will be other 'translators' within the team who straddle two or more quadrants at varying proficiencies who will serve as the middle ground between experts in Law+ skills and expert lawyers. Those at expert level may be referred to as 'SMEs' (subject matter experts), who are perceived to be at the same level of seniority as expert lawyers.

PART II

THE WHAT
THE LAW+ SKILLS

The four quadrants of Law+ skills are each split into two areas spanning the range of Law+People, Law+Business, Law+Change and Law+Technology. An understanding of the content of these areas can help you to identify and map the skills required of a modern legal team, and to understand what other skills may be missing or are present but are currently unrecognized. Consider this the first step on the path to achieving entry-level skills in each of the quadrants.

CHAPTER 4

Law+People

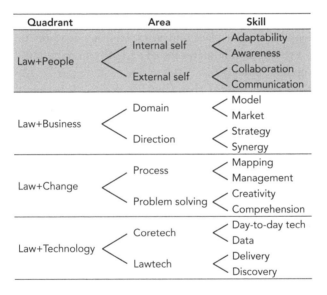

Quadrant	Area	Skill
Law+People	Internal self	Adaptability
		Awareness
	External self	Collaboration
		Communication
Law+Business	Domain	Model
		Market
	Direction	Strategy
		Synergy
Law+Change	Process	Mapping
		Management
	Problem solving	Creativity
		Comprehension
Law+Technology	Coretech	Day-to-day tech
		Data
	Lawtech	Delivery
		Discovery

This is the quadrant that I believe is the most important. Every single one of your clients is a person (or is represented by a person). Everyone you work with is a person. Every member of your team is a person. And, of course, you are a person too.

This is the foundation upon which all the other quadrants stand. A large part of the reason for trying to understand Law+Business is so that you can comprehend the business drivers and reasons for the activities undertaken by the people in legal teams and their clients. Law+Change involves the processes with which people engage. You cannot discover those processes unless you ask the right questions in the right way, and you will certainly not get anyone to change without selling the people affected by it on that change. Likewise, project management inevitably means managing people, and to manage people well you need to understand them. The application of Law+Technology skills to advise clients requires an understanding of how that client is going to use that advice, and if we are to engage people with new technologies we first need to understand their positions and how they might react to the way in which technology works. Even those who consider themselves experts in technology and artificial intelligence are required to interact with people in order to understand the requirements of creating the technology in the first place and to explain how it works to others. There is a reason that 'human-centred design' is an important element of developing technology.

It is for these reasons that Law+People is split between people skills associated with the internal self, i.e. ones that we can cultivate within ourselves and that affect our own mindset, and the external self, i.e. those that affect our interaction with others. Basically put, Law+People skills are either 'to me' or 'to you'.

Case study. The O Shaped Pilots

During 2019 and 2020, the O Shaped Lawyer group conducted seven real-time practical O Shaped Pilots with some of the most progressive in-house and private practice teams in the United Kingdom.

The pilots gave the teams time and space to explore how they could be most aligned to create a 'one team' approach that provided the business customer with the best possible legal service. Each pilot focused on one of the three buckets of the 'O Shaped Attributes': (i) building relationships, (ii) creating value and (iii) being adaptable.

In terms of their impact, one pilot involved a top-twenty law firm and a FTSE 250 client. The pilot comprised teams of different experience levels from both the law firm and the client attending fourteen 1.5-hour sessions together during the course of a client legal matter. The aim was to embed the O Shaped Attributes into the day-to-day relationship between the client and their legal advisors.

Working through the three buckets of skills, and under the supervision of a member of the O Shaped Steering Board, the group openly and proactively explored areas in which they could improve their service to the end user. With the support of Pirical, the HR data analytics experts, measurements of performance against the buckets were taken ahead of each session. The findings were that there was a significant improvement in awareness and skills development for the participants in all three buckets. The process resulted in fundamental changes to the relationship between the client and the law firm, including the introduction of

- regular post-transaction reviews and feedback sessions,
- joint meetings between all levels of seniority at both the client and law firm,
- joint training sessions, covering both technical and business skills,
- an increased number of social events, and
- peer-to-peer mentoring programmes.

See www.oshapedlawyer.com/the-pilot for more information on the O Shaped Pilots.

AREA 1: INTERNAL SELF

Adaptability

I have said several times already that the legal profession is changing and will continue to do so. Being able not only to cope with change but to thrive upon it is a skill that is vitally important to legal professionals. Of course, this has always been a key skill for lawyers. The law itself is constantly updating, and business situations can rapidly shift with little to no warning. The pace of change has picked up in the last decade, however, and the changes have expanded beyond simply being about what the legal rules are and now extend into questioning the way in which legal advice is delivered.

I have had the benefit through my time in legal education and practice to ask groups of students, lawyers and in-house counsel – in many different and varied settings – which skills they think are most important for the legal team of the future. It has got to the point where I can predict the answers before the audience vote, and there are two skills that are always guaranteed to be at the top of the list. One of those is adaptability – that is, being equipped to respond positively to change. The other is commercial awareness – something that forms part of Law+Business (see page 54).

As with many people skills, adaptability comes naturally to some. I work in an area of legal services – innovation – where people are always looking at what comes next and are excited and inspired by change. But not everyone is, and that is OK. It would be a boring world if we were all the same. Just because something does not come naturally to you, though, does not mean that you cannot ever improve. The skills contained within adaptability are resilience and independence, which combine to allow you to see change as an opportunity rather than an obstacle and to help you build the mental health and well-being needed to thrive in the legal profession.

Resilience

One of the key elements of being adaptable is being resilient. Often seen as being as difficult a concept to define as adaptability, resilience is the ability to effectively recover when one suffers setbacks, meets obstacles or encounters failure. As Bruce Lee once said: 'Do not fear failure. Not failure, but low aim, is the crime. In great attempts, it is glorious even to fail.'

Why is resilience important? Because trying new things means encountering failure. If people want to achieve a goal, it is incredibly rare that success 'just happens'. There is no magic pill or genie that can make wishes come true. Instead, it takes hard work and the ability to recognize failure.

Look at the Wright brothers, for example. Orville and Wilbur did not simply jump in an aircraft and have it fly. It took them years of trying and failing. It is not enough to just fail, of course. Anyone can fail. We must *learn* from that failure. When an aircraft did not work, the Wright brothers did not just try exactly the same thing again. They made adjustments and learned from that failure how to do things better next time. Even in the classic film *Chitty Chitty Bang Bang* the inventors recognize that you should be grateful for mistakes because they ensure that you will not make such a mistake again. That film may have been released in 1968, but this point is still very valid today.

The fear of failure is a problem in legal services. Law students are taught from an early stage that lawyers exist to *prevent* failure. They are given high-stakes assessments and, depending on their career trajectory, they are told that a single failure in any of those assessments means losing their job. There is a lot of pressure. And this does not stop once a lawyer is in practice, either; there are always deadlines, and having complex and intense matters to work on is a constant. It is as if lawyers carry with them the persistent spectre of failure – a Sword of Damocles hanging above their heads, with no clue of when it will fall. The culture does not help, of course – we do not have *time* to fail when every hour is being billed.

Let me tell you a secret. Every single lawyer you know – no matter how senior they might be; how much of a hotshot they are – has failed. For me, the failure I most remember was not getting every signature at a closing, meaning a frantic chase to beat a client to the airport so they could sign before they got on a plane.* Others have accidentally copied people into an email that they should not have, or sent the wrong document to the wrong place, or missed a filing deadline. Whatever the failure is, you can bet it was one we generally learned from and never did again. The problem is that nobody really talks about this, and as a result the willingness to fail seems to be the one thing that eludes the legal profession. The first element of being resilient, then, is to try new things and to learn from them when things go wrong.

The second element of being resilient is being able to recover from setbacks. Every time lawyers work on a matter, there are multiple rounds of reviews, feedback and amendments on every single document. Being able to take on board that feedback without it completely

---

*I got there in the end, so everything worked out.

ruining your day is something that is vital to your work. No draft of any document is ever perfect, and entire sections of documents will be rewritten and deleted before a matter is complete.

A huge number of people in the legal industry suffer with imposter syndrome, which is the feeling that you are a fraud who does not belong and who is always on the brink of being 'found out'.[1] This is easy to understand when your work is constantly being subjected to major and minor amendments that can make you feel like you cannot even grasp the essentials. However, these feelings are often unfounded: if you have made it into the profession, you belong there.

Looking beyond failure, if you were to ask a number of lawyers what resilience is, they would tell you that it is the ability to thrive in the high-pressure environment of the legal profession. Although this assessment of resilience is not false, I am reluctant to say anything like 'there are long hours in law, so you better get used to it', because it does not always have to be this way. There are many legal teams outside of larger law firms that do not have to work those long hours. But I am also not going to deny that long hours are sometimes necessary. Not because I had to go through those hours and I want to inflict them on someone else, but because there will always be deadlines in the fast-moving world of law. There is always going to be a company that wants to list on the stock exchange and realizes it needs to do so before its accounts go out of date, or an organization that needs to deal with some litigation within a court-mandated timeline. If you can cope under these conditions – indeed, if you can *thrive* under them – then you are going to be a better lawyer.

Independence

The term 'independence' is a catch-all for skills that are named variously as courage, the ability to take initiative, and actively seeking feedback. There is often an element of hesitation within legal to do something new. This is understandable: the power behind legal advice is that it is based on years of precedent and rules, and there is often little sense in reinventing the wheel each time when there is already a set of agreed-upon terms and processes that make business run smoothly. This can be all well and good, but what if the wheel we are failing to reinvent is *actually* square? Having the independence to think differently can set you and your organization apart from the pack. Take easyJet, for example, who changed their law firm pitch process in 2021. Instead of the standard pack of lengthy documentation, the company decided to review its roster of external advisers by giving all of the prospective legal teams a simulated Himalayan mountaineering expedition. They were looking for teams with whom they could work comfortably; teams who communicated well and worked together. It is no surprise that the easyJet general counsel Maaike de Bie was awarded the GC of the Year at the 2021 Legal Business Awards.

It is difficult to take action in the face of fear or uncertainty. I recall that I started in practice shortly after the implementation of the *Mercury* case.[2] Without going into a long discussion of the case, it basically changed the way that documents had to be signed in England and Wales: signature pages could no longer simply be signed in isolation – potentially before the documents were even complete – but had to be connected to the final version of an agreement. I remembered hearing about this in an update delivered by the knowledge management team, so when a partner asked for signature pages in a closing in a manner that was not compliant with *Mercury*, I was pretty sure that was not allowed. It took a *lot* of steeling myself and overcoming self-doubt before I felt able to confront the partner about this. As it turned out, I was right. But the fear almost led me to say nothing – something that would have meant risking the whole deal. People need to feel they can speak up and be heard, and likewise firms need to reward curiosity and independence of thought.

If nobody says 'Why am I doing it this way rather than that way?' nothing ever improves. Likewise, if someone does not feel like their voice is valued in an organization, that will hinder their motivation and encourage them to move elsewhere. Retaining people means building a culture in which people feel like they can explore alternative avenues to completing their work. Courage is not something that applies only to junior lawyers; new ways of working are sometimes not explored because more senior lawyers do not have the courage to talk to their clients and ask them if they can help in other ways. If we can build an environment in which lawyers feel able to ask their clients such questions, we can more readily discover the challenges that exist in individual matters and the profession as a whole and find ways to solve them.

Actively seeking feedback is an important part of progressing in your career, and it is especially important in law. With senior associates and partners under time pressure to complete matters and move on to the next job, they can forget to give feedback on the work completed by juniors. It is all too often the case in practice that first-draft documents prepared by juniors are received, amended and sent to the client by a senior lawyer without the junior being involved in that process. The final document that is sent can often bear little resemblance to the document as it was first drafted. Having the confidence to ask for feedback about that document at an appropriate time means gaining the opportunity to understand where the issues were and to improve next time, which is something that benefits both the junior and the senior in this situation. It can be hard to ask for feedback, but if handled appropriately it is always well worth it.

Awareness

If adaptability is the ability to cope with failure and with new ways of doing things, then awareness is knowing yourself and continuously looking to improve. This is a skill that goes hand in hand with adaptability; the more you learn, the more equipped you are to deal with change.

Mental health and well-being

If nothing else, the pandemic did a fantastic job of showing us how much we need interaction with other people, with restrictions on seeing people cited as one of the major factors in deteriorating mental health during the Covid-19 period.[3]

Mental health is one of the key issues affecting the legal community, and this was true even before taking into account the extra issues that the pandemic brought about. The 2021 LawCare 'Life in the Law' survey found that 69% of legal professionals had experience of mental ill-health in the 12 months prior to completing the survey. Similarly, research from McKinsey found that top post-pandemic priorities in 2021 for those planning to leave their jobs were the need to 'restore work–life balance (65%)' and to prioritize 'physical and emotional well-being again (63%)'.[4]

Knowing your own limits is important, not only so that you can be your best self at work, but also so that you have good mental health, meaning that you will live a longer and happier life. With the high pressure and the reluctance to fail in the legal profession comes an unwillingness to expose vulnerabilities and to talk about problems. When I encountered mental health problems while working in practice I did not feel like I could talk to anyone at the firm about my issues, but I am sure there were plenty of people who would have helped had I asked. The problem was that the environment at that time was not one that encouraged me to do so. We need to be better at recognizing our own limits and at seeing when we are under too much stress. We need to find ways to cope with that stress and to manage relationships with others so that we can support each other. There is often a perception that business and emotions do not mix, but the more we understand ourselves and those with whom we work, the more likely we are to be able to communicate and collaborate in a way that is best for everyone. Learning about mental health and being aware of our own emotions is vital to interacting with others and ensuring that we are motivated and productive at work.

Growth mindset

Despite the opinions of some I have encountered, a 'growth mindset' does *not* refer to financial growth. Instead, a growth mindset is where someone is voluntarily attempting to develop themselves by learning new things, seeking feedback from others, and embracing the new. Someone who possesses a fixed mindset, on the other hand, believes that their knowledge and talent are fixed, and they therefore do not seek to progress.

To give a real-world example, I have encountered many lawyers who have said something along the lines of 'I do not do numbers'. I have met an equal number who have decided that they 'cannot do technology'. These fixed-mindset people believe that their intelligence level and their skill set are defined by the 'lawyer' box, and that they cannot acquire new skills. It is as if the brain were a glass jug that is currently filled to the brim with 'law', meaning that pouring in any 'business' or 'technology' is going to cause all the law to overflow and be lost forever. Adopting a growth mindset means increasing the size of the jug while retaining *all* its water. Because those with fixed mindsets believe that the snapshot of your current skills and intelligence is all you ever get, they are often afraid to divulge that they have encountered *any* failures and instead seek to prove that their intelligence is higher than anyone around them – even when it is not.

Those who possess a growth mindset tend to engage with 'lifelong learning'. There is no magic to this term: it just means continuing to seek out development of knowledge and skills throughout our lives – something that is a fundamental part of acting on a growth mindset. It is a term that is popular in the education sphere, where there is a recognition that the knowledge and skills that we acquire during our period of compulsory formal education are no longer sufficient to maintain a lifelong career in most professions, which are continually changing and evolving. Law is no different.

It is important to note that *all* of us have some elements of a fixed mindset. There are always things that make us uncomfortable, or subjects on which we already believe ourselves to be experts, meaning we are therefore afraid to dig any further lest we learn that we are not as expert as we believe. Those who know the least about a subject can often talk the loudest. This is known as the Dunning–Kruger effect. The Dunning–Kruger effect, as examined in psychology, is where those with limited knowledge or competence in a particular area drastically overestimate their own level of knowledge or competence compared with others. The more we know about ourselves, the better we are going to be at our jobs, whatever that job may be. An awareness of the Dunning–Kruger effect is important, as it is the first step to recognizing that none of us knows everything. Those who can accept that fact are more readily able to work with others who possess the expertise that we lack. It is also important that people who think they are experts while being anything but do not tout that expertise to clients, who will be disappointed and frustrated when the truth is revealed. The general rule is that the more all-knowing someone claims to be in an area, the greater the chance they are not. I have encountered junior lawyers who describe themselves as experts in their areas of law, and I have spoken to partners in that same practice group who admit that they are only scratching the surface of what there is to know.

How does this apply to legal services and finding new ways to solve problems? Well, if we look at the way lawyers talk to clients, there is often an unwillingness to let those who specialize in areas other than law speak to clients. I know for a fact that there are a sizeable number of relationship partners and associates who are not asking their clients about new ways of doing things because they are afraid that the response will be outside the realm of what they know, and this will somehow reveal the lawyer as lacking in some way. This is despite the fact that they are a leading practitioner of the law and know more about law than a project manager, for example, ever will. I am not sure exactly what it is they are afraid of, because the average lawyer is *more* than happy to admit they know nothing about tax law, and that does not seem to make lawyers doubt their intelligence level. It is as if they think the client will be so disappointed that they will instantly stop instructing the lawyer, or will at least think less of them because they do not know everything.

Having a growth mindset, then, means recognizing that we all have shortcomings in our knowledge and skills and continuing to seek out learning opportunities in order to evolve throughout our careers.

Empathy and emotional intelligence: part 1

Empathy is often confused with sympathy. The difference is basically that sympathy is when you feel bad for someone else, or when you share their emotion – usually sadness – about something. Empathy, on the other hand, is the ability to put yourself in someone else's shoes even when you do not feel the same as they do. While empathy affects how we interact with others, it is a skill that we must first cultivate in ourselves, and we must therefore be aware not only of how *others* may feel or how they might like to be treated but also of our *own* feelings and emotions and how those come to the fore when we are communicating.

According to Daniel Goleman – a leading scholar in the field of emotional intelligence (EQ) for organizations and leaders – there are four elements to EQ: (i) self-awareness, (ii) self-management, (iii) social awareness and (iv) relationship management. The first two relate to reading and comprehending our own emotions; the latter two are connected to our interactions with others.

Self-awareness is fairly simple in its definition: it is being able to understand, accept and reflect upon the emotions you feel and the ways in which you act upon those emotions. This means, for example, identifying why receiving a heavily marked up contract from a supervisor makes you feel upset. The reason this is important is that it can help to guide the way in which we act in our business interactions and how we understand others. The better we comprehend how emotions can affect the way in which we and others act, the better we will collaborate. So, if you find yourself on the receiving end of a draft contract that has been almost entirely rewritten by your supervisor – in red pen, no less – you can acknowledge that you are upset and angry about the situation and can reflect instead of overreacting and doubting your own abilities, which may affect your future performance.

In his book *The Emotionally Intelligent Workplace*, Goleman found that emotional competencies were twice as prevalent as technical skills and cognitive abilities *combined* for staff in all kinds of jobs.[5] Further, he stated that the more senior you are in an organization, the more EQ matters. Understanding our emotions gives us an awareness of the fact that different actions have different emotional consequences, and it also adds to our understanding of how those emotions might develop and affect others.

An increased comprehension of our feelings, drivers and emotions allows us to have more control over the direction of our careers. This is the self-management aspect: not letting emotions overwhelm you and decide your course of action. Rather than being rational, your reaction to a given workplace situation might be the result of your brain going into 'fight or flight' mode. The issue is that this mental defence mechanism was designed to keep us physically safe by shutting down complex emotions, so that we either run or stand our ground. While this reaction might be really useful if you are up against a hungry predator, it is not so great when you are in the workplace and that threat is emotional in nature. Appreciating this can help you take a more measured response that benefits you more in the long run.

Think about a negotiation over a draft of a contract. Seeing changes to inconsequential language by the other side can make you feel furious. But if they do not change the meaning of the contract, should you really be wasting your time and energy on disputing the changes? Would your client want you to do that? We lawyers are often quite competitive, and that drive to 'win' can get in the way of good business. Thinking again about the earlier example of an amended mark-up from a supervisor, self-management can help us to stop before responding off-the-cuff in an unprofessional manner that is fuelled by an immediate emotional reaction.

The skill of being able to understand yourself and how you react is called reflection. Being able to reflect upon the past and being aware of where you went wrong or did well previously is an important step in doing better in the future. Reflection is not always easy, but it adds to resilience and it can encourage us to understand how others might react or why they react the way they do to certain situations. It was an ancient Greek maxim that you should 'know thyself', and it still rings true today. A reflective practitioner is one who is more aware of the feelings and motivations of others and who can therefore adjust their own approach in line with that awareness, resulting in the delivery of advice in a contextual manner.

AREA 2: EXTERNAL SELF

Collaboration

Empathy and emotional intelligence: part 2

The last two elements of Goleman's four dimensions of EQ are social awareness and relationship management. Understanding others and their organizations can help us to work with them, to guide them, to influence them, and to build connections between people. I think we can all agree that all of those things are important for legal advisors.

The general perception of lawyers is that they are not always great at understanding the perspectives, drivers and emotions of others. Take the Princeton University study in figure 5, which mapped out various professions on a warmth–competence scale based on responses from the public. I have made one of the circles black to help you find the legal profession. Spoiler: it does not come off well.

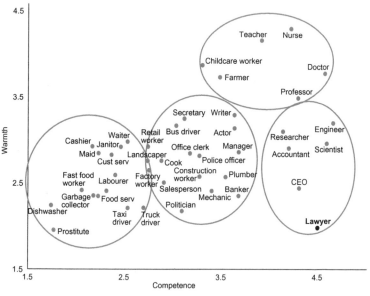

Figure 5. The competence and warmth of different professions.[6]

As you can see, the legal profession is perceived as one that ranks highly with regards to competence but much lower in terms of warmth. Even when grouped with others of the same ilk, such as accountants, scientists and engineers, lawyers rank by far the lowest for warmth. Because this was a survey that involved the public at large, it might seem easy for those in law firms and legal teams who are working in more commercial settings to dismiss the findings, but clients are invariably human (or represented by humans), and given the findings of organizations such as the O Shaped Lawyer group, this perceived lack of empathy resonates as much with clients as it does with the average person on the street.

Even if you accept being an unfeeling robot in your personal life, you might be wondering if being unable to understand the emotions of others really affects you at work. The answer, I am afraid, is yes. Being able to put yourself in the shoes of your client – whether that is an external client or an internal business client – is vital when providing legal advice. We cannot advise in a vacuum. Laws look neat and clean on a page, but in the real world their implementation is messy, with the position of our clients a major factor in how they should be applied. For example, a client whose business is on the verge of going bankrupt is in a very different situation to a client whose business is growing. A piece of advice for a CEO should not be delivered in the same way as a submission to a judge. I cannot tell you how many times I had to tell a student in an interviewing assessment that the proper response to someone who has just gone through a messy divorce is not 'great, that's fantastic'. They were so focused on getting the facts that they forgot the person. Possessing EQ can help us to appreciate the positions of our clients and can enhance the delivery of advice by factoring in the realities of the situation at hand. If that is not enough to convince you of its importance, then factor in that understanding the emotions of others also means being able to comprehend their perspectives and agendas in a way that can be useful in negotiations or adversarial situations. It will help you to anticipate how others will react. It can also be useful when making a sale – whether that is selling additional legal services, a new product, a particular legal position or a continued business relationship. To put it simply: understanding the emotions of ourselves and others makes us better advisors.

And, of course, possessing EQ also makes us better colleagues and teammates, with a greater ability to appreciate the skills and knowledge of others and the ways in which we can best interact. Only those who are unable to understand the emotions of others would use the term 'non-lawyer', for example, as it immediately defines that other person using a negative, showing that they are not valued to the same level as a lawyer no matter how much of a specialist they are in their own profession. We need to consider the relationships that we cultivate within our own organizations as well. All too often have I seen junior lawyers be dismissive to secretaries, for example, despite the fact that not only are those secretaries humans, just like them, but they might have been with the organization far longer and understand it much better too. We have to accept that we are more than just our business roles and that the level of seniority at work does not equate to level of importance in life.

Teamwork

Teamwork takes many forms, but at its heart it is about working effectively with others both in the short term and in the long term. This means being able to work with those within our organizations but also with our clients and even, dare I say it, with our competitors. In terms of working with clients, collaboration means identifying shared objectives when delivering legal advice. Those who excel at teamwork are able to pull together teams that might be diverse and cross-disciplinary to solve problems. That means quickly identifying times when a client might need a solution that is more than just law and working out who therefore needs to work on that matter. Those who are good at working in teams can engage in collaborative problem solving to achieve positive outcomes.

The benefits of collaboration are also greater than the simple sum of the parts of those working together. The founders of the Bionic Lawyer Project often talk about the 'economics of collaboration', which essentially boils down to $1 + 1 = 3$. So how does that work? Well, when you bring two people together with two points of view, you do not just get two perspectives. What you instead get is the two individual perspectives and a new *shared* perspective that combines elements of both. In fact, $1 + 1$ can sometimes equal a whole lot more than 3, because in collaborating and sharing their points of view, those two people might come up with lots of new ideas that they never would have explored had they approached the problem on their own. All too often when we work alone we are convinced that our ideas are right without checking with anyone else.

But what about working as a team with our competitors? The economics of collaboration come in here too. Think about it: right now, a lot of law firms and legal teams are seeking to do business in new ways and to find new services and methods of delivering those services. They are setting up focus groups and think tanks and thought leadership initiatives, and they are employing new technologies and techniques that have not previously been used in law. That means that many teams are trying out things that other teams have already tried and seen fail, and it means that clients and third-party suppliers are having to collaborate with their lawyers in a huge variety of ways. For a large in-house team that has a panel of lawyers, having twelve different extranets, all housed in different technologies with different data standards and rules surrounding permissions, is not the most helpful approach. What if that information was shared? It would introduce standardization, saving legal teams time and effort.

For those worried about sharing, this is not about handing over confidential client information or anything business sensitive. If we are honest, it is not as if one law firm is going to suddenly achieve some sort of innovative nirvana that other firms cannot even touch – a breakthrough that will give that firm such a competitive advantage that it will render all other firms useless. We need to progress together as a profession for our clients. With that in mind, can we all just get over ourselves and start to think about this together? Look at the decision in Europe to make USB-C the standard format for charging. We do not usually choose a smartphone for the way it charges, but having the same charger for all of our devices makes our lives easier. You can apply this to clients who are currently receiving data about spend and matters in different ways. They are not choosing their firms based on the data format, so we really should just agree one method for everyone.

The oneNDA project and the resultant Claustack community are a good example of cross-legal collaboration. It would be great to see more.

Case study. oneNDA and Claustack

The oneNDA project started with a single question: What if we all agreed to adopt one identical NDA template? This question was posed on LinkedIn in January 2021 by Electra Japonas, the CEO and founder of TLB. The reason she asked the question was because research conducted by TLB had found that while 63%

of their workload was in reviewing NDAs, that work accounted for only 7% of revenue, and they were pretty sure they were not alone in this.

The project quickly gained traction, with a website set up in February 2021 for people to express interest hitting 100 participants within 12 hours of launch. By the end of February that number was 330, and by July, when the oneNDA document was finalized, there were more than a thousand participating organizations, including both law firms and in-house teams from across the world. After establishing a Steering Committee, and in collaboration with the oneNDA Founding Club and oneNDA members, a standard-form NDA was created in just five months.

Since its launch, the initiative has attracted global interest: the oneNDA document has been downloaded more than 8,600 times; more than 600 organizations have adopted oneNDA as their organizational standard; and 10,000 people have signed up to the mailing list. As of March 2022, the group has launched a new version of the oneNDA and a new M&A-specific oneNDA form called 'oneNDA + M&A'. The group behind oneNDA have also established Claustack, a standardization-focused legal community platform where members of the legal community can download existing documents and participate in future standardization initiatives by providing feedback or spearheading an initiative of their own.

It is not just in standardization that collaboration with competitors is important: it would also be beneficial in traditionally contentious activities such as negotiation. Yes, believe it or not, negotiation *is* a form of collaboration. All too often – especially during the early stages of training lawyers – negotiation is perceived as some sort of competition that can be won. After spending a few years in the world of business, however, it is patently obvious that this is not the case.

I had first-hand experience of this in my time teaching corporate finance. During the course, we used to teach a session in which we negotiated a loan agreement. I taught this session in various forms for eight years, for both full-time students and part-time ones. Although the groups were not entirely homogeneous, full-time students tended not to have worked for any long stretch of time in another career, while those in part-time study either were switching from established careers or were in the world of work (necessitating the part-time model). The negotiation proceeded very differently between these groups.

In the activity, one group was representing a fictional bank while the other was representing a fictional corporation who wanted to borrow money from the bank. The balance of power in the relationship was fairly equal, but the majority of power was held by the bank. Each group was given instructions from their client about what needed to be achieved. What was not in those instructions, but which was supposed to be abundantly clear given the scenario, was that the loan was something that both parties wanted to happen.

The full-time students used the whole of their two-hour session finding ways to 'win' – sometimes by trying to sneak in extra clauses to catch out the other party, sometimes by haggling over something their client had not instructed them about, sometimes by just flat-out refusing changes. Honestly, between teaching and practice I have probably spent more of my life than is healthy listening to people argue over whether somebody should be giving their 'best' endeavours or just 'reasonable' endeavours.* In many instances, no accord was reached. The part-time students, however, often spent, say, fifteen minutes agreeing what seemed like commercially sensible provisions and the negotiation was then complete. Spoiler: all the suggested amendments were commercially sensible.

This difference between the groups was because, on the whole, the part-time students appreciated something that the full-time students missed: by the time the parties were approaching lawyers they had already decided that the relationship they were entering was one they both wanted. This was not a case of a company somehow forcing a bank to lend them money, nor was the bank trying to sneak into the company and dump a load of cash in their safe without them noticing only to then charge them interest on it. The point of the lawyers in this situation was not to win, but to negotiate a suitable position for their client in the event that anything should go wrong, with both parties hoping it would not, and that if it did it

---

*What is more, I am still not sure I entirely understand the difference!

would not be their fault. This meant that 'catching out' the borrower did not help the bank because a forced early repayment messed with the bank's projections for its money flow. In the same vein, the client somehow managing to escape ever having to pay interest because of some creative drafting might be a success for that particular loan, but that is a ruined relationship and the company is going to struggle to borrow money in the future if it is needed.

Contentious litigation aside, the majority of the parties in the types of business transaction that this book focuses on want the transaction to happen. The destination is the same; the role of the lawyers in negotiating is to decide how the path reaches that destination, and maybe to see just how much it can meander in their client's favour on the way. There are opportunities for lawyers to become involved in those initial business decisions, of course, but at the time of negotiation the role of the lawyer is clear: get the deal done and make sure the client is protected if something goes wrong. Achieving that requires working as a team with the other side.

Influencing

A lot of time and effort in practice is devoted to the training and advancement of future and junior lawyers. This is understandable: they are at the start of their careers, and they need to take on a lot of information about their chosen profession while also being inducted into the legal team and into how everything works. As a result, the skill of influencing is often not considered in as high regard as other skills when looking at the legal skills of the future because it is one that becomes more important the more senior a person becomes, and at those later stages of a career the concerns of actually doing work tend to trump learning about new skills.

A person who is skilled at influencing can gain the trust of others and can guide, encourage and persuade those people through their actions. This is a vital skill for lawyers to possess as the delivery of legal services requires 'trusted advisors' whose advice is taken on board by clients. However, it is also important when applied to wider legal teams in building relationships and working with others. Those who can influence others are also skilled at diffusing tension and dealing with difficult conversations, whether they are with clients or with other members of the legal team. Basically, those who can influence others are better at getting everyone to pull together, meaning that there are fewer disagreements and that when disagreements do occur, they are usually dealt with in a way that is satisfactory to all. For those in more senior positions, influencing is a core skill. If people do not trust you, they are unlikely to follow you, especially when you are instigating change.

Communication

Delivery

There is great power in being able to deliver a message in a manner that resonates with your audience. As lawyers, the message we have to deliver is often a negative one: somebody is not permitted to do something, for example, or certain arduous rules have to be followed in order to do that thing. The method of delivery of that message is therefore hugely important.

When teaching, one of the activities I used to give my students was to research whether a company was able to issue shares, i.e. sell a portion of its ownership in order to raise money to avoid bankruptcy. Understanding whether the company could do so required some in-depth research about the relevant law and the structure of the company in question. Once the research was complete, I asked the students to feed back to me as I role-played the client. The interactions more often than not went something like this:

Me: So, what did you find out in relation to our problem?
Student (proudly): We have figured it out and you cannot issue the shares.
Me: Sorry?
Student (still proudly): You cannot issue the shares. As you can see from Rule ...
Me (interjecting): So, we need to raise money to avoid bankruptcy and you're telling me we can't? How does that solve my problem?
Student (now not so proudly): Er ...

The technical ability was there, and the answer was correct; the company was not able to issue the shares in the manner in which they intended to do so. However, there was little thought given by the students to the client or to their situation, despite having been notified in advance about the bankruptcy issue. It is possible to deliver that same 'you cannot do it' message in a very different way – one that suggests a way in which the issue of shares *could* go ahead. There is power in thinking about the message.*

This sort of behaviour is not restricted to the classroom. When I have had the opportunity to speak to in-house teams about their interactions with their law firms, they almost always have something to say about the method of delivery of advice. The complaint is usually about receiving hundreds of pages of advice that the in-house team then has to turn into a handful of slides to present back to their CEO in the format that the CEO prefers. I have never spoken to a client who starts off by complimenting a law firm on getting the law right; they expect that. To say that a lawyer is a great advisor because they always get the law right is like saying a pilot is amazing because the plane has never crashed. Dig a little deeper, though, and you might find out that the pilot in question often takes off from the runway late, consistently takes strange routes that add hours onto flight times, and flies so erratically that the constant turbulence makes everyone sick. Delivery is important. So it is for clients, who are often presented with encyclopaedic explanations of the law without any consideration given to the reason they needed to know the law in the first place. Both the method of delivery and its content need to be carefully considered.

Those skilled at communication should be able to clearly explain the legal concept they are trying to convey in a manner that is suitable for their client. Let us take the example of a US company that needs to know the status of Covid-19 return-to-work laws across all fifty states. The traditional format of delivering legal advice for something like this would be a voluminous Microsoft Word document running

---

*I should clarify that my classrooms were always very safe spaces where these points were discussed in detail, and I did not delight in trying to catch out students.

to tens of pages. If the client is lucky, there might be a table within that document, but that table cannot be easily filtered or reordered. The correct method for delivery depends on how the client is going to use the information, but it is unlikely that a static table is going to be the best option. If the company just wants to check one or two states every so often, then they might be best served by an interactive database where they do not have to see all the information at once and can instead filter results as required. If they are trying to see when they can get people back into the office and they therefore need to compare multiple states at once, they might like a traffic light solution that colour codes the status as red, green or amber depending on the law in a given state. If the information is needed as part of a large-scale strategic analysis of a business model, then it might be appreciated in a clean data set that can be combined with other data the company is using. The skill of communication – whether it is in written or oral form – is not simply being able to clearly articulate a subject, but being able to do so in a format that is appropriate for the audience.

Another vital skill when considering communication is being open and transparent. It is also in keeping lines of communication open. At the end of any legal matter a client is going to be receiving a bill. Generally, that bill will include the time spent on various portions of the matter. If you have not kept up to date with the client on the running fee, for example, that cost might come as a surprise. Likewise, if you are engaging in months of back-and-forth negotiation with the lawyers on the other side without including the client in those communications, they are either going to think that you have stopped working on the matter altogether or they are going to be annoyed that they are charged for those months of work without having any evidence that you actually did anything during that time.

This is not just important externally, of course. For law firms and for legal teams sitting within an organization, failure to keep communication open means a more siloed firm/organization that is potentially engaging in counterproductive practices. For example, if different practice groups or departments are not talking to each other about tech products they are working on, the firm may end up with two or three products that all do broadly similar things.

We certainly do not allow this type of siloed division from a conflicts point of view, with legal teams having strict rules about who they can advise and what to do when conflicts arise, but we are not always so good at keeping track of all the different pet projects being worked on across the organization, and this may mean friction when it all comes to light. And hey, the more you know about what is going on across your organization, the more you can join the dots, which means you can borrow learnings from others when engaging in projects. To put it another way, when drafting a new type of contract you hope there is a precedent within your organization that can be built upon, and in just the same way you should be able to expect to build on completed work when engaging in new ways of solving problems.

Content

If you are pondering how important communication can be, you only need to look at what happened to WhatsApp when it announced a new privacy policy in 2021.

The facts are these. As part of its strategy to integrate its various messaging apps, Facebook (now Meta) announced an update to the WhatsApp privacy policy that allowed information from WhatsApp to be shared with Facebook. It also removed an option that users had possessed in previous privacy policy updates to 'not have your WhatsApp account information shared with Facebook'. The privacy policy was mandatory, and it was delivered using language that people felt was a 'take it or leave it' ultimatum. So what happened next? Well, a lot of people chose to 'leave it', causing a surge in popularity among other non-Facebook-owned messaging apps and a decline in WhatsApp users. There were swift moves by WhatsApp and Facebook to clarify that the changes applied only to businesses and that they would not apply to users in Europe, where data privacy laws are stricter, but the damage was done. And it was all because of the content of the communication. Miscommunication causes problems.

Applying this to legal content, falling back on legalese and Latin is usually not appreciated in a business context, and nor is extensive detailing of the relevant case and legislative or regulatory citations

– unless you are communicating a point in a court of law, of course, which requires such information. The client tends not to care about you 'showing your working'; what they care about is the answer to their problem. The audience is important. I have developed solutions that are ostensibly for an in-house legal team but were actually going to be *used* by a procurement team. Suddenly, a whole bunch of assumptions that the intended audience will understand any legal language used has to be disregarded and everything must be written in plain English, with additional information and explanations provided so that the content can be understood. If it is not understood, it will simply not be used.

One of the biggest issues that supervisors have with their juniors is in their drafting. University and law school courses that have a focus on essays do not tend to create concise writers, instead cultivating those who take pride in over-analysis and the use of flowery language. There is a reason that the language used in contracts tends to be concise: it reduces the opportunities for misrepresenting or misunderstanding the intention of the agreement. A good communicator knows when to draft in a concise legal style, when to use plain English, and even when legalese might be required. I already talked about the 'bridges' or 'translators' that straddle the Law+ quadrants, and a major factor in collaboration is in speaking the same language and conveying it in the appropriate way.

CHAPTER 5

Law+Business

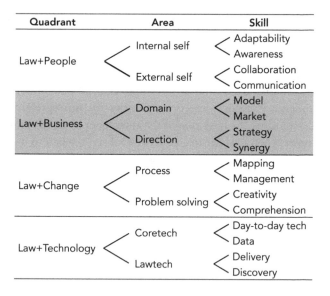

Quadrant	Area	Skill
Law+People	Internal self	Adaptability
		Awareness
	External self	Collaboration
		Communication
Law+Business	Domain	Model
		Market
	Direction	Strategy
		Synergy
Law+Change	Process	Mapping
		Management
	Problem solving	Creativity
		Comprehension
Law+Technology	Coretech	Day-to-day tech
		Data
	Lawtech	Delivery
		Discovery

When you work in a law firm or a legal department, you work for a business. Whether they are structured as limited companies, publicly owned companies, partnerships, limited liability partnerships or sole proprietorships, they are still expected to turn a profit. Even not-for-profit organizations need to make money to keep functioning. There is a temptation, however, to hold law up as somehow being *apart* from other professions, as if the application of the law can be separate from the world of business and be unaffected by it. But I am afraid there is no way to avoid the fact that legal advice in the corporate world is always framed within the realm of business decisions. Businesses need to consider returns on their investments, strategic directions and goals, and how to continuously evolve in order to stay relevant.

With all this in mind, legal departments are being put under increasing pressure to be more than a cost centre and to have input into the wider business while being mindful of expense. Gone are the times when a lawyer was able to sit and wait for a client to bring them a legal problem, only to dispense advice and then vanish into the mist until needed again; lawyers no longer get to be a Batman-type figure, waiting for the bat signal before they act. Instead, we are being asked to understand more of our clients' business and to proactively look for solutions. Rather than just having to point out the potential hazards on the road ahead, we are being asked how to navigate through them. That means we can no longer ignore concepts around business management, strategy and finance.

Like all the other quadrants, Law+Business is divided into two halves. The first is 'Domain', which means understanding the concept of a business – whether that be for a law firm or otherwise – including the structure of that business and how it makes (or loses) money. The second half is 'Direction', which looks at the strategies adopted by businesses to encourage growth and at the connections that we can forge from a business perspective to build and maintain good relationships – and by extension become good business partners.

AREA I: DOMAIN

To understand how a business functions, you need to boil things down to two key areas: the model of the business itself, and the market within which it operates.

Model

The law firm as a business

My time in education was spent not just lecturing but also drafting and updating curricula for courses. One of these courses was called the 'law firm as a business' module. The module was designed to teach students more about why law firms make the business choices that they make, and to help students understand their place as an individual within an organization.

There is a simple example that showcases why understanding how law firms operate is important. It tends to take senior lawyers less time to complete tasks than their more junior counterparts because the latter are still learning. Indeed, there is a reason that the first two years in a law firm in England and Wales has traditionally been called the 'training contract'. Lawyers at this stage of their careers are still learning, and part of that is taking a little more time to find their way through tasks. It is all too easy to see how a junior lawyer thrust into the world of business might fail to record all the hours they worked on a particular matter because they feel bad about how long it took. Although that might feel like an altruistic thing to do, the more you understand about how law firms function, the more you see that it is not the right choice.

The key thing to understand here is that lawyers are required to record their time, usually in six-minute increments. These increments are recorded as a running tally and 'released' (confirmed) by individuals before being reviewed by the partner running the matter and then billed to the client. This method of billing by the time spent is known as the 'billable hour'. It is telling that the first time I realized this concept existed was not during my actual professional legal education but in a fictional book about a lawyer. It was the first time I had ever come across the concept of time recording or seen how an actual legal office might function – and yes, I read the book after finishing my law degree. It is important to know this because I was certainly not the first law student who did not know about time recording and the effects that individuals can have on the bottom line of the law firm as a business, and I will definitely not be the last.

Getting back to our example, there are two reasons why time should not be under-recorded. Firstly, not all the time that is recorded is passed on to the client, so you are not necessarily saving anyone any money by misrepresenting your hours. There is a process of 'writing off' time before billing a client that will look at things such as time taken on simple tasks compared with the quoted fee, and an appropriate amount of hours will often be deducted from the bill. Secondly, the law firm uses those hours calculations to assess how long tasks take, regardless of the amount that is eventually billed to the client. Knowing how long tasks take can help with future pricing or with identifying where further training may be needed. Nobody is going to be looking for efficiencies in a process if the data shows that it takes only half the time it actually takes, and in the long run this might mean the firm losing money. This is a simple example but it shows how awareness of the wider business can inform the practices you undertake every day when working. Now, it is true that the time of a junior associate costs much less than that of a senior associate, but this just emphasises that we need to spend time making sure the right people are spending time on the right tasks.

For those who are more senior, the more you understand about how a law firm works as a business, the better prepared you are for managing that business. This understanding is perhaps even more important for those from outside the legal sector and for hybrid professionals who will have to straddle the worlds of law and business and understand where the two intersect.

So what should you know about how a law firm functions as a business? In terms of model, a lot of people talk about law firms as 'partnerships', with those who own the business as partners. Dig a little deeper, though, and you will find that there are various ways in which law firms are structured: from limited companies to limited liability partnerships (LLPs) to sole practitioners. Some law firms are even publicly listed on the stock exchange, meaning that anyone can buy shares in the firm. Regardless of their corporate structure, there is increasing diversity in the way in which law firms are organized internally. There are partnerships with, and investments in, software companies, for example. Some firms have established subsidiaries who handle consulting or legal technology services in order to build additional revenue streams. Other firms have allowed partners to be drawn from business services professionals rather than lawyers, opening up new options for people, while many are using outsourcing to assist with tasks. Law firms can also exist as parts of other businesses, such as accountancy firms.

The final thing to be aware of when considering the law firm as a business is that a law firm is more than just its lawyers. There are often large numbers of professional services or business services staff who are available to assist – a fact of which some lawyers are not always aware. Maybe there is an innovation team who can assist with new technology solutions, or a learning and development team who can train your team or your clients' teams. Perhaps you have access to a legal operations team that can help you project manage your matters or assist your clients in managing their team. Knowing that there are business professionals as well as legal professionals in a law firm is key to providing the best legal services to clients. Those business professionals are as expert in their areas as the lawyers are in law.

Law firm metrics

As well as thinking about the structure of the business, it is important to understand the metrics by which firms monitor themselves and on which they judge their success. If you are part of an in-house team, it is good to know how your partner firms can be and might be structured, just as law firm lawyers should understand their clients.

Utilization

Utilization is basically how much time you spend on billable matters. So, for all the time you have recorded, your utilization is the percentage of that time spent on billable activities, i.e. anything that can be charged to a client. To round out the picture, non-billable activities are those undertaken during work hours that are not generally charged to a client, such as training, firm events and business development. Individuals tend to have utilization targets, which is why law firms that want to encourage their lawyers to spend time on building Law+ skills need to consider how to factor this into an environment in which more hours mean more success; they also need to think about whether this metric is always the most appropriate one to use for bonus calculation purposes. It is worth noting that different firms will have different targets and bonus structures.

While some may reward only time recorded on billable activities, others may have minimum targets for billable activities and apply a bonus based on hours spent doing different types of task, such as knowledge management or pro bono work. Some firms have even experimented with removing hours requirements altogether.

Realization

If utilization is how much time you spent on billable matters, realization is how much you got paid for those hours. Law firms are not always paid (or paid in full) for their time. There may be discounts in place, or time may be written off for a variety of reasons.

Gearing

In a business context, gearing refers to a company's debt (the money it receives from taking out loans and borrowing money) relative to its equity (the money it makes from issuing shares).

In a law firm context, however, gearing (also known as 'leverage') is one of two things: either the ratio of hours worked by associates to those worked by partners, or the staffing ratio of how many junior associates there are to each partner. High gearing means a high number of associates or associate hours compared with partners or partner hours; low gearing is, unsurprisingly, the opposite. The more associates a law firm has, the more work can be delegated down from partner level. This frees up time for the partner to bring in more business and to bill more time on matters. Without that delegation, the firm would be utilizing a high-cost resource that the client would not be willing to pay for if the task is not suited to that level of seniority. But while higher gearing tends to mean more money for the firm, there are exceptions: where partners are needed for complex work, for example, or where their involvement is requested because of an existing client relationship or the type of industry in which they work. Partners should also be able to spend time cultivating and strengthening client relationships. Gearing is a factor worth considering when thinking about how law firms hire people or promote people.

Pricing

Pricing is an increasingly complex area for law firms, many of which have entire teams who are dedicated to pricing matters, and a range of tech tools and methods is available to support those teams.

The popularity of alternative fee arrangements (AFAs) to the traditional billable hour model means that legal services providers need a range of ways of pricing legal matters depending on the team involved, the time it will take, the complexity of the solution, and a whole bunch of other factors. AFAs can take a variety of forms, such as (i) fixed fees (in which a price is quoted and will be charged regardless of time spent), (ii) fee caps (billing by the hour up to a certain maximum), (iii) volume discounts (where the more work the law firm does for the client, the bigger the discount) and (iv) blended hourly rates (a single universal hourly rate assigned to anyone working on the matter). The pricing arrangement that is entered into can and does change the way in which a matter is staffed and how it is handled. For example, in a fixed fee or fee cap arrangement, efficiency is important, as is accurate pricing. It does not look great if a law firm has to return to its client asking for extra money. For other matters, efficiency might be less important because there is no time pressure or fee cap. Either way, these factors are another reason to properly record time: if you do not record your hours in a timely manner, the view of how close the firm is to the fee cap or how much to charge for a task is going to be wrong. This is doubly the case in instances where the client is given a view of the daily or weekly fees in some sort of client-facing dashboard.

Margin

The margin is the money raised by working on a matter versus the cost of that work. Most businesses show their profitability by taking their revenue (all the money earned) and subtracting their expenses (all the money spent). In law firms, though, that calculation can become complex when looking to calculate the margin, as some of the fees for which they bill may not be collected. Some firms show their profitability based on fees *billed* while others calculate according to fees *collected*. This places a different onus on the lawyers when a law firm is looking to increase profitability. Depending on when the financial year-end takes place, law firms who show profitability on fees collected are going to spend a good portion of the last month of the financial year making sure their clients actually pay what is owed, while those who focus on fees billed are going to be looking at billing more in that last month, with collection coming later.

Profit per equity partner (PEP)

First things first, it is worth explaining what an 'equity partner' is for those who might not know. Whatever a firm's structure, this still tends to be the most popular term used for those in the most senior positions. Basically, equity partners are the most senior lawyers in a firm, and they share in the profits of the firm as well as being able to vote on business decisions relating to it. The reason for this is that they have invested money (equity) in the law firm in exchange for these rights. The other type of partner is a salaried partner, who is paid a fixed sum and may or may not have voting rights in the firm.

PEP is calculated by taking the revenue of the firm minus its costs (rent, salaries, etc.) and dividing the result by the number of equity partners. It is one way to look at law firm profitability, and with this method, the higher the revenue and the fewer the equity partners, the better the firm is doing. While this may not always necessarily be true, hopefully you can see why this, combined with the concept of gearing, has led to the traditional 'pyramid' structure of law firms, with a few partners at the top and more people at each level the further down the seniority chain you go.

The client as a business

Whether you are a law firm who has external clients or a legal team that sits within an organization, you are providing legal services to a business that has its own strategy and financial considerations. It is exceedingly rare that a client is asking for legal advice just out of interest; it is because they have something that they want to do, and in order to do it properly they need to know the law. That means that they very rarely want the law for the law's sake, and the more that you as a provider of legal services can comprehend the world that your client inhabits, the better you can provide those services.

This also means understanding where the in-house team fits into that wider business model. In this book's introduction I mentioned the various effects on businesses over time that have led to them being more rigorous in analysing the spend of their legal teams. It is a driver that can affect the amount that clients are prepared to pay and, as a result, the way that work is priced for a client and the way that work is delivered.

Why do in-house teams care about data, and why are they increasingly asking law firms to price in consistent ways? It is so they can easily track and compare their spending on external counsel. They need to do this because at some point they are going to have to justify that spend to their own business. I believe this is why we are going to see more in-house teams creating their own technology and efficiency solutions in coming years; at the moment they are looking to law firms as their traditional providers of legal services, but at some point the business (or the in-house team itself) is going to question why they do not use their existing in-house resources to build these tools. When law firms create tools for clients, there can often be a lengthy series of hoops to jump through for both client and firm in identifying appropriate security controls. This added time and effort could be avoided by clients building the tools using their own systems. As traditionally risk-averse organizations, I predict we are going to see law firms losing out unless they can find ways of getting comfortable with providing clients with innovative solutions as well as speeding up risk-checking and information security processes. If one firm will not do it, another one will; and if no firm will do it, the clients will be forced to take matters into their own hands.

Being able to understand things like how the client makes money, their current financial standing, who *their* clients and customers are, and how the legal team integrates with the rest of the business is essential to understanding the client's financial situation. The only link a law firm has to the business is usually through the legal team, so if law firms can understand how legal teams are given and use their budgets, this can help them deliver legal services. Every financial year, business departments need to plan and forecast their budgets for the coming year. Not every business runs to the same financial year or budget timing, so understanding how and when your client makes these decisions can be vital to ensuring that any new solutions are pitched at the right time.

Your advice is also going to differ depending on the financial status of the business as a whole: those businesses that are struggling financially are going to have different priorities to those that are not. For example, settling a litigation case may be an option for a business that is making plenty of money and that wishes to avoid lengthy litigation that might end up in the press. On the other hand, a company that is struggling financially may have no option but to fight a case because settling or losing means financial ruin. To take another example, financial insitutions are increasingly having to set budgets over six-month periods as opposed to the one-to-two-year timelines they previously kept to. This means they need up-to-date information on the legal landscape in their market; if a lot of banks are being sanctioned then they may need to set money aside for sanctions, for instance. Knowing that information, a legal advisor might offer to a client a service that provides updates on sanctions in the banking market in real time.

Like it or not, legal services usually cost money – the very thing a business is trying to make. It can be difficult to prove your worth when what you are doing is stopping anything bad from occurring rather than actively making good things happen, no matter how important that service might be. The more that you, as a legal services provider, can understand the types of businesses you advise and their financial position, the more valued you are going to be to your client. As a primer, here are a couple of foundational things you need to understand.

Profit and loss (P&L) accounts

A P&L account is a record of a business's revenue, costs and expenses over a specific duration. The P&L account can be used to see how the business can generate further profit by increasing the revenue, reducing the expense, or doing both. Basically, this account shows the money the business made over a given period and the money it spent – and, therefore, the amount of 'take home' money.

Balance sheets

While a P&L account spans a certain time period, a balance sheet is a 'snapshot' of the assets held by a company, the outgoing liabilities of the company, and the amount of money invested in that company. Balance sheets help businesses understand what assets they possess and what they cost, and they are the basis of a number of financial ratios that contribute to assessing the success of a business. In short, a balance sheet shows what a business *owns* and what it *owes*.

Market

Commercial awareness

If adaptability is one of the skills people always say is essential for the legal team of the future, the other is commercial awareness. Like adaptability, commercial awareness means different things to different people. Maybe this is one of the reasons it is so popular: everyone who is writing it down is imagining commercial aware-ness as something different. To some it means reading the *Financial Times* every morning and understanding the stock market. To others it is appreciating the landscape of the profession and the direction of travel. To a few it might simply mean being able to explain what blockchain is.

A common definition of commercial awareness relates to under-standing how your business and your industry make money, but for legal teams, I am not sure that definition goes far enough. While it is important to understand how your profession operates, we have to advise a number of different companies on a number of differ-ent matters across a broad spectrum. Commercial awareness means understanding not only our own profession but also the world of our clients. For in-house teams, the range of industries is no smaller because the onus moves to understanding the clients or customers of the business within which they work.

This does not *necessarily* mean understanding financial state-ments. Most of the lawyers I have met are not particular fans of numbers or finance. Even if you do not like them, though, the very essence of Law+ is that there are skills at which you will only be entry level – and that is OK. Likewise, if you love finance and business, then that is an amazing skill to have and you are a vital part of the legal team of the future. But commercial awareness is *not* financial awareness. I would posit a different definition of the term commer-cial awareness: understanding how your business, your industry, and your clients and customers operate. There are many facets to our industry, and you need to find those that are of interest to you.

There is a reason I have taken the 'making money' part out of the original definition. Although making money is usually the pri-mary reason for a business to exist, there are other issues that will be vital to businesses when choosing their legal advisors, including diversity, equality and inclusion (DE&I) and environmental, social and governance (ESG) issues, all of which can form part of your commercial awareness. In addition, many of the skills discussed in this book are not unique to law, regardless of the fact that the legal profession often sticks the word 'legal' on the front of those skills to make it seem like they are. Many businesses are equally invested in finding efficiencies, applying design thinking to problems, looking for new opportunities to apply innovative technology solutions, and developing human skills. Having commercial awareness can there-fore include in-depth knowledge of the Law+ quadrants. Being able to talk in a language that resonates with the client will help when providing legal services.

Take me as an example. I am not fantastic at working with num-bers.* But while finance did not appeal to me, the world of innovation and technology was something I *was* very interested in when I was more junior. Commercial awareness in my context became under-standing that facet of the legal profession and the wider business world. It is a subject of interest both to law and to businesses beyond law, and it is something I have discussed with numerous people in

---

* I accidentally underestimated the cost of my own wedding by a not insignif-icant figure, much to the chagrin of my wife.

various contexts – clients and lawyers alike. The point of commercial awareness is to be better able to advise clients by understanding your own organization and its market as well as the business and market within which your client operates. Commercial awareness, then, is both more broad and more targeted than it may at first seem, and you do not need to panic and assume that it means having to track the stock markets on a daily basis.

Competition

The trend of global deregulation in the profession has led to an evolution in the legal market where, in most jurisdictions, in-house teams can choose to receive legal services from organizations other than law firms, depending on their requirements. The range of competition for law firms is wider than ever. No matter how good a law firm is, at some point or other it is going to have to compete to make it onto a panel for a client or to answer a tender for a specific piece of work. Understanding what the client needs is important to help identify where a law firm can best serve that client (and also to understand what other members of the client panel can handle). Is the client looking for a combination of bespoke legal services and high-volume work, and does the firm provide it? Is the solution technology based? What is important to the client, and how might it be delivered? In-house teams are seeking increasingly diverse panels; rather than having a homogeneous group of law firms that are simply used depending on who knows whom at what organization, we instead have clients compiling panels that involve lawtech companies, hybrid law firms and alternative legal service providers who might do both complex and simple legal work, all mixed in with the more traditional firms. Knowing this background and keeping up to date on the various entities that make up the 'legal market' is important because it affects how law firms are structured and what is available for in-house teams when looking for external services.

Knowing the state of the competition can also help with knowing how your own team or firm is going to evolve. As a traditionally risk-averse profession, legal teams – and law firms in particular – will often wait for someone else to make the first move before making a change themselves. What others are doing in the market is therefore always of interest, and it should be something you monitor.

The competition that our clients face – in this case whether our client is external or is the business in which the legal team is housed – is also key to providing legal services. I am not talking competition law here, just knowing the market. If you are advising or working within a large bank, for example, you need to be aware of the presence of challenger banks, what they are doing to the market, and how that might cause a change within your/your client's bank. Anticipating these changes by undertaking a horizon scan of the market can help you either spot problems before they arise or address unexpected issues more competently with prepared solutions based on your background knowledge. To give an example of this, if a client is in a competitive market during a crisis, they need immediate and up-to-date legal advice that can help them navigate that crisis and come out ahead of their competitors. A law firm that can offer such a solution would be highly valued. The more you know about the context in which your client sits, the better able you will be to help them by synthesizing information within the context of their business drivers.

Delving into the theory of competition for a moment, organizations sometimes refer to 'Porter's Five Forces' of competition. Porter's Five Forces help businesses to make decisions in their industry or profession by listing five areas that should be taken into account when making those decisions. The five forces are (i) supplier power, or how easy it is for those supplying products or services in the industry to increase prices; (ii) buyer power, or how easy it is for buyers to drive prices down; (iii) the number of competitors in the market that offer similar services; (iv) the likelihood that clients may switch to another similar provider of the same product or service; and (v) the threat of new market entrants.

I hope you will be able to see how these factors not only affect clients but also contribute to a lot of changes to the legal profession, where clients as buyers of legal services have more power due to an increased number of competitors in the market and new entrants caused by deregulation.

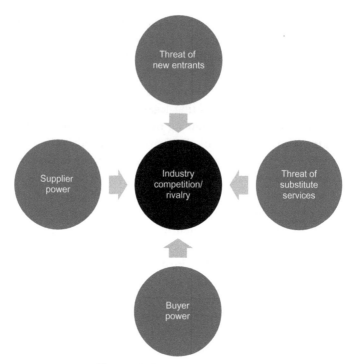

Figure 6. Porter's Five Forces.

AREA 2: DIRECTION

It is not just the current business landscape that is important; knowing where your business and/or your clients' businesses are going and why is a key factor to consider. This is all about the *direction* of a business; specifically, in terms of its 'strategy' and 'synergy'. In considering strategy, you need to be able to appreciate the strategic drivers of your organization and of your clients to make sure your advice fits within the broad direction of travel. Synergy is all about relationships: making them, maintaining them, and managing them. Building relationships is core to legal services, but unlike the collaboration elements discussed in Law+People, here we are more concerned with how those relationships affect the business of law. Business development and marketing are not always skills that people consider when thinking about lawyers, but they are needed; it does not matter how good your legal knowledge is if you cannot find anyone to whom you can sell it, and business development becomes a core part of your activities the more senior you become.

Strategy

Every business has a strategy. When I was a student, I took part in an initiative called 'Young Enterprise'. This was a programme that was designed to instil entrepreneurship and business knowledge into students, and there are variations on this theme all over the world. Even though we were just students, one of the first things we had to do when setting up our 'business' was to draw up a strategy. I cannot remember what that strategy was. Nor can I remember the name of our business, beyond the fact that it started with an 'X' because we were trying to be edgy. I cannot even remember what we sold. What is important about this story, though, is that even a business established by a group of students attempting to look professional had a strategy.

A business strategy is basically the way in which a business plans to achieve its objectives. Those objectives will differ from business to business, and strategies might be more or less complex depending on the goals that have been set by management. Within a single business there may be multiple strategies at different levels of the organization, with individual teams having their own strategies that align with the overarching strategy of the business as a whole. While every business will have a strategy, it is perfectly possible for those within a business to have absolutely no idea what that strategy might be. It is all too easy to get swept up in more immediate tasks and not think about what happens five years (or more) from now, or about how your work contributes to the wider goals of your organization.

Strategies are usually built around vision statements. A vision statement is a short statement outlining what you want from the business: 'We aim to be the best at providing corporate legal services', for example. From that vision statement you can create a business plan or strategy that describes how the business might get there, e.g. it might focus on acquiring new clients and hiring the best talent. A strategy is typically created by considering the strengths, weaknesses, opportunities and threats of a business (also referred to as a SWOT analysis), and by looking at how the resources of the business can be used to navigate these to achieve its vision. The inputs for a SWOT analysis tend to come from a 'PESTLE' analysis, which looks at the political, economic, social, technological, legal and environmental landscape in which a business functions. You will often hear the terms SWOT and PESTLE being used together for this reason.

Whether or not you are aware of it, almost every business (including law firms) has a strategy that usually covers a three-to-five-year period. Different organizations will have different strategies, of course, but some things they may choose to focus on are (i) reducing costs via efficiency or other methods; (ii) increasing revenue, whether by forging better relationships with existing clients or by taking on new ones; (iii) making better use of technology; (iv) moving into new markets and geographies; and (v) providing new products and/or services to clients. Those high-level objectives will drip-feed down into department-level strategies for different practice groups and for business services functions.

As an example, let us say that a law firm wants to forge better relationships with clients rather than acquire new ones. If that is the strategy of the firm as a whole, then the marketing department is going to have to form its own strategy that outlines how to strengthen existing relationships rather than finding new clients. This might mean doing more relationship management and less thought leadership in the broader market, or maybe it will mean focusing more on finding new work with existing clients rather than engaging in pitches for new ones. Similarly, for in-house teams the broader business will have a strategy, and in order to integrate with the business the strategy of the legal team should align with that. Does the business want to acquire a lot of companies in the near term? If so, the legal team should prepare faster ways of dealing with the legal work around acquisitions. Is there a new brand that the business wants to push? If so, the legal team should make sure the proper intellectual property is in place. By understanding the strategic direction of an organization, we understand our place within it.

Strategies are increasingly going beyond how an organization can make money, and you will often now hear businesses referring to their 'purpose'. What is a corporate purpose? It is something that an organization wants to achieve beyond the bottom-line: a reason to be in business that is about more than making money. Businesses who have a clear purpose expect those they work with to align with that purpose, and law firms should bear that in mind as it will shape how they advise existing clients as well as having an impact on their chances of getting onto panels for new clients. For in-house teams, the business may already have a purpose with which the legal team should align. Generally, a corporate purpose is a way of doing good in the world, such as having a focus on ESG issues and how ethical the business is, for example. For others, the primary purpose might relate to diversity and inclusion or to creating a community around the business. Whatever form it may take, a purpose allows people to feel like they are lending their time to something worthwhile.

Why does any of this matter to you as part of a legal team? If you are working as part of an in-house team, the business strategy might affect the resources available to your department or the sorts of matter on which you will be working. For those of you working in law firms, knowing the strategy of the firm can help when deciding where to focus your time. For example, does the firm want to acquire more clients? If so, it may be worth spending more of your time on business development. Or maybe the firm wants to save costs? If so, you should be talking with others in the firm who can help you find efficiencies in your work. If you do not take the time to learn about your organization's strategy, the work you are doing may be actively diluting it without you even knowing. A good example might be where a firm has decided not to produce any new legal technology products and in talking to a client you offer to build them a technology product; this puts the firm in the awkward position of promising something that it is against policy to deliver. Being able to see the road ahead allows you to spot opportunities for competitive advantage along that road, and to make sure that you are in the best place you can be in terms of the work you are doing.

Synergy

Business development and relationship management

Richard Susskind, among others, has argued that what people want from the legal profession is not lawyers but to have their problem solved and that – likewise – what people want from the medical profession is not doctors but to be healed.[1] The assumption is that if that outcome could be achieved without humans, it would be readily accepted by the public. As far as medicine goes, I feel like this ignores one essential aspect of healing: that is, to be made to feel better psychologically. Bedside manner is an important part of being a medical practitioner because people value connection, whether or not the activities the practitioners perform can be standardized/automated. In the same way, legal advice is designed not just to comply with law but to deliver comfort. Comfort that a business deal will proceed as intended, or that a case can be defended, for example. Comfort requires trust, and that means building relationships. If a relationship is built on some key metrics, then relationship management means ensuring those metrics are collected, monitored and communicated. If the important aspect of the relationship for a client is that they feel a human connection with their lawyers, then that might mean taking them out for dinner and taking the time to enquire about their personal lives. The recent interest in human skills in the profession shows that we are still far from irrelevant.

There are those who naturally flourish in the world of traditional business relationships and those who find it difficult and – sometimes – miserable. Generally, extroverts will enjoy networking and meeting new people while introverts will not. This is not set in stone, and to believe you cannot do business development because you are an introvert is to exhibit a fixed mindset. Take the example of lecturers. You might imagine that the vast majority of those who choose to spend their lives talking in front of roomfuls of strangers would be extroverts, but when engaging with personality tests at a team-building event I discovered that many of my lecturer colleagues were introverts. When asked about how they deal with being an introvert while teaching a class, one response that has always stuck with me was that they just *acted* like they were an extrovert; that is, the persona they adopted when teaching was not who they were in their personal lives. I therefore refuse to believe that you cannot improve at business development, even if you currently think you are terrible, or it scares you.

Of course, that is not to say that you have to engage with business development to the expert level in order to excel in the legal profession. Part of the rationale behind the Law+ model is that it allows you to specialize in those areas that appeal to you while working with other specialists in areas that do not.

While a law firm will have a business development team, every one of the interactions we have with our clients is an opportunity for further business development. For in-house teams, every interaction with the wider business is an opportunity to be more involved in the direction of the business by building new connections. The better we manage those relationships, the more fruitful they will be. Management of client relationships belongs to every level of an organization, whether you are a brand new associate, a senior equity partner, a general counsel or a managing director.

How those relationships are managed can be as simple as managing expectations about when or how work will be delivered. One quick example relates to a partner I used to work for who *loved* getting documents in a plastic sheet with a horizontal staple in the top-left corner of the page.* It took maybe ten seconds to clip a staple in anything I delivered to him and to then slip it into a plastic sheet, but it immediately let him know that I had listened to his preferences and acted on them. The result was that we maintained a good relationship and I did a lot of work with him that gave me some very senior client engagement at a much earlier stage of my career than I might otherwise have expected. I am not saying that obeying every whim of every partner you work for is the way to succeed at work, though. I am just saying that listening to others and acting on what they say is important in building and maintaining relationships.

If we are considering Law+ as a model for how holistic legal teams of lawyers and other specialists work together effectively, business development and marketing professionals need to feature more prominently in those teams. Those who are proficient in these areas can monitor client interactions, collect data relating to feedback and how relationships might be improved, coach lawyers on performing in pitches, and handle the 'sales' aspect while lawyers focus on the legal advice. This is an area in which the Big Four accountancy firms

---

* The answer is no, I do not know why I remember this in such detail more than a decade later.

have got the jump on law firms. They often promote marketing professionals to partner level, and while most larger law firms now have a Chief Marketing Officer role or similar, it is still often seen as more of a support function instead of one that is key to knowing your clients. Having functions that are able to focus time on this area is only going to become more important as the legal services market becomes more competitive and as clients are looking for law firms to prove themselves against key metrics and human skills.

Some lawyers might read the above paragraph and baulk at the idea of getting coaching in how to react to pitches, but clients are starting to think differently about how tenders work. Longer-form documents that no one has the time to read in full are on their way out, replaced by interactive user-friendly technology solutions. Stock paragraphs about the experience of the team are being replaced by requirements from clients to engage with pitch interviews that reveal more about the humans involved, with mock scenarios like how the team might climb down a mountain together or deliver advice that can only be the length of a voicemail message. Slide shows full of static text – the cardinal sin of delivering a presentation – are now competing with slick interactive presentations, or app solutions, or (when teams are confident enough) presentations with no slides at all. All-lawyer teams are being rejected in favour of more multi-disciplinary teams, showcasing how the different elements will be brought together directly from the experts in those areas, rather than having that expertise filtered through the legal team who may or may not be expert in that area themselves. Even the types of work that clients are asking lawyers to deal with are extending beyond just legal advice, such as asking not only for legal advice on setting up funds in a bank, for example, but also how to improve the process of setting up those funds.

At its core, relationship management is really just understanding what your client or customer wants and giving it to them. I once attended a meeting in which a client mentioned she loved the pens that our organization provided at events as she had mild arthritis and the pens fitted her hand comfortably. Guess who got sent a box of pens? With clients demanding more transparency, some firms have created daily dashboards that bring together data about current and former matters in one place. Both of those examples are simple but effective.

And the same principles apply in-house. Fostering relationships with the wider business is important. Think about how the different business departments that you work with like to receive your advice. Is it in large documents? As slides? Online? How can you make their lives easier? Is it by reducing the amount of legalese in documents? Should you make it easier to contact you? Can you work with your external providers to empower other parts of the business with self-service solutions? The more you understand about the wider business, the better you can manage those relationships.

Managing expectations

As I said earlier, both law firms and in-house teams can reap great benefits simply from managing expectations. This works both ways: it means being honest about what you can do and by when, but it also means being truthful about the date by which you need something. At some stage or other, we have all completed some work for another person by their strict deadline only for them to not look at it until a week or so later. That sort of expectation mismanagement damages relationships by making us reluctant to give future work from that person the same priority level as other work we have. Some of you may be familiar with the term 'lawyer time': that is, however long a lawyer tells you a task will take, it will end up taking three times that long. The fact that such a concept exists does not say a lot about our ability to manage expectations.

At the risk of giving away some trade secrets about education, it is a common tip if a class if struggling with motivation that you should overestimate the time needed for the next activity. When they complete it early, the morale of the class increases. Finishing activities or classes a few minutes early and drawing attention to it certainly helped me build relationships with my students in my lecturer days. This does not apply exactly to the world of business – I would certainly not recommend routinely lying to your clients about how long a task will take just so you can do it quicker. But there is a tendency in law to feel like deadlines have to be *underestimated*. You would think that this would be likely to lead to a difficult conversation when a timeline had to be extended, but I have frequently been in situations when everyone senior involved in a matter expected it to go over the deadline. This came as a shock to all the juniors on the matter, who had been working all hours to hit what was a fictional deadline. A little more honesty – and communication – on everyone's part can help to manage expectation and can strengthen relationships. Imagine if a client always expects every legal advisor they work with to go over a deadline but in fact you hit it or come in under it? That sets you apart. It seems like a very simple thing to keep someone informed of progress and to be open about status, but it can make a world of difference.

CHAPTER 6

Law+Change

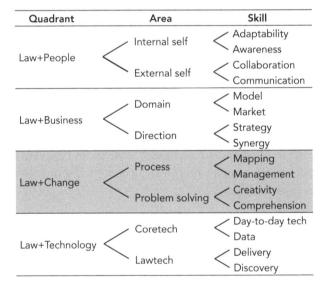

Quadrant	Area	Skill
Law+People	Internal self	Adaptability Awareness
	External self	Collaboration Communication
Law+Business	Domain	Model Market
	Direction	Strategy Synergy
Law+Change	Process	Mapping Management
	Problem solving	Creativity Comprehension
Law+Technology	Coretech	Day-to-day tech Data
	Lawtech	Delivery Discovery

Law+Change skills are often bundled up with other areas, like business or technology, but they are worth highlighting on their own as they are key to navigating the constantly shifting landscape of the legal profession.

Our profession is not unique in experiencing rapid transformation, and many industries and professions are increasingly turning to the skills featured in the Law+Change quadrant to find better ways to develop and deliver their products and services. Some of these skills help with identifying the incremental changes and evolutions that are going on every day in firms, while others can support large-scale transformation in how legal services are delivered. When you think of the kind of skills contained within this quadrant, you may picture big rooms filled with whiteboards and post-it notes – or, in this hybrid working era, virtual whiteboards and simulated post-it notes to replicate the real-life experience. For some, the exploration and reflection required to deal with change come as naturally as breathing, but for others it is a real struggle, especially when the driver for change – sometimes referred to as the 'burning platform' – is not always immediately obvious when you are focused on the day-to-day work you are doing.

Law+Change is divided into 'Process' and 'Problem solving'. On the former side, we will look at how there are many things we can do around the process of delivering legal services that do not remove the nuanced skill of providing the actual right advice. With regard to problem solving, it is worth pointing out that the very nature of giving legal advice is to identify and solve a problem. However, there are methods and tactics, such as design thinking, that are not regularly used in the legal sphere but are needed if we are to find new ways of solving the novel, complex problems encountered by our clients and our own organizations.

AREA I: PROCESS

Mapping

Process mapping techniques and methodologies had their genesis in product-based industries and have only fairly recently found their way into professional services and the law. A lot of what lawyers do is synthesizing information from various sources to find a legal solution that is unique to each client. This is creative and nuanced advice, and it is certainly not something that is readily amenable to being mapped in order to find efficiencies or a restructured process. When considering the application of process mapping to the law, I would encourage you to think of all the activities that take place *around* the delivery of the advice. Where do you find the standard form or precedent document? How do you recruit a team of lawyers to work on a matter? How do negotiations take place on the document? Each of these things involves a process.

I have both delivered and received training relating to process mapping with lawyers, and there is often an initial reaction from attendees that process mapping is not something that applies to law. This is partly down to the origins of process mapping. A lot of the methodology for process mapping started in product-based industries rather than in services, and the lawyers I have worked with have rightly pointed out that delivering legal services is not like building a car.

That is not to say that there is nothing that law can learn from other industries, though. Far from it. To take a wild example, there are many parallels between law and hairdressing. Yes, I mean it. Haircuts are a service. Although everyone who enters a hair salon is trying to solve the same problem – that they would like their hair to look better – the result that each person wants is wildly different. Even two seemingly similar haircuts (a short back and sides, for example) differ between two different people depending on circumstances such as the shape of the head, the texture of the hair, the placement of the crown. Hopefully you can see the parallels with contextualized legal advice here, which is unique to each client; a loan is a loan, but no two are the same as they depend on the commercial agreements between the parties, just like no two litigations are the same as they have potentially wildly different scenarios despite the cases going through the same steps.

Now, there is a balance to be struck between efficiency and quality in a hair salon. The faster a hairdresser can cut hair, the more people they can see in a day, and the more money they potentially make. But they also have to provide a good haircut or they will not get repeat business. Law is currently trying to find that balance too. Consider it this way: the most efficient way to cut hair would probably be a big headset filled with razors that you just pop on someone's head and lift when the hair is gone. Nobody is doing that because the quality will be poor and because everyone is different and will have different needs (in this case, because of the different shapes of their heads).

This leads me to my argument number 1: nobody is trying to take away the nuanced delivery of legal advice when they are talking about law as a process. However, this should be combined with argument number 2: just because the end result is different each time does not mean that you cannot engage in improving the process.

The cutting of hair is the core of hairdressing just as legal advice is the core of law. But around that core activity are processes that can be improved. For hairdressers, that might mean speeding up the way that people book their cuts, or how quickly a workstation can be cleaned, or how clients can be moved between the cutting chair and the sinks in an efficient manner. In the same way, while providing legal advice is the core of what we do in legal services, around that are a whole bunch of activities that are certainly processes.

Consider the process related to finding a precedent document, for example. It is rare that a lawyer will draft something new entirely from scratch, so how do you locate a suitable starting document? Do you contact your practice group with a 'pardon the interruption' email and hope someone has done something similar? Do you turn to a search engine to find the precedent you need? What about the process you go through in staffing a matter? Do you walk around the office and try to engage who you like or who you think is free? Is there a form of work allocation software that you use? As for the processes surrounding negotiations, do you work on a document with the other side via multiple emails back and forth, with a steadily increasing number of versions that need to be constantly checked to ensure the most up-to-date version is being used? Do you use a client collaboration or transaction management platform? Every single one of these processes sits around the delivery of advice and is one that could potentially be improved.

So there are plenty of processes in the delivery of legal advice. Going a little further, there are also areas of advice or guidance that can be mapped into some sort of process. For example, sanctions relating to road traffic offences tend to be applied in a very systematic manner, based on facts rather than any intent or motive. As such, the analysis of these sanctions and any defence that can be used against them has been automated by solutions like DoNotPay, the 'robot lawyer' that automates processes such as contesting parking tickets.

To take a more complex example, look at data protection law. I have previously worked with two data protection partners to create a process-driven legal solution for procurement teams looking to assess new suppliers for data protection issues. Data privacy is one area where the law follows some consistent procedural rules, the application of which can be ascertained by asking some key questions, e.g. where the data is coming from and where it is going. As each question is asked, the scope of potential laws that could apply is narrowed. There are edge cases that will have to be recognized for what they are, and they will require bespoke legal advice, but for the majority of cases there will be a similar set of questions leading to a finite set of results. The solution we created saved both the client's legal team and its procurement team time and effort. Even if these sorts of solution are only used as a starting point for a more in-depth analysis of the legal situation, there is a benefit to the increased consistency of the process and the time-saving for at least a portion of the whole matter.

Turning the application of law itself into a process is no easy task, of course. It requires a multidisciplinary team that understands not only the law but also how to map the processes and deal with any risk issues that may arise in giving automated legal 'advice'. But it is possible. Legal teams at Reed Smith, Mayer Brown, Ashurst and PwC, to name but a few, are doing it right now by developing self-service guidance tools for clients in the fields of data privacy, diversity and inclusion, the application of legal privilege, and compliance.

Mapping the process

So, what is a process map, and how are processes mapped onto one? Like many of the things I talk about in the book, the term has become shorthand for something very complex, with lots of different methodologies surrounding it. To reduce that complexity down into a simple definition, a process map is just a flowchart that shows how one process runs from start to finish. To create a process map you will need (i) those involved in the process; (ii) someone to ask the right questions; and (iii) a way of recording the process, whether that is pen and paper, post-it notes, virtual whiteboards or whatever else you have at your disposal. The more you learn about process mapping, the more you will learn about different types of map and the varieties of icon you should use – even languages that are useful in describing processes – but even when you are at entry-level proficiency, or below, it is possible for you to sit down and create one.

In order to map out a process all you need to do is agree on the process that is going to be mapped, figure out the first step and the final step, and then note down *all* the steps involved in that process between those two (including who does what and when). The level of detail is up to you and is about what works for the process being examined, but the key ingredient here is honesty. Those involved in the process need to feel they can share the bad bits about the process as well as the good bits. It may be embarrassing to reveal that in order to get a good precedent you need to email fifteen different people in four different time zones, say, but if it is not mapped it cannot be improved.

Those running the process mapping exercise will need to record every step and ask insightful questions to draw out the correct information. That means making sure that those present are representative of each level of seniority in the process and that they have first-hand information about the steps, and it also means going thoroughly through each step to ensure every detail is recorded. Having done a fair few process mapping exercises during my career, the simple action of just 'writing it all down' – and then seeing how their processes actually work – often comes as a shock to people. We deal with these examples in more detail in the next section.

What to do after mapping

There are a few things you can find out from a process map. In some instances, you will see that the levels of seniority are all wrong. You might find that a partner is currently doing the initial proofreading of a lengthy document, for example, while someone more junior could take care of that activity. You may discover that there are several extraneous steps to a process: for example, a team trying to get some data on client interactions may have to contact another team who can then access a database that reveals that information, when in fact it would be easier to just give the first team direct access to the database so they can get the information themselves. You might even find out that you are doing things in the wrong order: perhaps you only start to think about bundles in a litigation at the end, when in fact digital versions could be worked on right from the start to cut time from the overall process (appreciating that the final bundle will of course have to wait for the end of the matter).

What you do *after* process mapping is an equally important element of this skill. There are two major reasons to conduct a process mapping: either to make a process more efficient or to improve a process in terms of consistency and quality. Once a process has been mapped, you can start to apply analysis to it using different schools of process improvement. One of those schools is known as 'lean six sigma'. Lean six sigma is really a combination of two schools: (i) lean, which is focused on increasing speed and removing waste; and (ii) six sigma, which deals with standardizing processes and improving quality. In terms of identifying 'waste', or inefficiencies, in processes, there is an acronym that is used in lean six sigma. Although you may encounter slightly different versions of the acronym depending on the model used, the content is the same, so I will use the acronym TIM WOODS, which stands for the eight inefficiencies shown in figure 7.

The actions to take after process mapping might be transformational or they might only lead to minor gains. As a profession that records time in six-minute segments, the legal profession is one that should understand the value of small portions of time. Eliminating inefficiencies means speeding up processes, which means either freeing up more time to work on more matters or keeping fees low in a fixed or capped fee arrangement. It also means spending less time on a matter, of course. Where matters are billable by the hour and the client is willing to pay, it may seem that there is little incentive to speed up your activities, but in many jurisdictions the increased competition that law firms are facing from new types of entity mean they are having to prove their worth. Taking longer to complete an activity that the client knows can be done faster by someone else is not likely to impress. In addition, matters rarely work to a timetable that is considerate of the other work you have going on. Lawyers may be working on multiple urgent billable matters at once, in which

T **Transport**	Waste involved in moving things from one place to another, whether physically or digitally. This might mean printing documents and having to walk them back from the printer, or it might mean the back-and-forth of several document versions via email.
I **Inventory**	This is to do with information or items that the client does not receive. That might mean unanswered emails or voice messages, or bills sent too late.
M **Motion**	Unlike transportation, motion is to do with excessive movement, for example, excessive global travel or someone having to traipse to other floors of the office to get to a physical data room.
W **Waiting**	This is time wasted waiting for information to arrive. At some point in all of your legal careers you will have – or have already had – this in a matter, where you cannot act until the other side agrees something for example, but it can also mean something as simple as waiting for IT systems to load.
O **Over-processing**	Put simply, overprocessing means doing more work than is necessary. For example, having to get sign-off from too many people or having to ask a lot of people in order to get a precedent or standard form.
O **Over-production**	Overproduction is where work is done before it is needed or when it is not needed at all. For example, printing a whole bunch of documents for a closing when the signing is digital or doing more work than is necessary by providing a 300-page research memo when what was needed was an answer that can fit on a single page.
D **Defects**	These are mistakes and errors. It might be that information that is being manually copied across multiple documents is incorrect due to human error and needs automating, or that the initial pricing of the matter is often wrong, for example.
S **Skills**	The last waste means not using people at the level appropriate to their skills and intellect. This includes the example above where a partner is doing too many administrative tasks meaning they cannot be doing activities that require their higher seniority, or where lawyers might be doing work that should be done by professionals from other industries such as building technology solutions.

Figure 7. The eight inefficiencies.

case efficiency becomes important just so they can get the job done *on* time, regardless of how many hours they bill. In-house teams are usually unrestricted by the billable hour, so anything that gets the work done quicker is likely to be a bonus, provided the work is correct of course. As clients become more comfortable with using process mapping and similar efficiency methodologies themselves, they are going to expect the same of both their law firms and their in-house legal departments.

Also remember that not all the time that is recorded is billed to a client: much of it is written off, and not everything a lawyer does in a day is chargeable anyway – recording time itself, for example. While it certainly does not represent best practice, the current reality is that lawyers usually monitor time spent using automatic timers, and then at the end of the day they write a detailed narrative of the work undertaken. I have never seen a law firm that is 100% effective at releasing time on a daily basis. There are always people who forget – or do not have the time – to fill in the narrative. There is technology that can sit in the background on your computer and monitor the work completed, using artificial intelligence to pull together a first-draft narrative of the work undertaken. Not only can this speed up a process (time recording) that cannot be charged back to a client, but it can also uncover that lawyers are often underbilling their time worked, e.g. emails answered on a train or work completed in a non-traditional work setting, which is more prevalent post-pandemic.

Management

Project management

Projects – big ones and small ones – are *everywhere*. Planning a wedding is a project. Moving house is a project. Every matter a lawyer is working on is its own project. Project management is therefore not something that is reserved for grand company-transforming initiatives – it is something we all engage with at some point in our lives, and certainly in our jobs.

In law firms, the average lawyer uses project management to manage complex matters from start to finish, balancing fees, resourcing, capabilities and deadlines in order to make sure that the matter completes on time and within budget. They may do this with a specific project management team, but they usually do it without one. Despite this, lawyers rarely see themselves as project managers, which means they can neglect elements of project management methodology that could be helping them in managing matters. With clients scrutinizing pricing more closely, and with deadlines and outputs being monitored in terms of key performance metrics, managing matters is something all lawyers should be able to do in a structured and deliberate way.

It should be noted that what I describe above is often referred to as *legal* project management, but the term is merely used to refer to project management as applied to the legal sector so it is no different to the methods applied in managing projects in any other profession except for having to more carefully monitor hours spent on tasks due the nature of time recording and billing. Different schools of project management have published different methods for managing projects, but the most common are known as the 'waterfall' and 'agile' methods.

Historically, the waterfall method of project management was the most popular. Here, there are distinct stages in a clear sequence, with one following on from another and with 'milestones' that denote where one stage ends and another begins. The waterfall school of project management has fallen out of favour in recent decades, however, in favour of agile methods. Unlike the sequential steps of a waterfall, agile project management methods are formed of numerous smaller cycles of iteration in which the stages of project management are revisited again and again. Some common schools of iterative project management are Scrum, Kanban and Extreme Programming. For instance, my team uses a Kanban board to monitor projects, moving 'cards' that represent each project between columns called 'Backlog', 'Up Next', 'Active' and 'Complete'.

Many traditional legal matters align better with the waterfall method. There is not much call for going again and again until you get it right in a litigation, for example: there are key dates for filing and court appearances that have to be managed and met. Perhaps it is for this reason that lawyers can be uncomfortable with agile development methods, which are much better suited to finding new ways to solve problems.

Agile methods are often used for the creation of technology solutions or when plotting innovative solutions to problems, and as such they usually involve creating a 'minimum viable product' (MVP) that can be improved and iterated upon over time. An MVP is a 'bare-bones' low-fidelity version of the intended final solution that works in a similar fashion to that solution. Using an MVP can help people discover whether the final solution is viable for further development or whether they need to go back to the drawing board. The advantage of using a more basic prototype is that this assessment can be made without incurring the full cost of developing the final solution. Creating MVPs is not supposed to be labour- or time-intensive; instead, it allows all of those involved to 'fail fast', meaning that an idea that was never going to work can be ditched before it costs too much. It is worth noting that MVPs should not be 'high-fidelity' or professional-looking outputs. Although the legal profession attributes a high importance to perfectionism, if an MVP is too polished then people are reticent about giving their true feedback, worried that too much cost or time has already been invested. Using an MVP also allows for the collection of feedback from end users, meaning that the development of the final product can benefit from early opinions from its eventual audience.

To give a legal example of when an MVP might be used, let us imagine you want to use machine learning to identify and amend similar clauses in thousands of documents at once – updating clauses on the rate used in calculating the interest of a loan, say. While you might want to build the solution instantly in the latest artificial intelligence tool, it is possible you have missed some key considerations that mean the end result will be less useful. Maybe you are just updating existing clauses when the client actually needs to add some new ones depending on the type of agreement. Finding this out after you have already jumped forward to the solution will mean losing the time and money that was invested in the artificial intelligence tool. In developing an MVP, however, you might first run the idea with a few people making the changes manually to a smaller number of documents but working as if the system was doing it. This allows you to test whether the output is what the client has in mind and whether it will be useful to the client. You can even use pieces of paper or simple computer drawings to simulate dashboards and screens (known as 'wireframes') and to get a feel for what information could be useful to the client. This may feel counter-intuitive if you are used to delivering a polished final product, but it is better to get constructive feedback on a piece of paper and a few hours of manual work than on a multi-million-pound solution that cannot be easily changed.

The iterative development inherent to agile methods also means getting solutions faster. Take large-scale IT projects as an example. Creating a technology solution can take months. If the initial requirements are collected and the IT team go away and develop that solution for three months, then by the time it is actually delivered it may no longer be required – or at the very least the requirements will have changed. By creating a smaller version of the product first, the team can develop piece-by-piece, amending as they go. Indeed, some IT projects never end these days – instead we have 'software as a service', which is always improving and changing.

There are two stumbling blocks I have encountered when attempting iterative project management within the legal profession. The first – to which I have already alluded – is perfectionism. Working in a risk-averse profession means that a solution must often be 100% correct. Showing a work in progress or an MVP to lawyers, then, does not always lead to fruitful conversations about whether the core of the solution works: instead it can turn into a detailed conversation about all the ways it has to look better and have additional functionality. That can be an issue when trying to work in smaller steps. The second problem goes back to the communication and synergy elements of Law+People and Law+Business: lawyers can be reluctant to show clients things that are in a 'raw' form, even if it is only to get feedback before the final version. This reluctance can mean that solutions are developed into a near-final state without enough client feedback. At that point, any feedback is much harder to take on board, and indeed the client is looking at what they believe is a finished product so will feel like they need to decide whether they want it as it is presented, without any opportunity for feedback. Faced with that sort of ultimatum and a solution in which they had zero input, the answer will usually be no. As someone who has worked on projects that functioned in this way, that 'no' is especially disheartening when one has had repeated assurances from the lawyers that their clients will want the solution.

The steps of managing a project

No matter the school of project management, there are five broad phases to a project. They are called different things in different schools, they might be split up in slightly different ways, and you may revisit steps multiple times, but the essentials are always there:

- initiation,
- planning,
- execution,
- monitoring and controlling, and
- closing and reviewing.

Initiation

Initiation is the first phase of any project. During initiation you need to identify the problem, opportunity or goal that will serve as your objective. That objective needs to be properly defined, and a business case needs to be built around it. I have often encountered impatience at this stage, with people being tempted to just skip it and crack on with building something, but I have all too often seen this step being ignored only for the project to fail later. The reason for failure is usually that the project team failed to properly define the 'scope'.

The scope of a project is the parameters within which that project will run. For example, you might say that the objective is to build a tech solution that will automate employment contracts. It is important that everyone in the team has the same understanding of the scope. It is very tempting to spot new fancy features or have new ideas halfway through a project and want to throw them into the scope. This is known as 'scope creep', and it is one of the biggest dangers that projects face. Suddenly, something that started off as a small endeavour ends up taking three times as long and costing four times as much, and all because the team failed to outline a scope.

It makes sense to start small. For example, if you were developing the employment contract solution discussed earlier, then you probably would not want to start with every single jurisdiction and every possible type of employment contract all at once. That might seem obvious, but as you work through the project for one jurisdiction it might well feel natural to throw an extra clause for an additional jurisdiction in here or put another option in there. But doing either of those things costs time and money and pushes the end goal further and further away. You can see how agile iterative development comes into play here. Even when the end goal may be to produce an all-encompassing employment contract automation solution, starting with one jurisdiction means that any issues or bugs found when developing that first jurisdiction are easier to fix and it is easier to ensure that they do not occur in future iterations than if you had completed the project for all jurisdictions and *then* wanted to change something.

The usual way of defining a scope is for a set of 'requirements' to be collected from the stakeholders to the project. The stakeholders will be identified during this phase: they might be members of the team who will be working on the project, whether managing it or working on it; or they might be those who are invested in the outcome. The stakeholders should be properly recorded, along with their roles.

There are different ways of putting together requirements depending on the type of project, but if we are keeping it simple then requirements can be split into 'must haves' and 'nice to haves'. Whatever the project, you are very unlikely to achieve 100% of your aims, whether that is because of time or money constraints or some other issue. Splitting requirements in this way lets the team know what is essential and what could be changed or cut out in order to achieve the essential. The temptation is to make *everything* essential, but that is rarely a productive way to achieve anything. It is also worth pointing out here that requirements must be *certain*. A project is not going to work if the requirements are things like 'this will probably cover three or four jurisdictions'. Sometimes it can be difficult for lawyers to deal in certainties in the early stages of developing legal solutions, but it is essential that these are properly communicated.

Once the scope is established and the team is assembled, a 'project charter' can be created. This contains the project's goals, constraints, team members, budget, timeline, etc., and it should also contain the business case for engaging in the project. Business cases are usually required if you want any budget allocated to your project, and this is where having someone with Law+Business skills is handy. Servicing clients is the very essence of legal services, and clients may come to you with fantastic ideas for projects, but their desire alone does not a business case create. Unfortunately, a client wanting you to engage in a project is not enough on its own – new projects must be considered in terms of the time they will take, the resources they will use, how they tie into the broader strategy of the firm or business, and what the benefits will be to the wider organization.

Planning

The planning phase is where some organization is required. For more traditional project management methodologies, this stage can take up to half of the total time, although it is much shorter in agile project management. This is where you define the exact deliverables of the project, plan how long each deliverable is going to take, and decide how you are going to keep everyone up to date on what is happening. You should make sure that the deliverables for the project are specifically defined and are achievable within the time frame. If the goal of the project is to get to the moon within a year, then setting one of the deliverables to be 'build a ladder' is not really going to cut it. To help with planning, there are some handy acronyms that the project management community use. The easiest of these to remember is probably SMART, which relates to deliverables needing to be (i) specific, (ii) measurable, (iii) attainable, (iv) realistic and (v) timely.

In terms of the timeline for the project, this is where some process mapping might be needed in order to map out how to break down the project into manageable, deliverable chunks that can be achieved within the project's deadlines. Mapping in this way can help you spot the quickest way through the project, and it might assist in identifying stages that could, for example, be completed at the same time. There are a number of ways of tracking the timeline of a project, but two worth highlighting are the Gantt chart and the Burndown chart. Both might be used on the same project, and each works slightly differently.

Gantt charts show a breakdown of the tasks, who has responsibility for those tasks, the order in which they are to be completed, and when they take place in relation to each other. Burndown charts are much simpler and are most often used in agile projects. Put simply, a Burndown chart just shows the number of tasks left to be completed and the estimated timescale for completion. That estimate can change over time, and it can be mapped against the 'ideal' timeline for completion, although it does not need to be. Simplified examples of both of these charts are shown in figure 8.

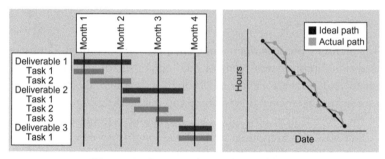

Figure 8. Gantt and Burndown charts.

Gantt charts are usually much more complex than Burndown charts, and they are useful for longer-term projects in which different tasks are to be completed at different times as they keep a record of everything that is going on. It is easy to see how this sort of chart could apply to a lengthy litigation, for example, including filing deadlines and tasks along with time taken for activities like collecting witness statements. Burndown charts are useful for showing the likely end date for a project and also for monitoring whether the project has gotten off track and/or fallen prey to scope creep.

Execution

At some stage in a project, you are going to have to actually do the work. This is in the execution phase, where the team work together to achieve the tasks that have been outlined in the planning stage.

Monitoring and controlling

This step really takes place at the same time as the execution phase, and it is where the project manager (unsurprisingly) monitors the progression of the project. This is where Gantt and Burndown charts can actively help in making sure everyone stays on track and meets deadlines. The project manager should also be monitoring whether the budget is still within its defined parameters at this stage.

Closing and reviewing

Closing a project simply means ending it. In the legal profession, this will usually be when a matter finishes, whether that is on the signing of contracts on a deal or the conclusion of litigation (by settling, victory or otherwise). Of course, deciding when to end a project can sometimes be difficult. Sometimes you need to 'fail fast' and accept that, say, the deadlines have passed or the budget has been spent, or perhaps the project team are not completing their tasks and are no longer engaged. In those cases, it is important to know when to shut down a project that is not working.

In firms that empower their lawyers to engage in knowledge and innovation projects, there is often a problem in defining the end of any such project. For example, the project may be to collect information about the current law on intellectual property in every jurisdiction for the purposes of providing an app to clients displaying this information. Those laws are always updating, though, so when do you say that the initial project has ended and that a project has ceased to be an 'innovation' project and is instead business as usual? This can be something that needs to be certain when hours are being devoted to certain activities. It also dictates which business services teams and specialists might need to work on the project. This is why the earlier stages are important: so that all the parties can agree upon a close.

The final thing to do after closing is to reflect on the lessons learned from a project. The intention here is that the next time you engage in a similar project you will not fall prey to the same pitfalls that befell this one (if there were any). It is a tricky thing to get everyone involved to take part in this sort of feedback – no one likes to spend time reviewing their failures – but it is a very important step and it is where being able to use the Law+People skill of reflection is key. More work is being done to automate the collection of this sort of feedback, but it is something you should consider doing before moving on to your next project or matter as it can help in the future.

An awareness of project management techniques is essential to managing any legal matter, but it is also a skill that anyone in legal services must possess. The reason for everyone to possess at least an entry-level proficiency in this skill is not only so that legal teams can appreciate the steps of their own projects and monitor their time, but also so that the individuals within those teams can gainfully engage with, and potentially manage, iterative development, which is commonly used by other professionals with whom they will interact.

Change management

It is not just projects that need managing: the very act of change itself is something that can be difficult to introduce into a business. For change to be implemented in a successful manner, the individuals in the business must feel like they are prepared for the change and that they are supported sufficiently to instigate and prosper from that change. Although communication is part of this, change management involves supporting people as they transition through the change, and also making them feel like the change is something they are involved in rather than something that is being done *to* them.

Managing change means, firstly, ensuring that everyone affected understands the reason behind the change and why it is good not only for the business but for the individual. If you give people a reason early on, they are more likely to support new developments rather than fight against them. Ignoring this step makes it more likely that your new change will be resisted and, even if it does go through, that there will be unwillingness to use whatever it is you have introduced. Change also needs planning. That means not only making sure that the change aligns with your organization's strategy and has a project plan attached, but that it is sponsored by someone senior in the organization and has the appropriate team assigned to it for a successful implementation.

Making change happen is a skill in itself. There are lots of people who have plenty of great ideas, but those ideas rarely make it much further unless there is commitment and dedication to enacting the change behind the idea. Implementing change means making sure that you have success criteria that you can meet for your change and that you manage the feelings of those involved in that change. It is here that Law+People skills can help with comprehending the emotions of others and making allowances for them. Change is not easy, and it can sometimes make people feel angry, displaced, worried and shocked, or put them into a state of denial.

Change management does not stop with the occurrence of the change itself: it must also include any necessary training and initiatives around increased awareness, including communications plans, those who will act as the agents and champions of the change, and how individuals will be supported throughout the change and beyond. A good acronym is always useful for keeping track when lots of factors are in play, as here, and one that is used in change management is ADKAR: (i) awareness of the change and the reasons for it; (ii) desire for change within the business; (iii) knowledge, in the form of training for the change; (iv) ability to set goals and adjust processes to successfully implement the change; and (v) reinforcement in monitoring the change and seeking feedback on its implementation.

AREA 2: PROBLEM SOLVING

Within the Law+ model, problem solving refers not only to finding the right legal advice for a client, but also to the right solution for an unexpected situation, problem, project, opportunity or challenge.

Tackling problems successfully usually takes two things: creativity and comprehension. Creativity allows us to find new ways of solving problems and to examine a problem from different angles. Comprehension is the skill of being able to synthesize information from various sources, and to undertake analysis and research in a way that leads to the best solution. Despite usually thinking of themselves as lacking creativity, lawyers are consistently asked to come up with creative ways to navigate tricky legal requirements – and anyway, just because you cannot draw does not mean you are not creative!

Creativity

Lawyers are creative people. Navigating solutions to legal challenges takes innovative thinking. The skill of creativity is one that allows us to question our approach and have the curiosity and confidence to wonder if there are better ways to solve the problems with which we are presented. As the world evolves and the law follows suit, this skill is one that lawyers and legal teams need in order to respond to new challenges and risks that firms, in-house teams and their clients will experience.

Design thinking

As with project management, the legal industry has adopted the term design thinking by sticking the word 'legal' on the front of it. Semantics aside, they are broadly the same thing, and they certainly use the same methods. Design thinking is simply an approach to solving problems. It has its roots in user-centred design, meaning that it involves the end user of the solution as much as possible in each phase of understanding the problem and developing the solution.

Quite often, what people ask for is not necessarily what they need. Knowing the problem you are trying to solve is as important – if not more important – than the solution you create. Einstein himself said that if you gave him an hour to find a solution to a problem, he would spend fifty-five minutes on the problem and five minutes on the solution. To take a more real-world example, you need look no further than elevators. A famous example of the application of design thinking relates to a series of complaints from a building's tenants regarding the slow speed of the elevators. If the problem really was the elevator speed, the only solution would be the costly replacement of the whole system. However, the building's owners took the time to understand why the slowness was an issue and found that the problem was not really related to speed but to boredom. Once the problem was properly 'framed' as relieving boredom, the answer was much simpler: install mirrors in the waiting areas and in the elevators themselves. The complaints evaporated almost overnight, because who does not like looking at themselves?

So how do you identify the right problem to solve? Well, we usually solve problems by combining three main elements: (i) the 'what', i.e. the thing that will be used to solve the problem; (ii) the 'how', i.e. the way in which the thing is going to be used; and (iii) the objective to be achieved by combining the 'what' with the 'how'.

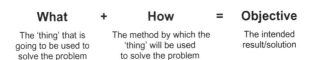

Figure 9. The problem-solving equation.

The way in which you identify and solve a problem might depend on which of these three elements you have already. For example, a law firm might have invested in a no-code piece of expertise automation software that can automate decision-making by asking the user questions that branch depending on the answers given. Having bought the software, the firm has the 'what' but now needs the 'how', as they are lacking use cases. Are they going to apply it to an internal process like the onboarding of new staff members, or are they going to use it with a client to automate their internal compliance decisions? Sponsored hackathons often work in this way, providing the 'what', in a piece of technology, and asking those present to solve a particular problem using that technology. Sometimes they might go one step further and also ask those present to identify the 'objective' or problem to be solved, but with that problem having to be one that can be solved by the technology.

The flipside of this is where a legal team knows the 'how' but does not know the 'what' that they are going to use to do it. For example, a legal team might know that it needs to automate the production of leases and it might even know that it wants to do that via a no-code solution, as they want the lawyers to develop the solution directly. What it does not know is what the 'thing' will be. This is where a legal team goes shopping for software after establishing a use case.

At its most pure, however, design thinking starts with *none* of the three elements. You do not know the 'what' or the 'how', or even the exact objective to be attained. What design thinking usually starts with is what is called a 'fuzzy front-end'. Essentially, this means that you have a messy start, without a clear direction or solution in mind, and instead you spend as much time defining (or framing) the problem as you spend coming up with and developing a solution.

This sort of approach can feel difficult the first time you try it, but it makes a lot of sense when you get further down the line to

designing a solution. To understand what clients need – the objective
– you need to conduct research and take the time to put yourself in
the shoes of the ultimate end user, perhaps by using your Law+People empathy skills. Take the example of someone asking for a new
database tool into which they can input relevant client information.
Without adopting a design thinking mindset, you may well just go
ahead and create one only to find that the reason that the data is not
currently being collected has nothing to do with technology and
everything to do with there not being a process for inputting the
data. If no user feedback mechanism is established, sometimes this
can mean going days, weeks, months or even years without knowing
that the solution was not successful and was never used.

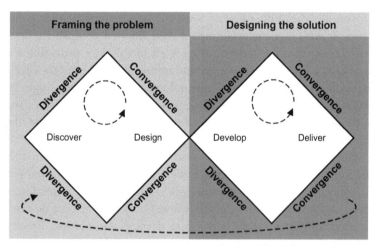

Figure 10. The double diamond of design.

The framework for engaging with design thinking is known as
the double diamond of design: see figure 10. Split into the two steps
of framing the problem and designing the solution, the reason for the
diamond shape is because in each step there is a period of divergence
in which lots of ideas are thrown around before everything converges
on a single one. Note the dotted lines in figure 10: they show that you
can move back and forth through these stages as required until the
right solution is created. A legal team that can engage in meaningful

design thinking can not only better design solutions, it can even identify challenges that their clients might not yet know exist. Obviously, I would not suggest using design thinking for everything – sometimes a client just needs an answer to a question, and they do not want to attend a physical or virtual workshop to explore their challenges – but it is a powerful tool when used correctly.

Framing the problem

When identifying a problem, there is a period of discovery. This stage is often overlooked in the excitement of creating a new solution, but it is well worth taking the time to complete it. This involves research, which ideally comes from the end users and those affected by the potential issue. This means that when designing a client solution, those who are developing the solution should also be those who are interfacing directly with the client. The lawyer and their relationship with the client are vital to this scenario, but by speaking directly to experts in the relevant profession – whether they themselves are lawyers or individuals that possess Law+ skills – a more effective solution can often be achieved, especially if those working on the problem are talking directly to equivalent professionals from within the client – IT professionals talking to IT professionals, say. Collaboration between the right people is the essential element here. For example, if you are creating a legal technology solution for a business's procurement team and you manage to have the legal team's IT professionals work with the client's IT professionals, you are more likely to successfully navigate any data security and integration issues. However, unless you involve representatives from the procurement team who are going to be using the solution, you are likely to miss elements that are important to them, and this will ultimately mean that it is less likely that the developed solution will be used. The team involved in design thinking should be multidisciplinary and collaborative, just like Law+ itself.

Lots of potential challenges to tackle may be discovered during the initial research, but eventually that information should be refined into a single viable challenge that is clearly defined and that is agreed upon by all those involved. This single problem might take the form of a 'how might we' (HMW) statement: for example, how might we simplify the process for contracting with new suppliers?

When designing an HMW statement, it is important that the problem being presented is narrow enough that it can be definitively solved but also wide enough to allow for a number of solutions. A version of the above HMW statement that is too broad would be: how might we make our procurement team's life easier? There are all sorts of things that might make that team's life easier, but the range of solutions that might fall under that umbrella are so wide as to be almost useless, and it is difficult to apply clear success criteria to any solution that is developed.

Meanwhile, a statement that is too narrow would be one such as: how might we design a product that will speed up each of the five steps the procurement team go through to onboard a new supplier? In this instance we are assuming that the current five steps – whatever they are – are going to remain in place and that the issue entirely relates to speed. This does not allow the solution team to investigate completely different processes, say, or to think of other methods of simplification that might not increase speed but might benefit the team in another way.

Designing the solution

Once a challenge has been defined, work can begin on designing a solution. Again, this stage is collaborative in nature, and the end users and those experiencing the challenge should be part of the team. As when framing the problem, the first stage of development involves an initial flurry of ideas before it is decided which one solution will be built, tested and implemented. Here is where techniques such as brainstorming and role play can be used to build an initial batch of ideas. In early design workshops, it should be stressed that no idea is a bad idea – the goal here is to get as many ideas as you can before narrowing down. As the saying goes: there is no one way to skin a cat.

There are methodologies that can help with generating ideas. One such method is the 'ten plus ten' technique. This involves members of a team sketching or designing several solutions on their own before sharing them with the team, with the aim being that ten potential ideas are created by the group as a whole. Next, the group picks one of those ideas and collectively sketches out ten versions of the idea. The aim is to make sure that every angle is covered, going both broad and deep with the ideas.

Sketching, drawing and storyboarding are all key parts of coming up with new ideas, although no advanced art skills are needed: a stick figure can work as well as masterpiece (and is much quicker to draw). Another way of producing ideas is by role playing a scenario. In our procurement example above, one member of the group could pretend to be the procurement team while another pretends to be a new supplier. As they work through the existing process, the group could explore where things could be improved. Examining a problem from a new angle helps to spot things that you might otherwise miss. When drafting exams, part of our sign-off process at my law school was to read the exam out loud to another lecturer. In doing so, we often found sentences that might not flow properly, or typos that we had missed when reading because our eyes read what we had intended to say, rather than what was there.*

Once an idea is agreed upon, work can begin on delivering a solution. While the rest of the design thinking process can proceed in quite a consistent manner, the delivery of the solution is very much dependent on what the team has chosen as that solution. Whether the solution involves people, processes, places, data or technologies, this stage should again be collaborative in nature and should involve the development of proofs of concept and early-stage MVPs before implementing the final solution. It is here that the school of iterative design from the 'process' area of Law+Change is useful in ensuring that the solution will be implemented successfully.

The triple diamond of design

You may sometimes see or hear people refer to 'triple diamond of design' thinking, rather than the double diamond we encountered earlier. Triple diamond models tend to leave 'framing the problem'

---

* No, I did not attempt the same thing when proofreading this book.

untouched but split 'designing the solution' in two, giving a whole diamond to coming up with the solution and another to the testing and implementation. The reason for this is to highlight the importance both of building out a proof of concept and of prototyping any potential solution before developing it. It can also ensure that any new solution is not just rolled out and forgotten, but is instead tested and iterated upon – something that is particularly important when implementing technological solutions.

Legal design versus design thinking

Although I have said that legal design is just design thinking with the word legal added to the front, legal design as a concept is usually described in slightly narrower terms than design thinking as a whole.

The realm of legal design has so far been closely tied to making the law more user-friendly and to making contracts more visual. While this definition sits more comfortably in the world of 'design' as the average person might understand it, the focus on the visual arts can mean that lawyers who do not think of themselves as creative and artistic feel ostracized and therefore miss out on the potential advantages of applying the concept to their day-to-day work. Visual contracts and user-friendly legal services are certainly things that can be tackled by undertaking design thinking and using connected methodologies, but you could just as easily use design thinking to analyse the pain points of a single practice group or to solve a specific legal problem for a client. In each case you still need to understand the challenges and develop solutions to them, and it does not matter that those solutions might have nothing to do with visual design or user experience. Design thinking is basically a tool for solving any problem, whether it is to do with a specific legal problem or disruption of the entire profession.

User interface and user experience

The terms user interface (UI) and user experience (UX) are being referenced increasingly in professional services, and there is good reason for this: they combine to ensure that anything we use is *actually* useful. While UI and UX are often used interchangeably, they are very different and they are both important. Put very simply, a UI is what something looks like while UX is what something feels like to use. These concepts apply equally to both products and services.

UI and UX can be used to guide users and to encourage certain actions. Take, for example, the cookies notification that often pops up when you are visiting a new website. The way in which these notifications are laid out is an interesting insight into the importance of design. Usually, the buttons that the website *wants* you to click (i.e. the choices that give the website owner access to all of your data) are in green while those allowing you to restrict such access are greyed out, as if they cannot be clicked. Likewise, if you click to clarify your choices, the options are usually presented in an overwhelming fashion that encourages you to click 'accept all'. Next time you get one of these notifications have a closer look at which buttons are highlighted, which are greyed out, and how the different pop-ups differ in trying to get you to give your acceptance. Design can shape behaviour.

On the whole, design is often one of those things that you never think about unless it is bad. I am sure we have all had the experience of using an app that did not let us do what we wanted to do, a web page that was not structured as we might have liked, or a frying pan that did not heat up quickly enough. The example that springs to my mind involves a mug I bought a few years ago. You may think that a mug is fairly simple from a design point of view: it has to hold hot liquid without burning the holder. So far, so simple. It has probably never occurred to you that another requirement is that the mug should not stab you in the eyes. This seems like it might be an obvious point. One that does not need expressing. However, my mug decided to play fast and loose with convention and … stab me in the eyes. How? Well, it was a very cute little mug. It had a cat's face on it. To drive home the cat theme, it also had, as a nice touch, a couple of little ears. Triangular spiky ears that protruded from the rim. Triangular spiky ears that protruded from the rim opposite the side from which I drank, which meant the act of drinking came with a side order of almost blinding myself. This is a good example of the difference between UI and UX. The *interface* of the mug – the way it looked – was great. It was quirky enough that I was excited to purchase it. The *experience* of using it, though, was horrendous. I bought the mug, but I would never buy a similar mug again, and I would certainly not use it. You can see it for yourself in figure 11.

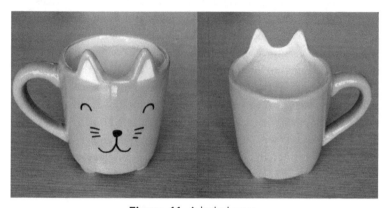

Figure 11. A lethal mug.

To take another example from the world of services, I am going to pick on the streaming service Disney+. The first iteration of the search interface for Disney+ involved the alphabet set out on a single line. To search for an item you simply clicked on the letters that spelled out the term you were looking for, and the suggested results would show up. It looked beautiful and minimalist, and the single line of text meant more space to show the suggested movies or series that were displayed as the search continued to narrow. But using it was an absolute *pain*. Why? Because although the UI was nice, the UX was not. Inputting a title on a TV remote or videogame pad meant having to scroll all the way from left to right. Take the Disney film *Raya and the Last Dragon* as an example. At the beginning of any search, the letter 'A' is highlighted. To search for 'Raya' I had to scroll all the way over to the letter 'R' only to then have to scroll all the way back to 'A' and then almost to the other end of the alphabet for 'Y' before finally returning to 'A' again. Now you would hope by this point the movie would have come up in the suggested solutions, but it was an annoyance to have to do this every time.

In both examples above, the UI was good while the UX was bad, but that is not to say that the interface is irrelevant. The importance of aesthetics cannot be denied. All too often I have seen lawyers and clients presented with a solution that does everything they want it to do but with a UI that is 'a bit dated' or 'too busy' or does not match their brand. Even if the *experience* of using it is good, it has already been discounted and the intended audience will feel less confident in using that solution or selling it to clients. Despite solving every problem and crafting a solution that can do everything, it will end up doing nothing if it is not actually used. Both UI and UX need to be understood and taken into account.

You might not think that these sorts of problem affect business decisions. In the case of Disney+, for example, it was a service I continued to use despite the interface. But that was because I could not get the content I wanted anywhere else. Where people *can* get the content in question elsewhere, this sort of annoyance is unacceptable to users. Research by Google in 2016 found that around 53% of mobile website visitors left a webpage if it failed to load within three seconds, and I would not be surprised if that percentage were much higher now.[1]

In a competitive legal market, clients can get legal services elsewhere. If you are seeking to sell clients a tracker that updates them on ESG law in competition with other firms, for example, then how easy that tracker is to use is going to be vitally important. Clients are not going to spend time inspecting if the laws that are being shown are correct – they expect that of a law firm – so the differentiators are likely to be price and useability. Likewise, businesses can choose not to use the tools, documents or methods produced by their in-house legal department. If an automated contracting solution developed by the legal department for the procurement team fails to work as expected, that team will simply not use it; it could sour relationships between the teams, and the problem the automation was responding to will certainly not be solved. Where there are other options, making an interface pleasant to look at and use suddenly becomes a priority. The UI and UX are as important as – and sometimes more important than – the content. Even a huge organization like Disney has since changed its interface, and has made a number of other 'quality of life' changes to the UX based on consumer research and feedback.

This also applies outside of pure technology. Let us assume that a client has asked you for guidance on the legal position on changing prices during the Covid-19 pandemic because their CEO wants to examine the viability of raising prices due to issues with supply chains. If you provide the client's legal team with a 500-page bundle explaining the rules and regulations, there is little chance they are going to read it even if it is nicely laminated or comes as a branded PDF – even if it is bound in a leather book. The UX for the intended use – advising the CEO on whether price changes can go ahead – is bad. Next time the client has a similar question, they will ask another firm or they will potentially find their own way of monitoring those legal positions, thereby cutting off a revenue stream for you. Both interface and experience need to be understood and considered when providing a client with any sort of legal solution.

Comprehension

The emphasis with problem solving is on human problems, and this is because the genesis of design thinking was in the school of 'human-centred design'. The idea behind human-centred design is that rather than assuming what your end users want, or even just asking them outright, you instead take the time to understand their position and the context within which their challenge sits. The goal behind this is to create better solutions that actually solve problems. The essential element in all of this is the understanding, which takes the skill of comprehension via research and synthesis. Comprehension is closely aligned with the Law+People skill of empathy: if empathy is an individual's cognitive, emotional and behavioural capacity, then comprehension is the combination of methods that individual uses in order to increase his or her understanding sufficiently to inform that capacity.

Research

Every lawyer undertakes legal research at some stage during their career. When I was a student this might have meant going to the law library and navigating various tomes in order to find the answer to a tricky legal problem. Now it is more likely to involve using the correct search engines, tools and terms. In legal education, though, these legal problems are usually simulated. Even if they involve role play, the actor with whom you are talking has only a narrow script outlining their situation, and everyone involved in developing that activity already has an idea of the solution you are going to reach. In the real world that is not the case. Often there is no answer to a problem. At other times there are *too many* answers! The one advantage with real-world problems, though, is that those who are posing the questions and problems actually do live in the world from which the problem or challenge originates, and they have far more contextual information than an actor or an activity on a page.

The aspect of research discussed in this section is not about how to navigate legal resources or how to find cases or legislation that are pertinent to the problem. Instead, we are looking at understanding the people and the context of the problem you are trying to solve in order to better craft and deliver your solution. You can undertake research at various stages of problem solving, whether that is to better understand your users and the problem, to come up with ideas taking inspiration from others, or to get feedback on what is being produced.

Inductive and deductive approaches

As mentioned above, rather than just focus on legal research here, I am going to examine research methods as a whole. Although there are lots of different types of research with which you can engage, there are two schools that define the starting point of that research: inductive research and deductive research. People often do not understand the distinction between the two, for which I partly blame Sir Arthur Conan Doyle. Sherlock Holmes is famously described as a master of deduction, but in reality he uses both schools of research, as you will see as you read about each.

Deductive research is the type we most often use in the legal profession. This is where you already have a theory or an idea and you want to test whether it works. For example, you could be asked if a company is required to comply with legal rules on pricing their goods. The parameters are set, and you know within certain boundaries what you are trying to prove.

Inductive research, on the other hand, is where you are seeking to generate a new theory based on the data you find from research. An example of this would be if you were to review the process and pain points of a practice group to look for opportunities for increasing profitability. You have no idea what the challenges might be or the solutions you might want to implement. Design thinking methods lend themselves to this type of research.

Knowing which approach you are taking can help you pick your methods and decide on the types of question you might ask. It also gives you some guidance about how the research is going to proceed – deductive research may finish as soon as a theory is disproved, for example.

Quantitative and qualitative data

Having looked at two *approaches* to research, let us now look at two *types of data* we can collect from our research. The first is quantitative data, which is revealed via structured research methods that give defined numerical or textual values; the second is qualitative data, which is more free-form and can lead to a range of different responses. A simple example of the difference between the two is that a survey that contains predefined options and ratings is going to give you quantitative data, while a sit-down interview with an individual or a free-text box in a survey is going to reveal qualitative data.

There is great appeal in quantitative data. It is easier and quicker to collect and it lends itself to being put into dashboards and charts that make for persuasive arguments when presenting the results of the research. However, the exact wording of the questions and the options given does need careful consideration to ensure that the results are meaningful, as they are devoid from any context and can be easy to misconstrue. Another danger with using only quantitative research is that you can use it to 'lead the witness'.* The way in which you frame a question can lead to quite different answers. For example,

---

*To use the legal terminology.

'How much of a problem did you find X on a scale of 1 to 10?' and 'How simple did you find X on a scale of 1 to 10?' can make very different impressions on the reader, implying that X is either difficult or easy before someone has even had a chance to answer. You should also be mindful of any scale that you use; it is tempting to ask people to comment on a scale of 1 to 5 or 1 to 10, but in both those cases people are much more likely to pick 3 or 5, respectively, as it is right in the middle and they do not have to make a clear choice. Questions should be clear, reliable and succinct. They should also be carefully timed. I am sure that at one point or another we have all been forced to complete a questionnaire on a website or after using a service. I can guarantee that some of you have not given honest answers to these surveys, just clicking on anything to get it over with. I know I have.

Qualitative data, on the other hand, takes a lot longer to collect and can be difficult to turn into scientific-looking charts and graphs, but what you do discover tends to be more meaningful. This sort of information is better sourced from interviews, focus groups and observation, rather than from directed questionnaires or surveys. You still need to be careful about how questions are framed, but allowing someone to talk openly can lead to more honest opinions. If you really cannot live without the charts and graphs, then after doing your open-format discovery you can engage in 'coding' – identifying and grouping similar words and terms and giving them defined values – to produce something that can be put into data sets and dashboards. For example, if you interviewed ten clients about their experiences on legal matters, you might receive three responses that state 'I got a lot of emails updating me on progress', 'There was a constant stream of communication' and 'I was always informed about the progress of the matter'. You could 'code' these three responses as each relating to 'communication' and you could therefore state that 30% of respondents praised communication during matters.

Quantitative research is better suited to the deductive approach (where you are testing a known theory), while qualitative research is better for the inductive approach (where the theory and answer are both being sought). However, a balance of both is always useful. Take as an example a new automated document solution for a client.

Speaking to a focus group of users can give you opinions on the solution's use, but you could also drill down into the data to see how many times people used it and for what purpose, or you could have a wider survey attached to the tool that asks for the experience of the user on a sliding scale. Thinking carefully about the way we conduct research can help us to better engage clients and others in the solutions we create.

Synthesis

Conducting research and ensuring attention to detail is useless if you cannot bring it all together with the legal and business knowledge your team possesses. Being able to synthesize means being capable of taking information from different resources and using that varied information to give advice or solve a client problem. Synthesis is all about being able to provide contextual advice and to understand the client and the information that is presented so that you can be a valued business partner.

After conducting your research, there are a number of ways you can synthesize your findings in order to ensure you are applying those findings in the most appropriate way to reach a suitable solution. I have highlighted a couple of those you may be less familiar with, but which can be useful in a legal context, below.

Personas

I love personas.* Why? Because they help you to better understand your clients and end users and give you a quick cheat sheet for checking whether a solution will work before you ever have to deploy anything. Building a good persona helps you to spot problems before they occur, and it can also build the empathy that is so important to Law+People skills. In short, a persona is a profile that represents a particular group or segment of your end users. This is built not on guesses and assumptions but on foundational research with which you have engaged.

---

*Yes, I am using personas as the plural rather than personae.

To understand how personas work, it helps to start by thinking of a dating profile. You will find a picture of the person; some key statistics about them, including their age and location; a short biography; and then some information about their preferences and frustrations, their goals and motivations. The persona will not be based on any one person but will be an amalgam of several real features you discovered in your research. The picture is to build an empathetic link and should be a stock photo rather than an actual person you interviewed.

To give an example of how personas can be useful, I was once involved in developing a solution for clients to receive automated advice on a range of smaller legal matters. Throughout the development process we had only really considered one use case: members of the in-house team using the tool to request and receive advice. What had not been considered was that the general counsel that ran that team wanted to use the tool in a different way: to look at how their lawyers used it and what advice was being sought, so they could better understand how often and in what situations external counsel were being consulted. And the lawyers in my firm wanted to use the tool in a third way: to be notified when the client posted a question and to be able to follow up on the automated advice from within the system itself. Once all this was understood we were able to take a step back and gain some good feedback from these different types of user and develop a persona for each of them. At each stage of development, we were able to return to those personas and see if each group were still able to use it as they wanted.

Maps

We have already talked about process maps in the 'Process' section above, but there are a whole range of maps that can be used when collating research. These include journey maps, of how a user might proceed through using the solution; system maps, outlining visually the relationships between different parts of a complex system, and where and when it intersects and integrates with other systems; data maps that show where the data goes and where it is stored in technology solutions; and stakeholder maps that show who interacts with the solution and where and when they do so. All of these maps help you to visualize how the tool will be used and to ensure that the solution will actually work. Much like process maps, they can be used to spot inefficiencies or redundancies in the solution before it is built. There are simplified versions of these maps in figure 12.

Jobs and stories

Using personas and maps is important because they help us create task lists of what to do when developing solutions. Once you know your users and how they will navigate your solution, you can start to ask important questions that will create your tasks or jobs. Two ways to reveal these tasks are by using the 'jobs to be done' framework and by crafting 'user stories'.

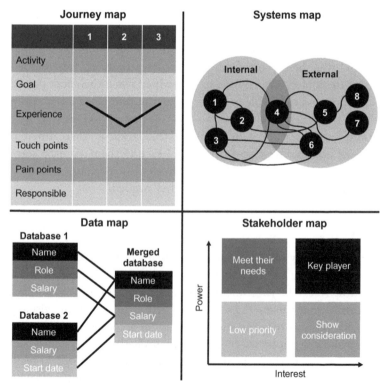

Figure 12. Simplified depictions of map types.

The jobs to be done framework looks like this:

When ... [situation], *I want to* ... [motivation], *so I can* ... [expected outcome].

A user story is similar, but it is framed as follows:

As a ... [user type], *I want* ... [action], *so that* ... [outcome].

These questions get right to the core of what is needed to solve a problem. In the example I gave in the 'Personas' section above, we might have used the following 'job to be done' example for the general counsel:

When I log into the tool, *I want to* see a dashboard of the queries my team have made, *so I can* see where they may need additional training.

In addition, we may have used the following user story for a partner in my firm:

As a partner in the firm, *I want* to be able to type my advice into the tool, *so that* the client can both log their query and see their advice in one place.

This user story could combine with one from a member of the in-house team that reads:

As a member of the in-house team, *I want* to see all my advice in one place, *so that* I do not have to log into several different systems.

It is important to stress that these methods are not designed to deal with the development of products, but are based on the school of service design, which is entirely dedicated to the provision of professional services. They are therefore entirely applicable to the delivery of legal advice.

CHAPTER 7

Law+Technology

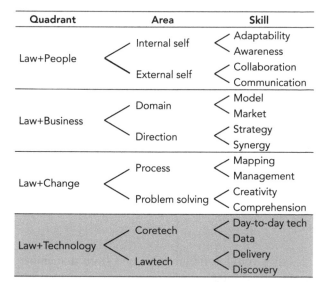

Quadrant	Area	Skill
Law+People	Internal self	Adaptability / Awareness
	External self	Collaboration / Communication
Law+Business	Domain	Model / Market
	Direction	Strategy / Synergy
Law+Change	Process	Mapping / Management
	Problem solving	Creativity / Comprehension
Law+Technology	Coretech	Day-to-day tech / Data
	Lawtech	Delivery / Discovery

For many in the legal sphere, there is a belief that legal technology – also known as 'lawtech' – is synonymous with innovation, and that the future of the legal profession is entirely dependent on the adoption of new technologies. According to database company Statista, the lawtech market generated revenues of $17.32 billion worldwide in 2019, with predicted revenues in 2025 of $25.17 billion.[1] A recent report commissioned by Lawtech UK estimated that the annual demand for legal technology in 2022 in the United

Kingdom alone is worth up to £22 billion.[2] Even more conservative estimates predict that revenue will rise to £2.2 billion by 2026.[3] Legal technology directory site Legaltech Hub[4] lists almost 2,000 different technology vendors that are working with legal teams across the profession. And yet despite all of this drive and investment, it is important to emphasize that technology is often no more than a solution looking for a problem.

What do I mean by that? Well, unless you understand the problem you are trying to solve and those who are encountering it, there is not much point waving technology in its general direction. If you automate a bad process, you still have a bad process – it just works faster. Although all four of the Law+ quadrants work best when they are combined, Law+Technology is the one that is most in need of the others if it is to have the desired impact. Those with Law+People, Law+Business and Law+Change skills are required to understand their clients and select the right solution for them. Empathy, adaptability, collaboration, communication, understanding clients' business drivers, mapping processes, managing projects and solving problems in creative ways are all necessary prerequisites for engaging with lawtech.

Lawtech is a big deal in the profession. There are multiple news sites, such as Legal Technology Insider, entirely dedicated to lawtech; there are numerous annual awards, such as the American Legal Technology awards; and there are scores of industry-wide initiatives, such as the Future Law Innovation Programme in Singapore. Despite being the subject of so much discourse, there is still much debate in the profession about what lawtech actually *is*, which requires a definition of both technology itself, as a concept, and the subset of technology that comprises 'lawtech'.

Law is not unique in considering this sort of question. During my master's in educational technology (which is known as 'edtech'), one of the first questions we tackled was the definition of technology itself, which is *very* wide if you go by the dictionary definition. Technology is essentially any tool that has been devised by knowledge/science and that is used to solve a problem. This means that, technically speaking, a chair is a piece of technology. It certainly solves a problem – not wanting to sit on the floor – and it was devised by knowledge. Of course, this is not what people are talking about when they discuss 'edtech', and it is certainly not what is meant by 'lawtech'.

Over time the definition of lawtech has been bent and stretched to cover pretty much whatever an individual wants it to cover. A common understanding of the term is that it is technology that supports, provides or changes legal services delivery. As a former lawyer who has never managed to shake off the profession's attention to detail when examining wording, it irks me that this definition is circular: it basically describes legal technology as 'technology in legal'. Does this mean the chair that makes a client comfier when having a meeting is a piece of lawtech? A chair is certainly technology, as we have established. It also (very literally) 'supports' the delivery of legal services: I cannot imagine that the client would be too impressed if they had to sit on the floor.*

Other definitions of lawtech I have encountered go wider than this definition and include elements of the skills contained within Law+Change, Law+Business and even Law+People, with people using the hype generated about the term to gain traction in discussing their own spin on it. The problem with defining lawtech too widely comes back to the fact that, for the average lawyer, the term 'lawtech' just means legal technology. This has led to the blurring of lines between innovation and lawtech, and it is part of the reason people think that innovation *is* technology.

For the sake of clarity, the definition of lawtech used within this book is as follows:

> Software provided primarily or exclusively to the legal profession in order to offer legal advice or to deliver legal services.

The reason for focusing on technology that is 'primarily or exclusively' provided to the profession is to differentiate lawtech from other technology that a legal team might use, such as the Microsoft suite of software, which is not exclusively used by the legal profession. The Law+Technology quadrant is therefore split into two parts:

---

* Except maybe if they were sitting on a beanbag in an innovation lab or hub.

(i) lawtech, defined as above; and (ii) coretech, which is defined as follows:

> Software that is *not* provided primarily or exclusively to the legal industry but that is used by legal professionals when offering legal advice or delivering legal services.

Case study. Legal Technology Core Competencies Certification Coalition (LTC4)

Formed in 2010, the not-for-profit global organization LTC4 was founded by a group of volunteer lawyers, legal technology trainers and IT specialists in order to develop a set of legal technology core competencies and to 'set the global standard for legal technology proficiency'. This led to the development of ten LTC4 'Learning Plans' and their aligned certification. They are all application and workflow-agnostic so as to allow tailoring for an individual organization. The LTC4 competencies are an industry standard foundation-level structure for legal technology training. The LTC4 global network includes law firms and law schools including Burges Salmon, Dentons, DLA Piper, Lerners, McKenzie Lake, Simmons & Simmons, Squire Patton Boggs and the University of Law.

The Learning Plans are designed to be incorporated into the internal policies of any law firm, legal team or law school, and for that reason they are scenario-based. They are:

- Working with Legal Documents
- Managing Documents and Emails
- Time Recording
- Collaborating with Others
- Client Relationship Management
- Security Awareness
- Hybrid Working
- Visual Communications
- Data and Reports
- Video Conferencing

LTC4 Certification has become a global industry standard for core legal technology skills. The plans are routinely reviewed by a wide range of volunteers to ensure that they remain relevant to practice.

Different organizations have taken different routes to certification of LTC4 skills, with some introducing LTC4 for new hires, while others are introducing the skills as part of wider professional development initiatives. The plans can be purchased individually, on an annual renewable basis, or as packages to address particular requirements. Each purchase includes the workflows and skills required to show competence, a pre-check of the training programme and assessment method by the Certification Pod, and two submissions of successful individuals for certification purposes. Learn more at https://ltc4.org/.

ADOPTION

In a recent study from Legatics, 95% of trainees and associates interviewed believed that 'it is important to implement and use new legal technology', and 75% of all partners interviewed indicated that lawtech was 'important for the future of their firm'. Despite these striking numbers, the report found that there are still barriers to introducing lawtech into the profession, including limited prioritization from organizations, a lack of knowledge about what is available and what its capabilities are, inadequate training for the technology that is in place, and a relatively small pool of role models or 'champions' showcasing how to use the available technology.[5]

How did we end up here? At the turn of the century, with clients asking for new ways of working and with increasing competition from new entrants to the profession, law firms were looking for ways to increase efficiency and deliver new methods of problem-solving. The issue was that traditional firms had not hired or invested in those with Law+ skills, so they sought the answer from external sources, which for the most part were technology vendors. The problem there was that those technology vendors were understandably invested in selling their solutions to firms and advertising the technology as a panacea to cure all ills, so we ended up in a market where everyone was buying technology and shouting about it in the press, while having no one with the skills to properly use it and with it potentially not solving a problem the firm was encountering anyway. The amount of technology a firm used or deployed became synonymous with 'innovation'.

The problem with judging success based solely on the amount of technology an organization owns is that prevalence often fails to translate to equivalent rates of adoption, usage or client satisfaction. Let us look at an example from another field: the One Laptop Per Child project. The project's intention was laudable: to transform education by (as you might have guessed) ensuring that every child in the world, and particularly those in developing countries, had access to a laptop. Although a number of factors contributed to its eventual failure, part of the issue was that success was based on the *number* of laptops distributed. Putting to one side some of the other criticisms of the scheme, this focus on the number of laptops delivered failed to appreciate the complexities of training children and teachers in using the technology and ensuring that the proper infrastructure was in place.

And we can see something similar in law right now: success is based on the amount of technology a legal team has, and adoption surveys and reports fuel the fire by equating number of tools bought with how progressive or advanced the legal sector is. What is *really* needed is an in-depth examination of how that technology has increased client and customer satisfaction, examining whether more technology really does equate to a better level of client service.

It may sound as if I am against the implementation of technology in law firms. Far from it. When properly planned, implemented and integrated in a manner that works for users – and when it is deployed in response to an actual problem – technology can and does achieve wonders. It is just that technology is only one aspect of the skills of the legal team of the future, rather than the totality of it. If the point is to better service our clients, then the medium should not matter.

AREA 1: CORETECH

Although law firms and legal teams are investing more into legal operations and technology expertise, there is still a lot of hype and misunderstanding about what technology can do. For example, much of what people perceive as 'artificial intelligence' is really just advanced search, or software following a simple structured process, as opposed to a computer truly reading and understanding legal language and applying reasoning to its decisions. Additionally, there are a lot more humans behind the scenes than people expect – people that are connecting the dots between the artificial intelligence and the inputs and outputs from it. This is unlikely to change in the future, with Gartner predicting that these sorts of 'human-in-the-loop' solutions will comprise 30% of new legal technology automation offerings by 2025.[6]

The fact is that you can buy all the technology you want but if you do not have people who understand it and can sell it internally and to clients, you might as well simply throw all your money into a big hole. Indeed, many of those firms spending six-figure sums on the promise of technology might be better off using that money to hire some capable people who can use the *existing* technology that their organization owns before investing in anything new.

A deeper understanding of the tools that you use day to day is important when considering how you might complete tasks and make best use of the technologies available to you. There are many people out there who essentially use Microsoft Word as a very expensive typewriter, for example, when it can do much more. A lot of what people want lawtech to do can actually be achieved with tools and technology that a legal team or law firm already possesses. Even if the tools that are already owned are not quite fit for purpose, they are usually more than good enough to create an MVP that can prove a concept and then spot any issues with a solution before spending a fortune on implementing new technology. I cannot tell you how many times I have been presented with a group who want to buy a new piece of technology without first identifying what problem it is that they want to fix.

A good example from practice is when I was asked to assist with a project to monitor the shareholdings of various corporate clients. The team wanted a new piece of technology into which they could input their data, but there was no current process to store all the data that was being collected. People were storing data in random places – sometimes in shared documents, sometimes in personal documents. After reworking the process, a centralized collaborative Microsoft Excel document was sufficient, from a technology perspective, to capture the data, and a connected Microsoft PowerBI data visualization dashboard gave a hub for clients to visit. Similarly, during the pandemic I encountered lawyers who were asking for new technologies that could assist them in viewing two different parts of a digital document at once – a problem unique to working from home, when printing reams of documents was not an option. The need to view two parts of a document at once was usually down to the fact that the definitions section of a legal document is essential in deciphering its clauses – the definitions section is sometimes longer than the actual commercial legal agreement in fact. While there were all sorts of new technologies that *could* have been used, a quick tutorial on the 'Split view' function of Microsoft Word was all it took to solve the problem.

The key elements of coretech are divided between (i) the 'day-to-day' technologies that we use and (ii) the way in which we identify and use 'data', which I believe holds the key to the future advancement of legal services.

Day-to-day tech

Legal teams have access to a raft of technology even before they purchase any lawtech. There are usually various standard 'office' technologies, such as Microsoft Word and Excel; collaborative tools, such as Google Docs; software that is being used by other teams (including business services), such as marketing and IT; and, for in-house teams, the technology solutions that are being used across the rest of the business. The lawyers are often unaware that this technology exists, but even where they are using it, there is often a lack of understanding about its full capabilities.

Part of the issue here is an assumption that 'younger people' will use technology effectively and that those who are already established within law can rely on newcomers to solve any problems. Speaking to law firms and in-house teams in the mid 2000s, I found that the majority of organizations I surveyed expected new joiners to change the technology landscape of their business in the next 5–10 years. We are currently beyond that horizon and it seems to me that we are still waiting for the revolution. Assumptions like this are reinforced by terminology such as 'digital natives' (describing someone who has grown up with technology and is intimately familiar with it) and 'digital immigrants' (those raised prior to the most recent 'information age' of technology and the Internet who are therefore treated as being less familiar). It is worth pointing out that the relevance of those terms has been soundly disproven, not only because they were terms thought of more than twenty years ago but also because there is no actual difference between the way the minds of supposed 'natives' and 'immigrants' work.[7] Instead, all these terms do is feed into a fixed mindset that allows people to assume they will never understand technology because they did not grow up with it.

The dangers of this assumption do not just go one way, either. Just as those currently in practice may believe themselves to be 'too old' or 'too conditioned' to use new technology, so too can those working their way through university and law school assume that they are already better with technology than those in practice, and that is not always the case. While it is true that younger people are likely to have grown up using different technology and that they might be more willing to experiment with technology generally, the problem is that the technologies they are proficient with are *not those that law firms and legal teams actually use.* To prove this I used to conduct a mind map exercise with my law students in which they would map onto a grid their level of expertise with a given piece of technology along with how often it was used in practice (as opposed to personally). Unsurprisingly, the average map looked like that in figure 13.

One can clearly see that the level of expertise the students had with the technologies they used in their personal lives was far higher than the expertise they could demonstrate when it came to technologies used in the traditional legal workplace. There are a few outliers, where the level of expertise is higher for technology that is mostly used in practice, but only because the university or law school was using those particular technologies. One conclusion we might draw from these findings is that law firms and legal teams are using

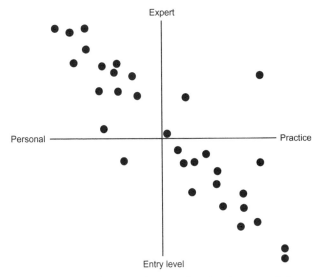

Figure 13. A student mind map of technology proficiency.

out-of-date technology or the wrong technology solutions altogether. Remember, however, that the Law+ model is designed to move the needle from where we are *now*, so we must first acknowledge the current technology stacks that legal teams possess.

This is a good moment to tell you a story from when I used to host innovation conferences for law students. During these conferences I would ask everyone in the audience who listed 'Microsoft Office' or 'Microsoft Word' as a skill on their CV/résumé to raise their hands. A *lot* of hands always went up. I would then ask those with their hands up to lower their hands if they did not know how to do something from a list I read out. That list included track changes, using styles, format painting, auto-cross-referencing, running a comparison and understanding metadata. By the time I was halfway through the list most hands were down, and by the time I had finished it there was usually no more than one or two students who still had a hand up. This is where the problem with assumptions is at its worst: the people joining the profession are professing to be experts in technologies, but the skills they have in those technologies are not equivalent to those that someone already working in a legal team would consider expert. I am concerned that this divide not only serves to reduce the adoption of technology in legal but is also one that people have not fully considered.

Working with documents

Lawyers spend a lot of time working with documents. Whether it is a prospectus, an employment contract, a loan agreement, a witness statement or a piece of advice, those in the legal profession are often drafting, amending, reviewing, combining or critiquing documentation.

Most legal teams and clients still use Microsoft Word when drafting. It is easy to see why: most organizations already own it, there is a low price point to entry, and Microsoft Office contains a number of different programs that are, for the most part, interconnected and generally work as advertised.

The fact that Office is widely used also means it comes in for a lot of criticism. Some of that criticism is well founded: pulling metadata out of a Microsoft Word document to try and glean some insights about what it contains is still a difficult feat unless you are prepared to learn and use a language that can be read by both computers and humans, such as XML. Some of it is not: there are a lot of people who complain about not being able to share or co-draft a Microsoft Word document, as they can in Google Docs, but that functionality does exist, at least in the Office 365 versions of Word.

This is not an argument for or against legal teams continuing to use Microsoft but is instead just explaining the reality: understanding the day-to-day of working with documents usually means being proficient with Microsoft Office. You will probably need familiarity with a technology that deals with PDFs too. Lawyers often share PDF versions of documents to ensure they keep the same formatting no matter what system someone is using, and to treat a document as 'final'. It is worth stressing here that PDFs can be amended, combined, signed and saved as word processing documents, and vice versa. They are not as locked down as people assume.

Whatever word processing software a legal team uses, it should be able to use styles in documents. By this I do not mean manually putting headings in bold and indenting paragraphs by pressing the space bar a few times. That sort of 'styling' can corrupt documents and make them very difficult to amend, and sometimes it can make them entirely unrecoverable. Law firms often have a house style that should be followed when drafting, which may involve rules on numbering, styles, fonts, etc. The reason for this is partially branding, with the idea being that a client can immediately see that a document is from firm X, but the other slightly more important reasons are consistency and certainty in the way in which documents are drafted and the language in them is used, and to avoid documents becoming corrupted.

While talking about lawyers working on documents, it is worth addressing document automation. While some may consider this 'lawtech', document automation is in use in a number of different fields to speed up the creation of first-draft documentation. Many legal teams use document automation in their day to day work, and there are plenty of tools that can automatically draft documents, such as Contract Express, HotDocs, Avokka, and more, and this is without mentioning open-source solutions or tools that include document automation as a small part of a wider offering. These document automation tools are becoming more prevalent in the legal profession, and legal teams should seek to understand not only how to use them to create automated documents but also how to automate documents in the first place. They should also get to grips with knowing what types of documents can be automated.

While people may think of document automation as automatically creating only a single document, whole suites of documents can be automated based on one round of inputs. This increases speed and consistency of drafting, removing the chance for human error when writing out the same information again and again. In terms of identifying appropriate documents for automation, think about whether you are either typing the same information into multiple documents on a repeated basis or whether you are regularly drafting an almost identical document. Both of these cases are ripe for automating.

Once documents are drafted they need to be saved, shared and searched for. Most law firms and in-house teams will have some form of document management system (DMS). A DMS is essential when managing huge numbers of documents. It can store and file documents, emails and other types of file in a manner that complies with the strict risk appetites of the profession by, for example, ensuring the right documents are archived and that they are discoverable in the event of a firm being asked for an audit of the location of all of their data. DMSs collect information about documents (metadata) that is specific to the legal sector, such as version numbers and matter numbers, and they usually have search functionality that allows legal teams to find the documents they need. This sort of search infrastructure, and being able to find knowledge, is a key part of the work of many a knowledge management and innovation team in the legal profession, and being able to use a DMS effectively is essential to legal practice.

An often-overlooked area when discussing documents is slideshows. We mostly think of documents as pages of written text, and many of the presentation slides I have seen in practice are just that: lines and lines of written text, rather than engaging presentation aides. Being able to produce effective presentations is important when engaging with clients, whether that be in a pitch, an update meeting or in the delivery of advice. There are lots of different pieces of tech out there that can help with the design of presentations, and truly understanding the technology can do wonders when it comes to adding finishing touches – whether that is knowing how to add and manage animations such as zoom and fade, making things move along motion paths, working with triggers that make slideshows interactive, or just understanding how to align shapes and use brand-specific colours. I know quite a few lawyers who have wasted many an hour working on a single slide or structure chart in a presentation, or on getting all the words and shapes to align and be in the client's colours, when it could have been done by someone proficient in a matter of minutes. This might not seem like a major skill, but it can save you a lot of time and it has always served me well, especially if you work in an organization without a large design team and therefore have to do things on your own.

Electronic signatures

During the pandemic, e-signatures became a piece of coretech that every business and legal team needed to understand. While the use of electronic signatures was more sporadic prior to the extended period of working from home, the use of e-signatures by legal teams is now not simply a preference but, in many instances, a necessity.

So what is an e-signature? Well, it is a signature that is electronic in nature, meaning you sign on a computer rather than on paper. The signature has the same legal standing as a handwritten or 'wet ink' signature provided there is compliance with the relevant jurisdiction's legal requirements. The use of e-signatures can make signings faster and easier, and many tools that assist with the drafting or managing of documents will now integrate with e-signature technologies so as to make signings simpler. Most law firms and legal teams now have e-signature software, and if you are not already familiar with using them, you should enlighten yourself soon.

Electronic signatures have been binding in various forms across the globe since the turn of the century, and this reflects the increasing recognition of business being conducted digitally; for example, the Law Commission in the United Kingdom has recently suggested methods for how international trade documents (which currently have to physically move from jurisdiction to jurisdiction) can be transferred electronically. This form of signing documents is not going away any time soon, pandemic or no pandemic, and it is an essential part of the future of 'smart' contracts that auto-execute upon the occurrence of certain events.

Time recording

Although this primarily applies to lawyers within a firm, it extends in some instances to business services teams in firms and to in-house teams. Regardless of whether you personally have to record time, somebody you work with is likely to record theirs, and knowing how they work and how they use this technology can help you work with them and understand their motivations. While in the past lawyer time was recorded by noting down six-minute intervals or dictating the way time was spent throughout the day to a secretary who would fill in the relevant forms, it is now mostly monitored online. Time recording can, ironically, take a lot of time itself, so being able to use technology to assist can be a massive boon. Despite being a piece of coretech, most law firms will use legal-specific time recording software. For some tools there are on-screen timers that can be pre-programmed with matter numbers, and colour coordination for different tasks. Some allow filing and pre-drafted narratives (descriptions of the work undertaken) to be completed automatically. There are now even tools that can automatically monitor the activities of the user throughout the day and then have a first draft of what was being worked on without any input from the time-recorder at all.

Recording time is so important to many firms that it is worth learning the basics of time-recording software at your first available opportunity.

Digital collaboration

Online collaboration and communication is now ubiquitous. The longer we worked from home, the less essential were the quick training sessions on whichever online collaboration software was being used – it was just assumed people were proficient already. Even the number of people speaking while on mute has dropped drastically, while the use of accidental filters* has plummeted. Everyone got good at it. Yes, there are still a few hiccups, but I think we can all give ourselves a pat on the back. We managed to make it work, business continued to run, and we all put up with the huge number of online quizzes we had to do with our friends and family.

As the office has become less of a physical place and more of a hybrid workspace for many organizations – within the legal services industry and outside it – the collaboration that started with video has now expanded into collaborative workspaces, cloud software solutions, digital whiteboards and a whole new world of working together via technology, whether through virtual or augmented reality. Being able to work with your peers and clients in an efficient digital manner is not just an option anymore, it is a necessity. That means getting to grips with the collaboration tools your organization uses. This might mean learning how to use systems like Slack and Microsoft Teams, or it could involve managing calendars and

---

* Such as cat filters. If you know, you know.

contacts. Sometimes it will involve working on documents in secure external collaboration sites (extranets), such as HighQ and Microsoft SharePoint, and at other times you might have to use virtual post-it notes in a workshop on a digital whiteboard such as Miro or Mural. While working collaboratively via technology used to mean simply being able to send appropriate emails, it now goes much wider than that. You should definitely take the time to master your email software too, of course – it is still an essential means of communication, with plenty of features that can make you more efficient and organized, such as the ability to create filing rules for different types of email.

Security

The more diverse the ways we work online – whether through cloud solutions or otherwise – the more important security and privacy are.

The weakest link in any form of digital security is not the technology, it is us. Humans are the biggest issue. This is not an insult, it is just a fact. I once watched a documentary about hackers in which a reformed hacker was shown the latest and greatest digital security on a computer and was asked how he could possibly hack such a state-of-the-art piece of technology. His solution? To threaten one of the workers until they told him the password. I also saw a different documentary about the military in which the camera crew passed through a room full of computers, one of which had the access password stuck to it on a handwritten post-it note. The system was hacked the day the show launched.

As legal teams, we are trusted with our clients' most sensitive information. It is therefore incumbent on all of us to understand how to keep that information safe. That means being aware of how we might be targeted via 'phishing' scams, where people contact us pretending to be someone else hoping we will visit a site or download a file that will give them access to our systems. It even means things as seemingly innocuous as not opening doors for people who do not work at our company and locking our screens when we are away from our desks, because if someone does manage to get through the door they could just sit at an unlocked computer and have instant access.

There are also, of course, more technical things to be aware of when considering cybersecurity. There is a reason that IT teams make you fill in lots of forms and do a big audit before you can use a new piece of technology: they have to ensure that there is no way that technology could be used to access sensitive client information. Whenever you are considering buying, using or implementing a piece of tech you should be thinking about what information you are storing in there and whether that place is secure enough for your clients. Being able to work with those who understand this world is vital, especially as all organizations are becoming more alive to security and data protection issues and are asking for specific evidence from law firms and legal teams that the technology they use complies with relevant security regulations.

Other day-to-day tools

Depending on your organization there may be other tools that you need to understand and use daily. Perhaps there is a virtual or remote desktop that forms part of the way in which you work, or maybe your organization uses a messaging service not talked about here. Whatever you use, it is highly advisable to learn more about the technology you interact with every day. For example, check if your organization has a directory of the tech that is in place – who knows, you might find something amazing you did not know about. It can only make your job – and your life – easier.

Data

The definition of data

Data affects everything we do, and in my opinion it has the highest potential of any technological development to change the future of legal services. It is part of your core technology use even if you do not know it. The legal profession collects a lot of data about clients. In a way, the whole legal profession is built on the concept of data: generally, people approach lawyers because they want an answer to a current problem based on existing rules and previous applications of those (or similar) rules. Lawyers use data collected in the past (judgments, laws, regulations) to predict the future. The legal profession is also in a privileged position in that we see a broad range of clients from different professions and industries. We could potentially use that data to find out new insights about the legal problems of our clients.

Data is a concept that some in the legal profession dismiss because they are under the false impression that they do not work with it. They are thinking of data as the stuff that lives in spreadsheets – numbers, pie charts, line graphs – but it is *so* much more than that. Data is just information, whether it is information in an email or a document, whether it is a clause in a contract or piece of legislation, or whether it is a time-recording narrative or a price estimate for a client. And the definition can be widened even further. Every time you work with software you produce data about your use. This is known as metadata, and it is all the (usually hidden) information attached to things such as emails and documents, including who drafted it, where they worked, the name of the file, and so on. Metadata is data *about* data. If your organization uses a more advanced taxonomy to collect metadata, you can structure your systems to collect specific information such as document type, region, etc., and this can later be used as the basis for search engines in DMSs and similar tools. It is also why law firms have those bits of tech that screen all your emails with attachments – they are stripping those documents of metadata so that you do not accidentally reveal something about the firm, or a client, when sending information outside your organization. Once we widen our definition of data in this way, we can see how understanding those things in more detail can help us to provide legal services.

Of course, not all the data I have talked about is useable. It is what is known in the technology sphere as 'unstructured data'. For example, a law firm may compile a list of regulations and laws that apply in the ESG sphere. That information is likely to be stored in a table in a Microsoft Word document. Within that table you will probably encounter different types of 'data' sharing the same space. For example, the date of a regulation and the content of that regulation, or information about the relevant jurisdiction, or the area of ESG, i.e. environmental, social or governance, that is covered.

In order for us to analyse and use unstructured data, it first needs structuring. This means putting it into a consistent logical format or a database so that it can be searched, compared, analysed, filtered and converted into dashboards and other visualizations. As well as being structured, data should also be 'cleaned'. This means fixing any errors, duplications or incomplete bits. Once the data is cleaned and structured you can start to use it to test theories or to find out answers to questions you did not know you had.

Going back to the ESG example above, we cannot create dashboards or insights from a Microsoft Word table, but if we took the information from that table and put it into a Microsoft Excel spreadsheet, we could then break up the data into separate cells, e.g. splitting out implementation dates from the content of a regulation, or separating the jurisdiction from the area of law. Once we have done that, we can run searches and comparisons. We could, for instance, start to see trends of when regulations were implemented in different jurisdictions, or filter our results to just examine those regulations and laws covering the 'environmental' aspect of ESG. We can then put all of that information in a dashboard or search engine that the client can access directly.

Taking another example, if we were to collect the results of court cases in a particular jurisdiction, we could go one step further and start to apply predictive analytics. Using information like the type of court, the judge, the facts of the case and even the time of year, software solutions have been produced that can predict things such as the cost of litigation or the likelihood of success on appeal of a case based on historical data. In this way we jump from analytics, i.e. simply collecting data and showing it, to predictive analytics, i.e. using data to provide some insight about the future. The latter is much more useful than the information just sitting in an email or a folder somewhere. It should be noted that you need to be careful with the use of predictive analytics. Because they use historical data to inform the future, it means they carry with them any inherent biases that historical data might have held. In the example of predicting case outcomes, for instance, predictions may be more likely to discriminate against certain ethnic groups because those biases existed in historical cases. We need to be very discerning about the data we choose to use and how it is applied.

One final example would be collecting all of the narrative data for all of a particular type of matter in order to break down those matters into discrete phases and analyse how long each one takes. That information could then be used to inform pricing the next time a similar matter comes along. We cannot engage in this sort of search without first collecting the data.

The biggest thing stopping the data revolution in law is time. It takes time and effort to structure and clean data, and without immediate gains it can be difficult to sell the advantages of taking this time to those who are responsible for collecting the data. The more that legal teams can give priority to the collection and use of data, the better equipped they are to tackle the future.

Data can be used to do some impressive stuff, whether it is reducing time spent in negotiations by having clear data on which clauses are usually changed and how, being able to more accurately price matters, or predicting the outcome of a case before it happens. The key to being able to do those things is to first *actually collect the data*. This takes a *long* time. I have seen it take three years for firms to put data architecture into place, never mind getting people to actually enter any data. Before engaging with any sort of enterprise data strategy for a legal team, you should first work with data specialists to ensure that you have an idea about (i) what your organization's 'single points of truth' are, i.e. in which system or systems 'correct' information should be stored; (ii) how data moves between the various systems that you have; (iii) who is using what data for what purpose; (iv) when and where people are entering new data; and (v) how data that moves between systems will be cleaned and structured so that it is usable. Unfortunately, you cannot simply fast-forward to the fun bit, much as you might like to. With that in mind, the best time to start collecting, structuring and cleaning your data is right now, if not earlier. Just as knowing yourself is essential to better connecting with others, data allows you to know your organization and your clients in order to better deliver services.

One area that is attracting a lot of interest is 'big data'. This just means data sets that are so huge that they cannot be reasonably worked with by a human, meaning they require the methods, techniques and tools used by data specialists. Quite often, analysis of big data requires artificial intelligence in order to make sense of everything. The more time that passes, the more big data is going to become available, and it is in the use of big data that we can start to see patterns and links that we did not even know existed. This will give rise to new legal issues to navigate, new potential services for legal teams to provide, and maybe even whole new areas of law.

Data scientists and analysts

Those who specialize in dealing with data are known as data scientists and data analysts, and legal teams should get familiar with these roles if they are not already.

But what is the difference between data scientists and data analysts? Put very simply, the former look at new ways of capturing, manipulating and analysing data, which can then be used by the data analysts. A data analyst's role is to make sense of the data and to report back on it. Both roles are key: the scientists to ensure that the right things are being captured, in the right way, and the analysts to relate the story that the data tells.

The combination of law and data is one that is becoming much more of a focus in the legal services profession, with law firms building data science teams and alternative legal service providers combining data functionality with law. In the field of education there are courses designed to enable lawyers and computer scientists to work together, and one of the important strands of those courses is learning how to use data. A lot of the technologies that we will talk about in the lawtech section below *need* good data to work, so the more comfortable you can get with capturing data and working with teams who can manipulate data, the better prepared you are going to be.

Spreadsheets

Working with data often means working with spreadsheets. If you love Microsoft Excel and the world of databases and spreadsheets, you are to be commended, but for an industry that is more used to working with large swathes of text, the strict parameters of spreadsheets can be difficult to work with. Learning about spreadsheets is vital, however, not only to work with data but to be able to understand the world of our clients. For example, financial information is generally stored in spreadsheets.

The tools used by data scientists and analysts to clean and structure data are not something that anyone at entry level – or even established level – will be expected to know, but a lot can be done with simple spreadsheets. That includes being able to do calculations beyond pure mathematical sums, such as counting fields and entries; searching for information about entries in a large database based on other information ('lookup' functions); combining information held in several different spreadsheets into a single cumulative spreadsheet (pivot tables); combining fields that live in different cells into a single cell; counting the calendar days between two dates; or even creating long conditional functions depending on certain values ('if' statements). My advice to you is that the next time you are tempted to use a table in Microsoft Word to store some information, put that information into an Excel file instead. It will make life easier if you ever want to use the information for data gathering or if you need to manipulate it in some way to filter and find information. You can always include an Excel sheet in a Word document if that is really the ultimate format in which you want the information to be held.

AREA 2: LAWTECH

Lawtech can be divided into two areas that cover its application to the legal profession: 'Delivery' and 'Discovery'. This divide draws a distinction between technologies that can improve the delivery of advice and those that can help in supporting or producing the advice in the first place.

Delivery

The drivers for improving the delivery of legal services have their roots in concepts such as human-centred design (discussed in Law+Change), empathy (Law+People) and an appreciation of the business context in which advice is delivered (Law+Business). While clients continue to need legal advice, the way in which they want to receive that advice is changing. Rather than being presented with traditional memos or reports, clients want to receive accessible, easy-to-use versions of advice that can be integrated with their own business systems and combined with other information as required by their organization. There are lots of different forms of lawtech in the delivery space, and I intend to address some of the main areas and explain why they are important.

Management

I am using 'management' as a shorthand for contract, case and matter management. To some extent the technologies in this area utilize techniques from the project management sector to give a visual representation of tasks and to show the progress of a matter in an accessible and user-friendly manner. The functionality of tools in this area includes the automation of checklists, responsibilities and capabilities; dashboards showing outstanding tasks and the progress of matters; the sending of notifications to parties on the occurrence of certain events; and a shared platform on which information and documentation can be accessed by the relevant parties.

Basically, these tools are trying to turn processes that have previously relied on multiple emails going back and forth, with an ever-increasing number of versions, and the printing and organization of reams of documents, into a single collaborative workspace from which all of these facets can be controlled and monitored.

When implementing these solutions for clients, success requires a collaborative approach to understanding the people involved and how they would like the process to run before introducing any technology. For in-house teams, any solution in this field should fit into the other areas of the business. Everyone in the business has *some* involvement in the legal world, whether it is contracts (agreements are the foundations upon which businesses are built, after all) or litigation that is affecting the business. That means involving the relevant procurement, sales and finance teams of the client's organization as much as possible when implementing solutions that affect those teams.

Extranets

Extranets are organization-specific intranets that can be accessed by registered external users. Basically, they are like limited-access websites. These areas are shared collaborative workspaces that might be used to store documents for a data room in a transaction, to monitor the financials of a matter or relationship, or to host one or more of the other types of technology talked about in this section within a single environment. For many legal teams, extranets will not be a day-to-day technology, and the functionality of what they can achieve will be used to varying degrees, with some firms treating extranets solely as a place to transfer documents and others using them as an interactive client collaboration portal.

The intention is that extranets serve as a 'one-stop shop' for all parties in a matter. The problem with extranets can be in who controls the administration of the site – especially where matters involve multiple law firms – and in making sure that permissions for access are given to the right people. It can also be a hassle for clients to have to access several different extranets – one for each of the law firms they work with – and to remember a different password for each. For this reason it is worth considering whether other ways of working might be better for the client or whether techniques such as 'single sign-on', or 'SSO' (which uses the client's network credentials to automatically sign them into a platform), can be used.

Expert systems and chatbots

In this context, an expert system or 'decision tree' is just a piece of software that uses the expert knowledge of legal advisors to automate a decision. This is also known as 'expertise automation'. For example, a client might like to know if they are signing a document in the right way. The legal team would then come up with a series of questions and answers that can be mapped into a process that the client will follow; it is basically a legal 'choose your own adventure' novel. The client in this example would answer questions such as 'What type of document is it?', 'How many parties are signing?', 'What are the roles of those signing?', etc. The system would then run through the process designed by the lawyers to provide the right answer and possibly the appropriate signing block.

Expert systems are not used only in law, of course: they are also what powers things such as online medical advice, where you input symptoms to get a possible diagnosis. The trick is to build the system in such a way that the correct result will be reached and to ensure the questions are easy enough for the intended user to answer. And this is me speaking from experience: I have used a number of these tools and am a certified engineer in the use of expertise automation software called Bryter. The other key element in building an expert system is understanding that you cannot just build it and then walk away. Each time the law changes, the flow through the system might have to be updated, and this is a consideration that is often over-looked when deciding to build one. The final issue to consider is the legal status of the advice in the system: law firms may be prohibited from offering legal advice through an automated tool, or they may only be able to do so with extensive disclaimers about the tool's use.

One particular area of lawtech that is popular right now is 'no-code' or 'low-code' technologies. The idea behind these is that lawyers or clients without training in software development can create new tools without having to understand how to code. These no-code solutions are often used to build expert systems. Chatbots are also a type of expert system – just with an interface that mimics interaction with a real person.

Using expert systems via no-code and low-code software makes sense in that it allows further collaboration between the legal advisors in a legal team and their colleagues, but a few factors should be considered when creating these solutions, including whether creating such a system is the best use of a lawyer's expensive time, whether assistance is needed to help users map out the decision tree that will power the solution, and what the requirements are in terms of training and expertise in the technology from IT or innovation teams. The firm's wider strategy should also be considered, as the creation of multiple solutions from individual lawyers without a joined-up approach to implementation can lead to a number of different solutions all seeking to satisfy the same problem in different practice areas in different ways. This can only lead to confusion and an unnecessary split in resources.

Potential issues aside, expert systems can empower clients to find out their legal standing on their own, and they can even be used by any team in a client organization, not just the legal team. This can, in turn, save in-house lawyers time and effort, avoiding the need to give the same advice repeatedly, and it can also ensure consistency of approach in tackling legal issues. The result given by the system also does not need to be definitive; in many cases it is a form of guidance that can then be built upon in collaboration with the lawyers, but with the initial questions already answered. For law firms, they can provide an additional service to clients that can help to strengthen relationships or they can advertise the existence of such tools as evidence of their expertise in a particular area of law. These tools can also be revenue generating, with clients being charged for using them on a subscription, per-use or one-time-payment basis.

Robotic process automation (RPA)

The more technology systems we have, the harder it is to shift information in those systems from one to another. Take, for example, a solution that requires a lawyer to find the latest legal developments relating to regulatory actions in a particular jurisdiction. This may involve the lawyer going to a website, typing in search terms, scrolling through the results, and then copying and pasting those results into another document that can then be sent to a client. RPA is a way of automating this activity.

The way RPA works is that a computer first observes and then copies the manual actions of a human user. The computer uses the exact same process as the human, but it is done much faster and, in situations where the activity has to be conducted hundreds or thousands of times, it can be done without a break. There is also less chance of human error, which can creep in when someone is asked to carry out the same task multiple times across multiple different systems. RPA technologies can help lawyers and in-house teams by speeding up tasks, although it is worth noting that they will not improve processes: as with any type of automation, if you have a bad process before, all RPA will do is speed up that bad process.

Smart contracts and blockchain

Smart contracts are contracts that self-execute upon the occurrence of certain conditions. For example, a contract for a mortgage might be set up to be automatically signed and dated once a credit check is complete. The idea behind smart contracts is that they can speed up transactions by cutting out intermediaries and quickly creating legally binding relationships. The majority of use cases so far have been for smaller-scale interactions that might happen multiple times. This makes sense, as for larger and more complex transactions the fact that you may not *need* a 'middleman' in the form of a lawyer or other advisor does not mean that you should not have one. Smart contracts are becoming increasingly popular as a method for doing business, especially since the pandemic, and a number of jurisdictions are looking into how to make their legal position more secure.

The reason blockchain is mentioned here is that the two often go hand in hand, with the idea being that smart contracts can be hosted on a blockchain. Blockchain has been a buzzword in law for a few years now. So what is it? At its simplest, a blockchain is technology that stores a shared version of digital information on lots of different computers at the same time. Unlike a database, which stores its information in various cells, blockchains store information in (unsurprisingly) blocks that are locked off when certain events take place (such as the passage of time, or a certain storage level being reached) and then connected to the previous block in the chain before a new block is created to record the next series of events. This creates a timeline of events that have occurred in that chain, and in theory those locked off blocks cannot be hacked (in practice, they are at least more difficult to hack) as the information is stored in lots of places rather than in one central location that someone could access. The 'information' most commonly associated with blockchain is digital currency, such as bitcoin. The ownership status of bitcoin is recorded in these blocks, meaning that ownership can be proved and those bitcoins can be spent or passed on to others.

In the world of legal services, there is not yet a compelling use case that directly affects the delivery of legal advice, but blockchain is being used by businesses for a number of purposes, including monitoring and proving the legitimacy of freight supply lines, share offerings paid for by crypto coin (known as initial coin offerings, or ICOs), and in the non-fungible token (NFT) market. As a result of this, legal teams should be comfortable with how it works, whether or not they accept it is going to change the profession as drastically as some believe.

Discovery

Lawtech is not just about the method of delivery of legal advice: it can also help to establish what the legal advice is in the first place, or to find issues for which legal advice might be needed. It should be reiterated here that the majority of complex legal advice delivered in a corporate context cannot be replaced by technology, but it can certainly be supported by it.

Artificial intelligence (AI)

Artificial intelligence is what powers a lot of the solutions that are getting people excited about the future of lawtech. It is worth pointing out, though, that the term 'artificial intelligence' is used extensively in marketing materials across the profession and often when the solution being marketed is not *actually* AI. In order to be able to spot where AI really is being used, you should first understand that there are two types: general AI and narrow AI.

General AI is the stuff you see in films, where software has true intelligence and the ability to apply that intelligence to its situation in order to solve any problem. In the cinema, this kind of AI usually leads to killer robots. What is more, it does not actually exist yet: we have so far developed only narrow AI.

Narrow AI is designed to solve a particular task but undertakes that task with no self-awareness or understanding of what it is doing. To demonstrate the difference, think of a narrow AI piece of software that can beat a chess master. That might be impressive, but the same software cannot follow that up by going to make a cup of tea. The AI is trained specifically on one thing. Narrow AI is entirely dependent on how it has been programmed, and it may not always work as we intended. To take an example from the world of business, a few years ago Amazon had to abandon an AI-powered recruiting tool because it acted on historical information and therefore discriminated against female applicants. Even when the algorithm was changed so that it did not take into account the gender of the applicant, the AI had learned to spot words and phrases typically used by women so that it could continue to discriminate against them. The technology was not doing this on purpose; it had no opinions either way on the difference between the gender of applicants. It was simply acting on historical data that showed that the majority of successful applicants had been men, so it was doing its best to hire what it had been trained to see as the most suitable candidates. This was obviously a major problem, and the system was discontinued in 2018.[8]

When people talk about AI in legal they are often referring to machine learning (ML). ML is a branch of AI that is focused on creating technology that imitates how humans learn, improving accuracy over time. When combined with data that feeds the system and helps it to learn, a machine learning system can be trained to classify that data or make predictions based on it. The learning that ML does can be broadly categorized as either supervised or unsupervised.

Supervised learning is where the system is trained to identify what to look for. For example, you could train a system to spot clauses that look like jurisdiction clauses in a collection of thousands of documents. In supervised learning, humans are involved in reviewing the results and in ensuring the right result is reached; all the AI is doing is speeding up the initial review. Over time, the humans reinforce the learning by confirming whether or not the system is correct. The longer the system is trained and the more data it is fed, the more accurate it becomes.

In unsupervised learning there is no specific output in mind. Instead, the data fed into the system is manipulated via statistical methodology and algorithms to glean new insights. An example of unsupervised learning would be if you were in possession of all of the structured data produced by a whole law firm and you applied AI to that data set to learn new things about how the firm works or about the relationships between clients or departments. For example, you might learn which types of clients are most likely to come to the law firm for what type of advice, or how client retention and fees relate to the frequency and timing of particular business development activities.

AI is being used in a number of ways in law, some of which I have mentioned already, like the automatic logging of time recording, and some which I have not, like voice recognition technologies. However, AI has mostly been applied in the profession in grouping, classifying, reviewing, searching and organizing documents. Doing this involves a few different methods but the most prominent is natural language processing (NLP), which is a fancy way of saying the computer can read your words. This is obviously a useful function of technology in a profession that spends so much time with the written word. There is much more scope for what AI can do in law but to see the greatest advantages we will need to apply that AI to good, clean, structured data.

NLP in eDiscovery and due diligence

One of the most common applications of NLP in law is in undertaking large-scale document review and analysis. Electronic discovery, or eDiscovery, involves identifying, collecting and producing electronic information in a litigation or investigation. As you can imagine, what used to involve searching through reams of physical files and reading every document held by an organization in person is now pretty much impossible. Organizations nowadays produce a huge amount of data contained in emails, messaging systems and DMSs, not to mention all the other systems that they might use. Reviewing this data using human eyes alone would take far too long, so instead eDiscovery software analyses it and finds duplicated and redundant information. For example, there may be thirty-four emails in a chain but only the final one needs to be reviewed as it contains the chain of the previous thirty-three emails. The eDiscovery software could automatically filter out the thirty-three previous emails as a result, helping to make the review process more manageable.

eDiscovery was one of the first real applications of technology that legal teams adopted due to the scale of the possible time and effort savings it enabled, and it has now become the standard for use in litigation. Similar technologies are now being deployed in transactional situations to review large data sets during due diligence and to extract the required information. For example, AI-assisted document review can analyse hundreds, or even thousands, of documents to find a particular clause or to compare documents in order to locate clauses that might be unacceptably worded compared with others.

This is useful in instances such as the recent phasing out of the London Interbank Offered Rate (LIBOR) (i.e. the interest rate at which banks lend to other banks). These ML technologies can identify all the LIBOR clauses among the various contracts a company has signed and can then even change those clauses to instead refer to a different rate. Like those referred to above, these solutions should be fed data in the form of similar agreements so that they can learn how to identify certain clauses. Legal team members can then review the system's results and confirm whether the right clauses were identified so that the software is better trained for the future. Another use case for this technology is when two companies are merging. You may need to review the various contracts that are in place for each company, including employment and supplier contracts, and find similarities or differences between them. This technology can help to spot patterns and highlight unique or problematic clauses.

Exploring and evaluating lawtech

There are many more applications of technology in the world of law that have not been mentioned in this book – from client relationship management systems and business development tools to e-billing software that can digitize the process of charging fees to clients. The worlds of technology and law are more aligned than ever, and technology skills – particularly when it comes to day-to-day technologies – are becoming an expected minimum standard in effectively delivering legal services. But there is a lot of technology, and it can be difficult to understand all of it, especially when faced with a vendor who is selling something that seems to answer all of your hopes and dreams.

When you find yourself in the situation of purchasing lawtech, I would keep the following points in mind.

- Do you fully understand the challenge you are trying to solve?
- Have you considered whether the solution could be reached by people or by introducing or changing processes rather than by using technology?
- Can you use the solution more widely across the organization, whether in other practice groups, in business services teams or in other locations?
- Could the solution lie in a piece of technology that you already have?
- Once you have found a piece of software that you are interested in, can you see a live – rather than a prerecorded – demo?
- Is the vendor able to explain in very simple terms what their technology does? If they explain it and you do not understand, never feel that you are an idiot if you have to keep asking questions. A good vendor should be able to sell the technology to those who do not understand it, so if you do not understand it, the fault lies with them, not you.
- Can you try the technology out for a proof of concept or pilot?
- Can you speak to others who have used the technology?

Once you have dealt with the above points and you have had an opportunity to compare the technology you are assessing with other technologies and you have received feedback on any proof of concept or pilot, *then* you can start thinking about making a purchase, going through any procurement procedures that your organization may have in place. I do not want to imbue you with too much scepticism, but if technology is going to improve the delivery of legal services and is going to support the advice being given, then it needs to be properly considered and implemented. At one time or another we have all been burned* by a technology that did not work as it should have, souring us on using a similar solution again. To avoid this happening with lawtech when rolling it out across the profession, exercise some caution in making sure that it will do what it is supposed to do and that it it likely to be used by those for whom it is intended.

---

* Metaphorically, I hope.

Law+ in action: an example

The best way to bring a subject to life is to see it in action. When I worked in legal education we would often give a fictional case study in order to provide context and aid comprehension for the students. A simulated example of the application of Law+ skills to a real-life scenario is similarly useful. Taking a leaf out of the learnings that apply to the development of user personas in design thinking, this scenario is not based on one real-life situation but is instead an amalgamation based on my own experiences.

THE SCENARIO

The procurement team of Whoopee Limited (Whoopee), a large whoopee cushion manufacturer,* has to work with a number of suppliers for different elements of their whoopee cushions, from the rubber to the noise box to the distribution services. Ben runs the procurement team and knows that it is a legal requirement for new suppliers to comply with data privacy regulations. He knows a little about data privacy law from clicking through cookie settings every time he visits a new website, and he knows that while every jurisdiction has different data privacy laws, they all boil down to one essential principle: be careful how you use or transfer people's personal information.

---

* I could not make this *completely* serious.

In order to find out whether new suppliers comply with the relevant data protection laws, Ben usually emails Agatha, the general counsel. Agatha contacts Colleen, her team's data protection specialist, who will then analyse the supplier to understand (among other things) (i) where they are based and (ii) how they are dealing with any data provided to them by Whoopee. Based on that information, Colleen will know whether data protection laws apply and, if so, which data protection agreement is needed to protect that customer data. Colleen will tell Agatha, who will in turn pass this information (as well as any relevant documentation) on to Ben. This current process is taking too long for a legal team who are already busy on other matters, but they have to ensure that this assessment takes place.

We have three players on the client side so far: Agatha, Ben and Colleen. There is a fourth individual, Dani, who works for Whoopee's IT team, but she currently has nothing to do with the process. Following some recent changes in data privacy law, Agatha is concerned about the current process and instructs an external law firm to help Whoopee navigate the uncertainties.

On the law firm side, we have the relationship partner Wallace. After receiving Agatha's email, Wallace goes to the data protection practice group where Xavier works. It is here where Law+ starts to come into play. Having recently seen a presentation from the law firm's innovation team, Xavier approaches Yukio, the law firm's innovation lead, and Yukio then brings in Zheng, a member of the IT team.

Having assembled all of the players, let us map our Law+ skills to see how they will work together. Again, in each case the individuals are based on the features and skill sets of real people and roles from the legal profession. The team has been simplified here: for example, Xavier (the data protection lawyer) would in reality be represented by a team from that practice area that comprised various seniorities, but for the sake of this example we are imagining that each of these individuals possesses skills that might come from a larger group.

The relationship partner Wallace understands the business of his client, and he knows that the whoopee cushion market is currently in decline. As a result, he knows that Whoopee needs a solution that can save them money and free up some time for Agatha and Colleen

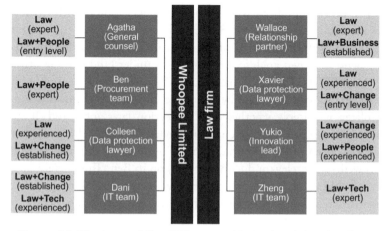

Figure 14. The Law+ skills of Whoopee Limited and their law firm.

to work on other things. Wallace understands both the market in which Whoopee operates and the individual position of the company thanks to his Law+Business skills. It was when discussing these issues with Xavier that the latter suggested bringing in Yukio.

Yukio had previously worked on similar solutions. With an understanding of Law+Change and knowing that the current process is not as efficient as it might be, Colleen works with Xavier to frame the problem: the procurement team are taking up too much of the legal department's time in asking about data protection issues with new suppliers and/or they are engaging in inconsistent practices around those new suppliers and not involving legal at all.

FRAMING THE PROBLEM

Xavier and Yukio use their Law+Change skills to run some design thinking sessions with Agatha, Ben and Colleen so that they can understand the problem in more detail, and they learn that the procurement team would greatly prefer to handle the data issues themselves rather than going back and forth with legal. The legal team, on the other hand, need to keep track of who the new suppliers are and where they are sending data, and they have to be able to get involved when there are 'red flags', i.e. where data is being sent to jurisdictions that are considered a risk to data security. This boiled down into the following 'how might we' statement: 'How might we ensure a consistent process for approving suppliers while also saving time?'

Among the different solutions suggested were specific email inboxes, ticketing systems, seconding a member of the legal team to the procurement team and vice versa, but the one that appealed most to all involved was the development of an easy-to-use web application that would empower the procurement team to automate the assessment of new suppliers for data privacy purposes while also collecting data that would reassure the legal team and notifying the legal team in a high-risk scenario.

BUILDING THE SOLUTION

When the solution team is being built, Dani and Zheng are brought into the fold early on. Given the need for the solution to deal with complicated legal advice, Zheng suggests using a no-code software solution so that Xavier and Yukio can build the solution together. Dani has concerns about the security aspect of the solution, so Dani and Zheng agree to work together to ensure that single sign-on is possible so that the procurement team can use the same login details that they use for their organization when logging into the solution. They also discuss the necessity for integration, so that any automated documents or reports are saved to Whoopee's DMS automatically, ensuring that there is good data being collected in a structured fashion.

Before building the solution, Yukio arranges a session with Wallace and Agatha to report back on the decision and to ask if it meets the requirements of the business. Both agree that it does, and work begins on an MVP that is a simple process map (remember, essentially a 'choose your own adventure') that contains questions that draw out the legal information required in order to create an initial assessment of a supplier for data protection purposes and the resultant guidance based on the answers to those questions. Without using any technology, this map is presented to Ben and Colleen, who test it with a few examples from past supplier relationships to check that the right guidance is being given based on real answers to the questions. While Colleen is happy with the flow of the questions, Ben finds it difficult to understand the complex legal terminology used. Yukio relates this feedback to Xavier, and together they work on rewording some of the questions so that they can be better understood by those in the procurement team, removing any complicated legal phrases and concepts as well as making sure that where such terms and concepts have to be used, they are accompanied by clear explanations. Once these problems have been ironed out, the team can work on the first iteration – turning the process map into an interactive solution – while Zheng and Dani work on the security and integration aspects.

A first-draft solution is presented via Ben to the wider procurement team, and this is used on a test basis for a month, after which feedback is received and the solution is further refined. The development of the tool is iterative, beginning with one jurisdiction and only expanding to others once the tool has received good feedback combined with an analysis of the usage statistics to ensure that the feedback is backed up by actual real-world use. Xavier is appointed project manager and uses a Burndown chart to track progress (see chapter 6 for more information on Burndown charts), working closely with Zheng and Dani to ensure that sufficient time is allocated to testing and implementation.

The final solution is a no-code decision flow hosted on a website that is accessed via single sign-on in a cloud location for Ben's team. By answering a few questions, the procurement team can find out if they need a data protection agreement for a new supplier and, if they do, it will automate the first draft. If the questions reveal a high-risk scenario, a notification will automatically be sent to the legal team for their involvement and the procurement team member will not be allowed to proceed any further.

This solution saves the legal team time by not having to respond to queries, ensures that consistent practices are followed by the procurement team, and empowers that team to do their own assessment, thus halving the timescale for onboarding new suppliers. Yukio uses the success story to find opportunities with other clients by communicating the success internally and externally.

To build the solution, the team involved needed (i) the legal knowledge to inform the assessment, (ii) the necessary people skills to work with and understand the requirements of the client and to ensure that the solution worked for the end users in the procurement team, (iii) the ability to analyse the business of the client to spot the initial opportunity and need, (iv) the expertise to map out processes and manage the technology project, and (v) the technology skills to build the software tool. In short, it needed not only law but Law+People, Law+Business, Law+Change and Law+Technology. Projects like this are happening all the time, and the more diverse viewpoints we can bring to them, the more successful they will be.

Perhaps you will find some similarity with your own organization in this example, or perhaps there is some part of it that strikes a chord. Even if you do not see any of your own practices in the example, you can see how Law+ skills can be combined with legal knowledge and skills to provide clients with solutions that may not work in the traditional ways in which advice has been delivered.

PART III

THE HOW
BUILDING LAW+ SKILLS

U nderstanding the content of the various Law+ skills is important, but so too is knowing how to build those skills. This is
an issue that is relevant to individuals, universities, law schools, law
firms and in-house teams when considering learning, training and
development, and each of these viewpoints will be considered in
this part of the book. For organizations looking to implement Law+
skills as part of their framework, the exact method used to build
those skills is going to differ depending on established processes,
assessment methods, working styles and available resources, but the
basic fundamentals remain the same.

A pertinent issue for anyone building Law+ skills is the way in
which the education and training that takes place prior to any career
in the legal profession matches up with the continuing training and
development that goes on within that career. At present, the unfortunate truth is that the fields of legal education and training should
be much more closely intertwined than they currently are, and this
is without even considering those who study other subjects and come
to the legal profession later in their career journey. At present, pretty
much wherever you are in the world, the education delivered prior to
becoming a lawyer is mostly divorced from the path of training that
takes place after becoming one. That may once have been acceptable, but when lifelong learning forms such a key part of continuous
improvement in a career that is subject to accelerated change, it is

definitely not acceptable now. Lifelong learning should not be based on disconnected silos with the individual having to fill the gaps; it should start with organizations bridging that gap and supporting their employees in learning more. We are in a highly volatile job market, embroiled in a war for talent at all levels of the legal profession. Being provided with a path of continuous learning and training that picks up seamlessly from education is the least that new joiners should expect, but unfortunately it is not what they are likely to experience right now.

That, then, is my first bit of advice: find a way to connect education and training. If you are currently a student, keep a log of the skills you are building and the areas you find interesting. As you progress in your career, reflect on those skills and specifically ask your learning and development department how you can build on them further or make progress in a particular area. This applies whether you are a law student or you are studying another subject and want to transfer into law in the future.

If you are a university or a law school, reach out to employers and ask for help with building courses and assessments where possible. In England and Wales, the Legal Practice Course that was used to professionally train lawyers ready for qualification remained untouched for decades, and by its end what was being taught had little connection to modern practice. If the intention of your course is to prepare students for the world of work, then you cannot afford to let it become so divorced from that world. Continually seeking engagement and validation from those in the profession can only be a good thing. I assure you there will always be someone in the profession who will help in these endeavours, whether that is borne out of a desire to usher in a new generation of lawyers or simply to be able to put it on their CV/résumé or LinkedIn profile.

If you represent a law firm or an in-house team, then try to connect with education providers. Where the model of education is such that you have the power to dictate elements of what is studied, then put pressure on your educational providers to include a more rounded set of skills. Even where you do not have that power, you should ask your educational providers for a framework of the skills and knowledge that the students should possess upon completion of the course. This framework can then be used as the first step of a training plan within your organization, allowing you to identify gaps and build on foundations rather than going over the same ground or jumping too far ahead. If you are able to obtain a breakdown of your future joiners' attainment scores, you can even start to identify early skills specialisms within the groups, which can help you to encourage people down different paths as required.

If you think that your existing education and training model is not working for you, then I recommend looking to other professions and their methods of training. Accountants, for example, are much more likely to be working while learning, and because of this they are much better able to contextualize their education and apply it in real time to the work they are doing. There is plenty that law can learn from other professions.

CHAPTER 9

Building Law+ skills as an individual

Now that you have an appreciation of the various skills and proficiency levels that make up the Law+ model, you might be wondering how you can go about cultivating those skills within yourself. The good news is that there are plenty of things that you as an individual can do in order to build Law+ skills in whatever quadrant is of interest. There are numerous educational courses, one-day training sessions, seminars and conferences online that can teach you about these areas. Courses can be found for free on websites such as Coursera[1] or via Massive Open Online Courses on sites such as MOOC.org. Alternatively, you can engage in paid courses at universities and law schools in order to build these skills. Support from your organization for that training is something I talk about in chapter 13.

When looking at enrolling onto educational courses, I would advise that – at least for your foundational studies – you should find one that is not couched in the world of law but is a more generic course that is applicable to a number of businesses. Why do I suggest this? First, because you will get to learn about the Law+ skill in the same way your clients have learned about it; and second, when reflecting on its application in the law you may find connections that others have not. Remember that I first learned about design thinking not through the medium of legal design but through a course in educational technology that introduced the broad concepts of design thinking rather than starting from a very 'legal' standpoint. This allowed me to see the similarities to and differences from its use in law and to understand why the concept was so important to my clients.

Another great way of finding out more about the Law+ quadrants is by locating individuals who have expertise in these areas. There are many in the legal industry who either started as lawyers and then turned to these Law+ skills, or came from another profession and joined law. Finding these people on social media and engaging with them – at the least by simply following them; at the most by asking them to mentor you – can give you an insight into the skills and their application. If you do follow people or organizations online, then as they quote other groups and people you can start to follow those too and in so doing build yourself a network to increase your understanding.

Finding, or becoming, a mentor is well worth the effort. Mentoring is a mutually beneficial relationship between two people in the same company/profession/network in which the mentor formally or informally assists the mentee in working towards predetermined goals. While the relationship usually involves a senior mentor and a junior mentee, this is not always the case – the concept of 'reverse mentoring', where more junior individuals in an organization mentor those who are more senior in skills such as technology, is increasingly popular. Having a mentor can help you to structure the path you want through your career, and it allows you to learn from someone with more experience in a specific area. Being a mentor can help you cultivate leadership skills and understand a new perspective.

For both mentor and mentee there is an opportunity to improve communication skills and advance their careers. While there may be established mentoring programmes within your organization, there is nothing to stop you seeking out your own mentor in order to move your career forward. You could consider finding mentors from other Law+ quadrants to help you build skills in your area, for example. Rather than simply aiming to be a mentee, there is a lot to be said for being a mentor. Not only will you be valuably building the career of another person, but you will also be acquiring skills yourself; often the best way to learn a subject is to teach it.

Of course, learning about Law+ skills does not have to involve anything as formal as a course of study or a mentoring relationship.

Lots of legal services providers now put out whitepapers and reports on various Law+ skills; whether from vendors, law firms or alternative legal service providers. You can also find discussion of the different Law+ skills on various specialist news sites, such as Artificial Lawyer and Legal IT Insider, and even traditional legal news websites such as The Lawyer and The American Lawyer have entire pages dedicated to the quadrants in some form or other, and that is without mentioning focused articles and reports from sites like Legal Cheek or the *Financial Times*.* Finally, there are tons of sites that host shorter bursts of learning and awareness, such as Crafty Counsel and 3 Geeks and a Law Blog. Lots of the organizations I mention in this book are also rich sources of information; if you are interested, find their websites and sign up or enquire about learning more. There are plenty of conferences, meet-ups, groups and events going on in every corner of the globe, whether you prefer a Legal Geek conference full of TED-style talks on the innovative side of law; David Cowen's SOLID series, which focuses on those who have enacted real change and how they have done so; or even an in-house festival in the park, such as the recent Crafty Fest in London. Almost all of the people I have met in the Law+ and innovation spaces are open and willing to help others learn more about their chosen specialty, me included!

If you are interested in the Law+People quadrant and the psychology of law and business, then look at what the latest journals contain, read up on mental health and well-being, download reports and look at the solutions that people are implementing to help people. Perhaps take a closer look at education and training, and the application of teaching and learning methodologies to the legal profession. You can undertake courses on education or speak with learning and development teams; maybe that could become a focus of your outside interest. You could also look at techniques for collaboration and communication and choose to learn from other professionals who specialize in this area, such as marketeers.

For Law+Business you should strive to better understand how businesses work and make money. Read the financial press. Take the

---

*Note that some of these publications have subscription fees so may not be accessible to all.

time to talk to business services teams in your firm, such as pricing and billing, to understand how a law firm works as a business. Learn more about how your clients function and what their strategic goals are. You might even want to get a business qualification such as an MBA (master's of business administration). If you are in a position to do so, you could engage in a secondment or placement with a client, or – for in-house teams – you could try working in another area of the business.

Those of you interested in Law+Change will find a plethora of training in project management and change management. Much of this training comes with the chance of gaining additional qualifications. You can also work towards certifications and qualifications in process engineering, and in methodologies such as lean six sigma.

Finally, Law+Technology enthusiasts have a wealth of websites and journals that you can check that talk about the future of law. You could teach yourself coding in your spare time to understand how that works, or try out some no-code software building or data analytics courses. If you are not yet in practice, you could seek out work experience or placements in lawtech companies. Wherever your interests lie, you should immerse yourself in that world to set yourself apart from others and to give you a wider view of how law might change.

In summary, there are lots of ways to build Law+ skills, whether you are just increasing your own awareness of the quadrants or seeking a deeper level of proficiency. Think of this step of your journey as being in the foothills, scoping out which peaks you would like to climb.

Case study. Design Your Delta

The Design Your Delta method is grounded in the Delta Competency Model, a progressive and agile competency model for the twenty-first-century legal professional. The Delta Competency Model consists of three competency areas that are foundational to the success of today's legal professional: 'The Practice', 'The People' and 'The Process'.

The model recognizes that twenty-first-century lawyers must start with a base of deep legal knowledge and skills: The Practice.

Building off the concept of a T Shaped Lawyer, lawyers must also understand the impact of technology and digitalization on their clients' businesses as well as on their own delivery of legal services – appreciating the power of data, technology and process improvement: The Process.

THE PEOPLE

Understanding and
relating to clients,
colleagues and
ourselves

THE PROCESS

Delivering legal
services efficiently
and effectively

THE PRACTICE

Knowing, researching
and clearly
communicating the law

Figure 15. The Delta Competency Model 4.0.

But with the increasing reliance and utilization of technology and machine learning, lawyers must also encompass emotional intelligence, communication and collaboration skills to effectively work with clients and colleagues: The People.

The Design Your Delta method involves offering a model, a framework and the tools to build these skills and to progress as an individual or an organization. For more information see www. designyourdelta.com.

LAW+PEOPLE: INTERNAL SELF

Adaptability

Becoming adaptable when that is not something that comes naturally to you can feel impossible, but like any skill discussed in this book, learning it is a process that you can hone over time. The main starting point for increasing adaptability, in the form of both resilience and independence, is to request feedback. If you do not know what you are doing well and where you need to improve, you might not even know that you have encountered personal failures, never mind how to learn from them.

It is all too often the case in practice that if a partner or associate is unhappy with the work product of a junior, they will simply not work with that junior again, and all without the junior ever realizing what has happened. While this is certainly a failing on the part of those more senior lawyers in terms of their communication and collaboration skills, it is very rare that a junior lawyer asks for feedback on their work product. It should be common practice that if you send over a draft document and see that it was subsequently sent to a client (or you do not hear anything for a week or two), you should check in to see how the draft was received and ask about any changes that needed to be made. You might fear seeing one of your draft documents covered in red pen or with a huge amount of tracked changes. But unless you ask for feedback, you will never know how you did.

When I started my first seat in my training contract, I spent a huge amount of time marking up a contract and demonstrating my attention to detail by changing almost every sentence. What I did not realize was that most of my changes were made to the standard form wording for that client, so almost everything I suggested was ignored. In this instance I was lucky: the partner was helpful enough to tell me what had happened, so it was a lesson learned, and in the future I always made sure to check any standard forms or precedents before suggesting amendments. Had the partner not given me feedback, however, I am not sure I would have had the confidence to ask her, and I would have been convinced that all of my changes were just plain awful without knowing why.

It is not just your seniors that can give you feedback but also your clients. Getting over the fear that asking clients for feedback will invite criticism will help you forge better relationships with them. And let us be honest, if you ask for feedback from your clients and you do get criticism, then you can only improve that relationship. I am not saying that you need to check in with your clients on a daily basis, but as a service industry the legal profession is not always fantastic at listening to those they serve. Think about how often you are asked for feedback on your shop, or your experience on a website, for example. If you are interested in reaching out to clients, then make sure you work with the relevant relationship partner before trying to change any aspect of the relationship. Ideas to try might include checking in with the client at regular intervals, presenting the client with a dashboard of matters currently being worked on, or offering a regular catch-up session, regardless of whether you are currently working on a matter together. You might even like to engage in training together – whether as firm and client or in-house team and wider business – such as a course of study revolving around the O Shaped Lawyer.

Another way of building adaptability is to learn more about what is coming; if you are aware of upcoming change, then you are better equipped to deal with it. This means drawing on Law+ skills to research in your quadrants of interest; this may include learning more about the strategy and direction of your organization, meaning that you can plan initiatives aligned with that strategy, or it may mean checking in with the IT team on any upcoming technology tools that might be available. Curiosity can help adaptability.

Awareness

There are a number of ways to understand your own emotions and, in turn, the emotions of others. If you are looking to appreciate how certain situations make you feel, you could keep a journal describing the situations in question and your feelings about them. This can help you reflect on similar situations in the future and comprehend your response.

Another way of understanding yourself is to engage with a personality test. There are lots of different tests that you can take out there – some that define your personality as a colour, some as an animal, some as a series of acronyms. A useful one to get you started in this sphere is called '16 Personalities', and it has the distinct advantage of being free.[2] It is based on the Myers–Briggs personality test structure, and after completing the test you can read more about which of the sixteen personalities you most closely align with. For the record, I am apparently a 'campaigner', with 'extraverted', 'intuitive', 'feeling' and 'prospecting' personality traits. You might not agree with everything that is written about you; you are likely to see things that you identify with in a positive way and others that you may not feel so positive about, but this should all help you learn things about yourself. When I did the test I learned that, on the one hand, I possess a 'healthy dose of imagination, creativity and curiosity', but, on the other, I am also prone to overthinking, even when I should be paying attention to something else. Going one step beyond personality tests, there are business-focused tests that can map the talents of those in your team, helping people to find their 'flow', i.e. the type of work they like to do. Talent tests like these can also help an individual understand others in their organization and how to interact with them.

Quite often it takes intervention from an objective observer for us to appreciate traits about ourselves. This was certainly true in my role as a trainer for lecturers. We would observe sessions and regularly find that people were not actively aware of how they reacted to certain situations. For example, one lecturer tended to draw attention to mistakes they had made, even when they were inconsequential. This meant a running commentary along the lines of 'Oh dear, I have put the wrong slide up, let me go back' or 'I have pressed the wrong button again', and so on. This caused an issue in the classroom because the lack of confidence that was being expressed led the students to doubt the lecturer's knowledge, which was of course impeccable. Once the lecturer knew about their subconscious tendency to point out their own mistakes, they could actively control the situation and avoid it in the future. This translates into a business context too: it is easy to see how highlighting insignificant errors when presenting to a client might cause them to doubt the legal advice being delivered, and how understanding your own reactions can make you better prepared to deal with unexpected situations. With that in mind, you should ask your peers about your work product, and seek feedback from those you work with. This is easier if there is a specific mechanism for seeking feedback, such as an appraisal process. For those in more senior positions, you should actively seek out 'reverse appraisals', where your direct reports give feedback on you rather than vice versa.

In the same vein, it can be useful to pose questions to yourself that force you to confront how you react to certain situations. For example, you might like to ask yourself the popular interview question: 'How would your friends or peers describe you?' Addressing these questions head-on can be difficult, but asking them of yourself allows you to be a little more honest than you might be in an interview situation. It certainly helps to know that a chance of getting a job does not depend on coming up with an answer that somehow simultaneously demonstrates that you are amazing while also not showing you up as being too cocky.

In terms of your mental health and well-being, there are a few ways in which you can start to take care of yourself. This includes making time for breaks and 'me time'. This has become even more important in hybrid working environments, as it can sometimes feel less like working from home and more like living at work. You might consider blocking out some time in your calendar that you know will be clear and then using that time to take a walk or do something you enjoy. Remember, at work you would probably have spent time talking to colleagues and walking the floors, and you might have spent time commuting too. All of that is gone when you are working from home. The same applies if you work in an office, of course: you need to ensure you have clear breaks to allow your brain to rest.

I mentioned walking above, and physical activity is a great way to help us improve our mental health. For those who are working from home, consider taking a walk at the start and end of each day to break up your routine and get your mindset into and out of 'work'. Think of it as a miniature commute. We often feel like we are doing a lot because we are busy, but 'busy' does not equate to 'active'. Taking even just ten minutes of exercise a day can help your mindset.

Should you need additional support, there are organizations such as LawCare[3] that you should reach out to. These organizations can help you navigate times when your mental health is not as good as it might be. The final thing that can help is to connect with your friends and colleagues. Make time for a catch-up on a regular basis, even when there is nothing specific to discuss. Just talking about work (or an entirely different topic) can help to lighten the mental load, whether that is with colleagues at your place of work or with people you know from elsewhere.

LAW+PEOPLE: EXTERNAL SELF

Collaboration

Collaboration is something that gets easier the more you do it. The best way to build collaboration skills is by taking action. You should be actively seeking out projects that will require you to work with others – whether or not those sorts of collaborative project are in your comfort zone. Those in law firms could look for opportunities to work with business services professionals in the firm, for example. Those in in-house legal departments might try to find opportunities to work with other professionals around the business. Seeking out people from other professions and with combinations of Law+ skills that are different from yours can help you to understand how other people work and how to work with them.

Collaborating takes confidence; we have all been in situations where we thought something could be done better if we just did it ourselves. But that is no way to work, as we never learn anything new and we never help anyone else progress in their career. A business is only as good as its weakest link. Try to delegate work where you can, and seek work that can be delegated to you where you are in a position to do so.

Communication

The first communication skill you should look to improve is your ability to stay quiet. Listening is possibly the most important part of communication; if neither side is listening, both are just waiting for their turn to speak. I am sure we have all had a friend or acquaintance who we feel is not really listening to us and is just waiting to tell us another story about themselves. Imagine how annoying that is in a business context. When someone else is speaking, take the time to try to truly understand what they mean. Especially in the workplace, it can be tempting to feel like you have to prove yourself and be the person who is answering all the questions, but this can mean that other people's contributions become white noise as you formulate your next sentence in your head. Listening means getting out of this habit. This applies equally on video calls, where it is all too easy to start side conversations and work on other projects on a different screen while on a call. But the more you do this, the less you are likely to really hear the person with whom you are talking.

In terms of listening to clients, some law firms have set up specific 'client listening' initiatives or teams to centralize the activity, but there is an opportunity to listen every time you work with a client, whether you are from a law firm or an in-house team. If you do belong to a firm with such a listening scheme, try to find out who is running it and whether there are any insights that can be gleaned from it. You might even want to see if you can enrol your clients (if they are not enrolled already) or join some of the meetings, although these sorts of schemes work better when objective parties are doing the listening. While listening and feedback schemes within in-house teams are more diverse and varied than those within law firms, you should still take the time to find ways to listen to both your internal clients and the clients or customers of your business. This may mean tracking down the equivalent of a client listening scheme, or it might mean engaging with training on communication being run by the wider business.

Just as you should take a personality test to better understand yourself, before talking to someone you should think about what *their* personality is. Do they like facts and figures? Do they prefer an emotional or human angle? There are tools out there that can help you understand how others like to communicate (the Innovation Beehive's 'Cognitive Diversity Profile' is one[4]), which will enable you to tailor your communication accordingly. Once you know how your personality meshes with others, you are far more likely to deliver a message that resonates.

If you are yet to join the world of legal practice, make sure you pay attention in legal drafting and writing sessions. Not only will they help you produce better quality legal documents in the first instance, but they will also help you tailor your message for different audiences. This is a topic that some dismiss as they believe that they can already write, but one of the skills that lawyers consistently say that their new joiners lack is clear and concise drafting, so it is well worth taking the time.

LAW+BUSINESS: DOMAIN

Model

To effectively advise a client, you need to understand their business. One route to understanding more about the world of business is education. If you are already in practice, then MBAs are becoming more popular in the legal profession should you wish to undertake one. Alternatively, there may be training opportunities within your organization around business skills, such as the courses on understanding balance sheets that law firms often give. In-house legal teams are often closely connected with the CFO, and the finance team may be able to give similar crash courses and training.

Another way to find out more about business skills is to talk to the specialists in your organization. In law firms, this means talking to your pricing and finance teams about their work and what metrics are important to the firm and its clients. For in-house teams, it might be talking to that CFO or engaging more widely with the business to understand how the legal team fits in with the way other teams work.

Key partners	Key activities	Value propositions	Customer relationships	Customer segments
Who are our key partners? Who are our key suppliers? What resources do we acquire? What activities do partners perform?	What activities do our value propositions require?	What value do we deliver? Which customer problems are we helping to solve? What needs are we satisfying?	What type of relationship do we have with each customer segment? How are they integrated in our model?	For whom are we creating value? Who are our most important customers?
	Key resources What resources do our value propositions require?			

Cost structure	Revenue streams
What are our key inherent costs? What resources/activities cost the most?	What will our customers pay? What do they currently pay?

Figure 16. The Business Model Canvas.[5]

There are other techniques that can help you understand business models, such as the 'Business Model Canvas'. As you can see from figure 16 above, this model aims to give you information and insight into a business by encouraging you to consider and write into a table the partners, activities, resources, value, customers, costs and revenue of that business. There are lots of examples available online, but a good place to start is Medium's 'Business Model Canvas Explained' site.[6] You do not have to fill out the model for only your own business, either. You can apply the model to the business of your clients to further understand their position. The Business Model Canvas is not used only to analyse a business as a whole: it can also be used to analyse a particular new product or service. Experiment with using it!

Market

The first step in developing your commercial awareness is finding the area of commerciality that appeals to you, whether that is the financial aspects of a business, the marketing, the technology, the people or whatever else it might be. Once you have established where your interest lies, you can start to dig deeper into that area. For example, many sectors have industry-specific trade publications and websites, whether that sector is for grocers or for multinational banks. The more you can surround yourself with the language and the issues that are important to that area, the greater your commercial awareness will become.

My own involvement with commercial awareness of innovation in law simply started with research. As law firms that were working with my law school started to ask about innovation and technology, I volunteered to learn more. I spoke to innovators and technologists in practice and asked them what they believed the key issues were. I clearly remember scribbling down words such as 'blockchain' without fully understanding what they meant, promising myself I would look them up at the first available opportunity. As I learned more about the issues I started to gravitate towards websites and communities that were active in the innovation space. The more people I met, the more people they introduced me to, so my network grew. I did not come from a background in computer science or technology, and while I have since undertaken additional qualifications, the beginning of my career as an innovator started with nothing but an interest and a commitment to research.

Advice about building commercial awareness basically boils down to finding what interests you about your job and learning more about it. There is no wrong place to start because when you start with zero knowledge, the only way is up.

LAW+BUSINESS: DIRECTION

Strategy

There is a simple first step to understanding strategy: go and find out what your organization's strategy is. It is bound to be on your intranet, published in the annual report or stored *somewhere* in the business. Once you have your hands on the strategy, outline how the work that you do integrates with that strategy. What does your team do that supports the wider strategy? How do you fit into that strategy as an individual? If you do not currently belong to an organization, go and find your law school or university's strategy instead. It is bound to have one.

Business courses and MBAs can help with understanding strategy, but in terms of day-to-day work, try to get into the habit of prioritizing tasks and understanding the *why* behind the work you are doing. It is easy to get bogged down with the immediate tasks in front of you and not think about the wider perspective; get used to taking a little time to think about what you are doing for the wider organization. It might even help your motivation levels to know how you are helping your organization as a whole rather than feeling like you are dealing with just one little task that does not matter much.

You need to understand more than just your own strategy too. What are your clients' strategies? Are they on their websites? What matters to them, and how does the legal advice your team is giving fit into that? These are all important questions, and clients will appreciate you understanding their perspective and the context within which your advice is delivered.

Synergy

Building a business network means cultivating a personal brand. Our online activities leave a footprint that can be discovered by anyone who has the inclination to look; are you confident that the information that is available about you is the information you want people to see? You should make a plan of how you want to be perceived and how you might achieve that goal. Spending a little bit of time thinking about when you post and what you post can make all the difference to your working relationships. I am certainly not a personal brand specialist, but there are plenty of people out there who are.* There are also an increasingly large army of 'lawfluencers' – legal influencers – who work in different areas of the profession and share their experiences on social media.** You do not have to become an influencer yourself, but following such people online can give you ideas about how you want to present yourself from those who are already doing it successfully.

If you are cultivating a brand, then you can be sure that those with whom you work are also doing so. Looking at their social media, analysing their networks and finding out what is important to them will help you to build and maintain business connections. You should also learn about the brand your organization seeks to build online, as well as the brands of your clients' businesses. Are they professional? Friendly? Casual? Serious? Might this affect how you communicate with them?

Branding is only part of your toolkit of synergy skills. Another aspect is networking, which can sometimes feel like a tough skill to learn. As an activity, networking can sometimes feel like 'using' someone for business connections rather than seeking to forge a real friendship. But you should not think of your network as *just* business contacts. Friendships can blossom from networking relationships, and that is certainly something I have experienced. You can end up in new communities and initiatives that you never would have found had you not reached out. Of course, you do not *have* to make friends – there are plenty of people who understand that business contacts can be just business contacts – it is just that that is not a mindset I have ever personally adopted.

One of the best ways to get good at networking is to learn from others. Next time you are at an event, watch how other people move around the room. How long do they talk to people? When they talk

---

*You could start by following Helen Burness of Saltmarsh Marketing, for example.
**Chrissie Wolfe (Law and Broader) and Eve Cornwell (CreateiQ) are good examples.

to you, how do they break off the conversation in a natural way without leaving you feeling offended? If networking makes you nervous, then try it out at 'safe' events with people you know, or attend entirely new groups where you know no one if you fancy throwing yourself in at the deep end! Organizations such as Legal Geek sometimes put on speed networking events that can help you to hone these skills in an arena where everyone is doing the same thing.

If you are reaching out to people online, then it is easy to just add thousands of people all at once. However, it is best to be discerning about the people with whom you connect when you are building a network, especially when you are just starting out. While it is fine to follow a large number of people online, you should carefully select those with whom you engage further. When you are working on a matter, you should take the time to get to know the people with whom you are working, whether that is a client or those representing the other side. It is now very easy to find a wealth of information on people's work history and opinions via social media. You never know whether you might end up working together in the future, and there is no downside to having better communication with competitors. The network you build should align with the personal brand that you want to cultivate. If you start small, with a few good connections, you will find that your network will grow organically over time.

LAW+CHANGE: PROCESS

Mapping

How do you get better at mapping processes? You map processes! This might seem like trite advice, but getting into the habit of breaking down the work you are doing and presenting it as a flowchart can help to frame your thinking so that you start to identify the stages in every process. Maybe start with an old matter you worked on. For those of you who are not yet in practice, map out a process you go through – how you revise for an exam, say, or even how you make a cup of tea.* These small acts get your brain into the habit of break-

---

* Or coffee, if you are so inclined.

ing large tasks down into smaller ones that can be mapped along a process. This will make it easier when you are examining complex business activities and seeking efficiencies.

If you want to go further, you can start to specialize in one of the process methodologies. For example, the advancement structure in lean six sigma mirrors the system in martial arts, with the qualifications divided into 'belts': white, yellow, green and black, before you can be granted master status. Just as you do not need to be an expert in all of the Law+ skills, you do not need to be a black belt to provide value in this skill. Knowing the basics at, say, yellow belt level will give you the lexicon needed to work with other specialists and to identify opportunities to improve processes. Your organization might deliver this sort of training itself or it might sponsor you to engage with it, whether through apprenticeships or short intensive courses. It is certainly worth asking if you are interested.

Management

Project management is a skill in nearly every job, so there are *lots* of courses out there that can help you to better manage your time, yourself and your projects. If you want to start small, task lists and prioritization can help you manage your work. There is a balancing act in the workplace between what is urgent and what is important, and unfortunately what is important is often left to one side in favour of urgent tasks – until it becomes both important *and* urgent, anyway. Carving out a few moments before you start your day to appreciate the tasks you have and how they should be managed can give you clearer direction in your work.

Project management software (such as Planview's Projectplace or Microsoft Project) can help you to manage projects, but the fundamentals are probably already available to you in simple products that your organization or educational establishment is likely to have. Make a timeline in a Microsoft Excel document, for example, or draft a checklist in Microsoft OneNote. Create a bullet point list of tasks and responsibilities in Microsoft Word or a collaboration space in Slack. You do not need the latest project management software to maintain and share task lists or to prioritize tasks; you need to get into good habits first before you apply technology to those habits. There is a tendency to believe that technology can solve problems even if you have not laid the foundations for solving those problems in the first place. While it is true that technology can help, it cannot change your frame of mind to make you actually manage projects effectively in the first place. Even creating a daily to-do list is a good start.

LAW+CHANGE: PROBLEM SOLVING

Creativity

As I have said, being creative does not mean being able to draw or paint – it means questioning the way you currently do things and thinking of better ways that they could be done.

As a profession, law can be reliant on tradition and history in the way in which it approaches problems. This is understandable, as lawyers are often engaged by clients to give the correct solution based on precedent. While lawyers regularly find new ways to navigate the law on a case-by-case basis when delivering advice, the profession has historically viewed all the processes around giving advice as being set in stone, with new joiners having to stick to the ways in which things have always been done rather than suggesting an alternative.

As a recent example, I have encountered newer lawyers who started their working life during the pandemic, and who have therefore mostly been working at home without access to the facilities of a full office, being told that 'best practice' when reviewing documents is to print them off and review a hard copy. These people have been reviewing documents on screens for two years but as soon as they are back in the office we tell them they need to revert to the old practices. Especially when you are more junior, you should question whether the way in which you are being told to work is the best method. Is there a new and better way? You should identify those in your organization who think differently already (such as innovation teams or leading lights in your practice) and see if they can give you some advice about their own experiences and how you might go about suggesting new ways of working.

The creative concepts of legal design and design thinking are, as I have already said, based on human-centred design. A good place to start when it comes to legal design is with Margaret Hagan's book *Law by Design*.[7] One way that business can put into effect design thinking is by engaging with 'design sprints'. Put simply, a design sprint is a time-constrained series of interconnected workshops focusing on applying design thinking techniques to a specific challenge. If you are interested in design sprints, there are resources from organizations such as Google Ventures and Stanford's d.school, and the book *This Is Service Design Doing* is also a good starting point.[8] Whichever resources you engage with, the fundamental core of getting to grips with human-centred design is asking questions and listening to the answers.

Building your creativity also means diversifying your learning. Look at how professions other than law solve problems; you will find that it is often through reframing problems that we find new solutions. For example, you might think that creating a Tube or subway map is something that should only be done by graphic designers, but the iconic London Underground map was designed by someone who was in fact an electrical engineer. The inspiration for the simplicity of the map came from the way in which circuit boards are wired. Another example is that of the town council tasked with solving late-night antisocial behaviour. They stopped examining the problem from the perspective of cracking down on pub leaving times or alcohol licences and instead reframed the issue as a *transport* problem. The issue was not people being drunk, it was lots of people being drunk all together in a town centre when they really needed to be somewhere else. When they looked at the problem from this perspective, the council took learnings from festivals, which excel in making sure people leave a venue in good time, and in this way they were able to solve their problem. The more you know about how other professions solve problems, the more you might be able to apply creatively in the legal profession.

To build creativity, you could apply the SCAMPER framework to solving problems. SCAMPER stands for substitute, combine, adapt, modify, put to another use, eliminate and reverse/rearrange. To break this down, it means thinking about where you could replace parts of an existing product or service (substitute), how you might bring together two different ideas or areas (combine), whether you can change one element of an existing solution (adapt), what parts of an existing solution you could alter slightly (modify), whether you can apply your idea elsewhere or take ideas from elsewhere (put to another use), if you can remove part of an existing process or solution (eliminate), or if you can reorder existing processes (reverse/ rearrange). In summary, the advice is to just keep questioning.

Comprehension

Research as a skill is something those of you who had a legal education will have been taught. Doing good research means seeking out a variety of sources, establishing the reliability of the sources, and synthesizing the results of your research into clear findings. Whether or not you have legal training, research is something that almost all of us do every day now, whether we are searching online for content or discerning between different points of view on social media. The real problem with research is making sure your own opinions and biases do not affect the results, especially where you are engaged in deductive research where you have a theory that you want to prove. It is very tempting to find results that only prove your theory to be true, but it is important that you seek out the right answer and are informed by the data rather than twisting the data to fit your own results. Sometimes the answers that you get from your research may not be the ones you want, but you have to accept the facts.

An example from my career relates to a video series I hosted on innovation concepts that I described in a few minutes. Despite my belief in the concept and the good feedback I had received from peers, I decided to do some research to see if they were worth the time I put into them. Unfortunately, once I pulled the numbers I found out that the series did not attract many viewers. It was not a nice truth to be faced with, but it gave me the impetus to abandon that project and to pursue another – hosting live online sessions about innovation – and these attracted hundreds of viewers. Had I not done the research and accepted the results, I never would have launched the live series.

Library teams and, by extension, the knowledge management team as a whole can be your friends here. Not only are library teams and professional support/knowledge management lawyers usually skilled in research and research methods, but they will also know what resources you have at your disposal to complete that research, and they may be able to offer some assistance themselves as well. Gone are the days when library teams were only about books and knowledge teams were only about compiling precedents, if indeed that was ever even the case. Instead, they are fundamental parts of the future of the profession.

LAW+TECHNOLOGY: CORETECH

Day-to-day tech

There are multiple ways in which you can learn more about day-to-day technologies. One is by engaging with the Legal Technologies Core Competencies Certification Coalition (LTC4) (see the case study in chapter 7) and purchasing and following their plans. In the event that your organization does not have access to the plans, you can find plenty of just-in-time training online that can help with Microsoft software and other products you use on a daily basis. Microsoft offer a Microsoft Office Specialization certification, for example, and there are tools and tests on sites such as LinkedIn that can showcase your abilities in different software.

The real trick to engaging with technology is to put aside the fear that pressing an unfamiliar button will make everything go wrong. Yes, there is the joke that moving an image in Microsoft Word a millimetre to the left can cause all your text and images to shift, four new pages to appear in your document, and sirens to wail in the distance, but there is always an undo button, and the more you experiment, the more you learn. At the risk of giving an anecdotal example about how to increase technology skills, I am going to talk about my mother. Realizing that computer skills were going to be important to her career, my mum went on a bunch of different courses to understand the fundamentals of IT and using computers, but nothing really helped. Eventually she got a laptop, though, and once she was immersed in the technology, she picked it up far faster. She was now actively using a computer as part of her daily life, and before you knew it, I was unable to get her off my social media timeline.* She did not break anything that could not be fixed. Simply trying out new technologies can help you become more comfortable with them.

There are always IT and/or innovation professionals who would be more than willing to show you how tools work, and for students there are usually groups and clubs within or external to your educational establishment. It is also worth remembering that the IT onboarding or training that you did when you first joined your organization – that you were probably so overwhelmed by that you immediately forgot in its entirety – is likely still out there and could be done again. Getting familiar with the day-to-day technology that your organization uses is increasingly essential in any role, so the better you can get, the more prepared you will be.

Data

Data is becoming a key part of the world of work, and lots of online courses that can help you build your skills in the use of data are therefore available – and only a quick internet search away. The first step towards understanding data, though, is to collect it. By going through the activity of collecting and structuring data, you will start to realize how it might help you. As was the case for technology, there are likely to be people in your organization, education establishment or wider community who are keen to help you understand data. Seek them out and work with them.

As far as data projects go, the key is to start small. You do not want to begin with, say, an overwhelmingly large data audit of your whole firm. Instead, see what data already exists and how it might be used. Take, for example, a system such as time recording, which already has a huge amount of data. What uses are there for that data? How can the data help you? Maybe you just want to look at the people with whom you work across an organization, based on their practice or business area. You could put their information into

---

* Sorry mum.

a spreadsheet and turn it into a chart showing what percentage of your time is spent working for different departments. That is information worth knowing, and it will help you to appreciate the processes around structuring and cleaning data, albeit on a small scale. Remember that you do not have to do this alone. that you do not have to do this alone. It is a good idea to work with others who are skilled in this Law+ quadrant as they can guide you in working with data and spotting insights you may not realize even exist.

Just try to think a bit differently when approaching problems. Maybe you know something is true or you have a hunch. Well, let the data back you up and give you evidence. It is much harder to argue against a sea of facts. Data is the foundation upon which so many of the legal technologies that we deem exciting are built. Get it right and you can build to that exciting stuff.

LAW+TECHNOLOGY: LAWTECH

Delivery

Many of the recommendations for coretech apply equally to lawtech solutions. Seek out and learn what technologies are out there by using websites such as the Legaltech Hub,[9] and build new skills with starter courses such as those provided by Lawtech UK in their 'Explore and Learn' sections,[10] which are applicable globally. Find opportunities to run small projects and pilots that test out these technologies, and establish who is skilled in this area so that you can collaborate with them. Make sure you seek feedback. What does your client really want? How can you deliver it? Knowing the answers to these sorts of question will help you establish which technology is the best fit.

You can also join organizations such as the International Legal Technology Association and the Corporate Legal Operations Consortium. Becoming a member of these groups gives you access to a wealth of knowledge, training and events that will help you find new ways of solving legal problems using your Law+ skills. Even if you do not want to become a full member, you can read articles or watch webinars put out by these organizations.

Discovery

New technologies and use cases are published by law firms and legal teams on a daily basis – so many, in fact, that it can get overwhelming. Rest assured that you do not need to know about every piece of technology that is launched, but you should horizon-scan the movements of technology in legal and find out how technology can best help your team with the problems they face. Remember, you do not need to know everything; instead you should focus specifically on the challenges your organization is encountering and what tools might assist with those. Do not feel like you have to buy a tool because everyone else has one if you cannot see a use case for it.

In the first instance, make sure that you understand the technology you are using. Ask vendors to explain how their AI system works. Seek out training from your IT or innovation teams. The more you know about these sorts of technologies, the more you will find opportunities to use them.

CHAPTER 10

Law+ skills in education: an introduction

Within a legal team we see the effects of education on every new joiner in every team, whether they come straight from university or law school or are hired from another organization. How we learn is important, and so is how all of those who join our organizations learn. To ensure that Law+ skills become prevalent in the legal profession, new types of skill need to be acquired not only by those who are already working in a legal team, but also by those who are currently in education. This is an important topic for all of us. Whether you are a lawyer, a business services professional, a student or a teacher, everyone has a part to play. If you are not currently a law student or if you have joined the legal profession from another industry, it is still worth understanding the genesis of lawyers within the profession as it will help you to work more effectively with them if you have some awareness of their knowledge and skills.

When considering how Law+ skills can be integrated with existing educational offerings, you first need to understand how people qualify as lawyers throughout the world. By examining the similarities between the various systems, we can identify key ways in which educational establishments can better implement Law+ skills in their existing curricula. The system in England and Wales is a good example to use here, because it is currently in the middle of the biggest shake-up of legal qualification (and thus education) in more than two decades. It is important to understand these changes because it will highlight some of the potential barriers to introducing a Law+ approach into legal education, and how those barriers might be overcome. By looking at the past and future of the English and Welsh legal education system you will see many parallels with the different systems for qualification globally.

THE QUALIFICATION PROCESS: ENGLAND AND WALES

In many jurisdictions the role of the lawyer is split between those who represent their clients in the courtroom and those who mainly do legal work outside of the courts. In England and Wales these roles are referred to as barristers and solicitors, respectively. Not only are the routes to qualification different for each role, but the way in which barristers and solicitors structure themselves from a business perspective also differs. The focus of this chapter is on the qualification of solicitors, i.e. those who work primarily outside the courts. Other jurisdictions, such as the United States and the Isle of Man,* do not have such a clear distinction, although they will have specialists who prefer one or the other.

In 1993 a new method for qualifying as a lawyer was launched in England in Wales: the Legal Practice Course (LPC). In order to qualify under the LPC, the following three steps had to be completed, in order.

Step 1. An undergraduate law degree or a non-law undergraduate degree followed by a one-year law conversion course.
Step 2. A one-year LPC.
Step 3. Two years of training at an approved legal services provider.

Under this system, traditional universities covered step 1 while specialist law schools tended to cover step 2 and law firms step 3. The teaching within universities primarily covered the academic aspects of law, while law schools taught professional skills for practice. By the time students had finished the three steps, they would usually have studied

---

* Being from there, I had to put it in the book *somewhere*.

- in step 1, the seven 'core' subjects of Constitutional and Administrative Law, Contract Law, Criminal Law, European Union Law, Equity and Trusts Law, Land Law and Tort Law;
- in the first half of step 2, the four 'core' professional subjects of Business Law and Practice, Property Law and Practice, Civil Litigation and Criminal Litigation, along with a Wills and Probate assessment;
- in the second half of step 2, three professional 'electives', with the most common for corporate law firms being Debt Finance, Equity Finance (not to be confused with Equity and Trusts Law) and Private Acquisitions;
- during both halves of step 2, the professional skills of legal research, drafting, writing, interviewing and advising, negotiation, business and solicitors accounts, and advocacy as pervasive topics; and
- in step 3, a six-month period in four different practice areas of a law firm.

After three decades of the same system, it was inevitable that some issues would arise, and arguably there were some there from the LPC's inception. In 2016, the Solicitors Regulation Authority of England and Wales undertook a consultation on replacing the LPC with a new system, and in September 2021 a new qualification route was introduced for lawyers in England and Wales. It was dubbed the Solicitors Qualifying Examination (SQE).

The SQE differs from the LPC in a number of ways, with the major difference being that there is *no prescribed course of study*. The SQE instead consists of a series of assessments combined with on-the-job training that, if completed, lead to qualification. In order to qualify under the SQE route, candidates must complete the following four steps.

Step 1. Any undergraduate degree.
Step 2. SQE Part 1 functioning legal knowledge assessments.
Step 3. SQE Part 2 legal skills assessments.
Step 4. Two years of qualifying work experience at up to four legal services providers.

While the traditional LPC route had to be undertaken sequentially, the SQE route can be completed in any order so long as the student passes SQE Part 1 before undertaking SQE Part 2. Although I have described the LPC as a historical artefact, the LPC route will still be available to those who started their course of legal study prior to September 2021, with a longstop date of 2032. However, many law firms have already moved over to the SQE route at the time of writing, and I believe most major LPC courses will no longer be offered from around 2026.

In terms of assessments, SQE Part 1 consists of two papers of multiple-choice 'single best answer' questions. Single best answer questions are questions in which every option given is viable but there is one that is 'more correct' than the others. This is a type of assessment that is often used by medics in diagnosis exams. The content of the assessment is not dissimilar from the LPC, covering roughly the same core topics.

SQE Part 2 involves a series of skills assessments – some oral and some written – within the context of an area of legal practice from SQE Part 1. The subjects covered are again similar to the LPC, comprising client interview and attendance note/legal analysis, advocacy, case and matter analysis, legal research, legal writing and legal drafting.

This is a big shift for the profession, and it has led to much discussion over the appropriate format for qualification, how education should prepare people for practice, and what should be done about the 'gaps' between the LPC and the SQE (such as the elective topics from the former). I have been party to many of these discussions, on all sides of the profession: designing new law school courses of study in response to the SQE, advising law firms on the most appropriate qualification route to develop, and talking to in-house teams about new opportunities for legal education with my O Shaped Lawyer hat on. Regardless of whether you prefer the SQE or LPC route, between the two they share features with the majority of qualification methods around the world. There are not that many different 'flavours' of qualification really: all essentially involve some form of traditional university education followed by law school and a period of professional training.

What almost all of the various qualification routes do share is a reliance on a single set of high-stakes examinations to judge preparedness for practice.

EDUCATION ≠ PRACTICE

No matter where you are in the world it is likely that your university and/or professional legal examinations consist of either multiple-choice questions, essay questions or role-play assessments, or some combination of the three. I would argue that all of these assessment types are inadequate for legal education, and that they are a major factor in why the legal profession has found itself slow to adopt new problem solving methods and Law+ skills.

While multiple-choice questions encourage quick problem solving that requires a deep knowledge of a topic, they bear little relevance to how problems are actually tackled in practice. There are certainly times where you might be put under time pressure, but in those instances it is unlikely that the client has given you a definitive list of options from which to work. It is also unlikely that you would be unable to ask further questions to clarify the position. One of the biggest issues with this type of question is cultivating a mindset where there is always a solution, and one that must be reached quickly. Indeed, for many multiple-choice questions, the more you know about a subject the less likely you are to get to the answer that the examiners want in the time required because you will spend too long thinking about the factors that might affect your answer. When looking at the new SQE Part 1 example questions, many of the lawyers and law lecturers I have worked with found themselves wanting to know more about the scenario in order to give the right answer, and as a result they spent longer on these questions than the short time usually allotted for them.

Essay questions – whether they are in response to simulated legal scenarios or are more traditional academic essays – give more of an opportunity for critical thinking and for showing the steps that a student goes through in answering a question, but the style of writing they encourage again bears little relation to practice. Firstly, essays – particularly at university level – require an answer that is not succinct or to the point. The standard way of answering essay questions is to start by reinterpreting what the question means to you and then to take a lengthy tour through each of the possibilities, with lots of references to show that you know what you are talking about. The whole essay is generally capped off with a lengthy conclusion that fails to choose one option, instead discussing the merits of all potential avenues. Many times I have been faced with an essay question and have spent the first few paragraphs interpreting what is meant by each of the words in the question before diving into any sort of answer. Clients do not have time for that sort of deliberation. In legal services you are either writing for a legal document, in which case being clear and concise is essential so that the intention of the parties is properly interpreted, or you are writing advice for a client, in which case it is your view that is needed first and foremost, with any evidence backing up that view often really included only so that the lawyer can show that the appropriate research has been done. Your point – and your findings – should be clear right from the off. I am sure we have all done that thing where we are faced with a question we do not *quite* understand so our answer includes some words that are roughly related to the question in the hope of getting a few marks.

Another type of essay question that is worth mentioning is the problem question. Problem questions involve students being presented with a simulated case study or fact pattern and having to give advice based on that fact pattern. This type of question is used extensively in post-graduate legal education. Problem questions do not usually suffer from the issues of deliberation and question reinterpretation that apply to traditional essays, targeted as they are to a specific set of facts, but they have their own unique problem in that the fact pattern is necessarily fictional and can therefore either be completely out of step with how law is currently practised or be too simplistic. While many law schools employ former practitioners to make sure the fact patterns stay relevant, questions in any exam do still need to be assessable and markable, which means, for example, that unclear or complex points of law can often be ignored in favour of those that can be examined. For example, a question that involves several different issues for a client across several practice areas is not easily marked or delineated into a single subject area, and as a result you will find that single clients have singular problems boxed off into one single area of law.

Whatever the type of question, essays encourage students to explain both sides of a problem before reaching their conclusion. To put it another way, we are all trained to sit on the fence and not make any sort of definitive decision. Again this is understandable, as it is a way of showing that you have understood the entirety of the problem and have not just picked a side for no reason. Those who mark exams need to see that evidence in order to give all the marks available. But this approach to problems is, once more, not what clients want to see when they need an answer that will allow them to conduct business. I have seen the after-effects of essay writing all too often in practice, with contracts full of lengthy run-on sentences and client research memos that expand the question being asked to examine as many angles as possible and include in-depth references to laws that the client neither needed nor wanted, therefore taking three times longer to draft. Even though law schools generally eschew more 'traditional' essay questions, to expect the (usually one-off) 'legal drafting' and 'legal writing' exams that students complete in law school to combat years of essay-style writing is like expecting a toothpick to dam a river.

What clients want from their external legal advisors and their in-house teams is a business partner. They want people who make decisions. Yes, lawyers are risk averse, and our entire job is to help people avoid legal issues, but in the corporate sphere we cannot do this in a vacuum, without considering the person to whom we are delivering advice. One of the main reasons for the popularity of user-centred design is the simple fact that people like using things that are nice to use. Legal advice presented along the lines of an essay question is decidedly not nice to use, as it meanders through all the possibilities on its way to a conclusion across pages and pages of text. Essay questions do not adequately prepare future lawyers for the world of work they are entering, and quite often they actively work against them by training them in a style of writing that is wholly inappropriate for their chosen profession. It is interesting that the SQE does away with essays altogether as they remain a feature of many other qualification routes.

Role-play assessments are undoubtedly better than essays, but they still have issues. Before going into those problems, it is worth pointing out that I am totally sympathetic to the pressures and realities that universities and law schools are under here. I have written, delivered and marked all the types of assessment discussed so far. I know what it is like to try to ensure there is a consistent practice for students and to try to make sure that everyone gets the right mark – one that represents how that student performed. I know that role-play assessments are notoriously difficult to assess because they often take up a lot of time and are delivered on a one-to-one basis, unlike a written assessment, where a single invigilator could be charged with monitoring hundreds of students. The nature of role-play assessments being singular also means that individual examiners will have slightly different views about what should and should not be given marks, and to effectively moderate them, someone needs to take the time to watch the role play again (provided it is recorded). It is for these reasons that, despite role-play assessments being the most appropriate assessment method for practice that we have looked at so far, they are the least used of the assessment styles.

You will find role play being used only where there is no other option for testing the student, e.g. with interviewing or advocacy skills. Role play does at least provide some sort of facsimile to the real world of work, and for that it should be applauded. The assessment method normally involves bringing in a trained actor, providing them with a scenario, and then taking the student through a live performance. The fact that the assessments are dependent on the opinions of an individual examiner when marking means that a level of standardization needs to be applied to the marking method so that examiners are kept consistent. And *that* of course means that there has to be an answer technique that can be adopted to excel. There will be certain words, phrases or responses that are expected. In case some readers are sitting there doubting this fact, I should point out that I once developed an automated chatbot client that could take a student through every step of the LPC interviewing and advising assessment and highlight where they had gone wrong. There is very much a process map you can follow to achieve success in these assessments – and indeed in all assessments. That is simply inevitable when you make something into a test that requires standardized marking.

There is a single major failure that all of the above assessment methods possess: they are once-and-done affairs. Do it wrong the first time and you fail. This sort of high-stakes single opportunity is not how life works, though. It also certainly does not chime with the mindset that is being encouraged in legal services today – a profession in which mental health and work–life balance were major problems even before the global pandemic. We all make mistakes. Seriously. All of us.

Let us revisit my biggest failure in practice, when I forgot to get a document signed at a closing. It was a rectifiable error, albeit one that required me to race to the airport to obtain a signature from the client before they left the country. My attention to detail skyrocketed that day because I learned from my mistake. The person who sends out incorrect advice can usually fix the mistake; I have seen a huge number of emails in practice that start with the phrase 'To clarify', which is code for 'I got this wrong in my last email so here is the right answer'. I have also sent a fair few of those emails myself. Had any of these instances been an exam scenario, I would have failed and that would have been it. I would not have had the opportunity to progress, and my career could have been over before it started. Sure, I could have resat the assessment, but the initial failure would have been 'on my record' and I may well have lost any job I had lined up or have had to explain the failure at any future interview.

The sum of our experience is not something that can be encapsulated in a single sitting. People are not snapshots; they are feature-length movies – three-hour long epics. Some might describe their career as a 'journey', although this is a word that has fallen out of favour in recent years. I can understand why; there is an implication in this word that we are all of us on a singular path from start to finish. It is certainly how law firms have been historically structured, with a very clear path of progression, but it is not really how we progress in our careers. We are each of us on *multiple* journeys. We are not going from A to B. Heck, I did not know what B was when I was a teenager. I did not even know what B was when I was doing a law degree, and I am pretty sure that most of you reading this have already moved from A to H or have gone from A to B, then back to A before moving on to D, then back to A only to end up at Y. We all progress in different ways; indeed, the Law+ model is perfect for those people who started with law and then decided to add another string to their bow and take on another specialism, or vice versa.

ASSESSMENTS FOR A NEW WORLD OF WORK

I do not believe that assessment and qualification structures that share similarities with the LPC *or* the SQE are the appropriate way forward for the profession. If we accept that lifelong learning will be an essential aspect of our careers for the foreseeable future, then we have to accept that we will continue to acquire additional skills and knowledge and that we might therefore naturally change our specialism. And if we can shift between specialisms and even careers throughout our working lives, then we need to consider exams in a different way.

It is often argued that lawyers are too risk averse, and that they are unable to embrace failure. If that is true, then the problem starts with the education system. As you have seen, the current exam structure demands that students provide the sum of all of their knowledge, appropriately referenced and reinforced, with failure to do so on the day potentially affecting job prospects for life. So how do you assess students while also preparing them for practice? The answer to this riddle has to be one that recognizes the progression and evolution of the individual. Something that can potentially provide a suitable handover point from education into the world of work and thus bring closer together the fields of pre-practice education and post-qualification training. It also needs to be something that is already recognized in the academic sphere. Ideally, it should be something that can assess both skills *and* knowledge and that can factor in elements from the Law+ model in the context of legal practice. The solution is portfolios.

Think about it: if as a junior you complete a piece of work, it very rarely gets sent straight out of the door without anybody checking it. As I have mentioned, a more senior colleague or supervisor will review the document, suggest changes and – in a perfect world – give you another go. So why can we not do this with our assessments? Why do we not let students attempt an activity, receive comments and then have another attempt? Why can they not then do a similar activity sometime later in order to cement the concept being tested?

This applies *doubly* when looking at skills. Under the LPC route in England and Wales, legal drafting was examined precisely once. One time. In one exam. Despite the majority of exams requiring written answers, the particular skill of drafting was assessed just once, and that skill is not usually a pervasive one that is being assessed in any other exams. How likely is that to cement a new skill?

As part of my training for practice, I was lucky enough to spend six months working in Tokyo. Before I went to Japan my firm paid for me to attend a series of Japanese lessons. These lessons took place once a week and I had ten lessons in all. Each lesson covered one topic relating to the language, and that topic was never revisited. For example, in one lesson we covered numbering, in another we looked at verbs, and so on. That would have been fine if my aim was to pass a Japanese exam and I only needed to retain that information for a short time. But no, after ten lessons covering each topic once, I flew off to Japan alone and had to navigate the country for half a year. I managed to retain three phrases: 'Can I have two beers please?', 'Sorry' and 'Shadow clone technique'.*

Now I was lucky, because Tokyo is actually a pretty good place for English speakers, and I was soon joined by a number of trainee lawyers from various firms, some of whom actually spoke Japanese fluently. But imagine if, instead of being sent to Tokyo, I had been packed off to a rural part of the country and was alone for the whole time. *That* is what it has previously been like for law students who join a law firm after a few drafting lessons and one drafting exam. In fact, it has been even worse than that, because lawyers usually joined their firms around six months or so *after* doing their drafting exam. If I only remembered three phrases out of an entire language after a couple of months, imagine how few of the techniques learned in that single drafting exam are retained after half a year.

---

* I worry this says a lot about me.

Portfolios are the most suitable form of professional assessment because they require reinforcement over time to show progression and evolution of a student's abilities. Portfolios also help to sidestep the issue of cheating (although this is only a minor issue in professional education) as it is far more difficult to feign sustained progression than it is to cheat on a single assessment. More importantly, repeated practice is better at helping people to retain information than cramming for a single exam is. The latter inevitably leads to knowledge and skills sitting only in people's short-term memory, disappearing after the assessment. Portfolios can show skills evolution rather than just snapshots. Having one bad day in a portfolio assessment structure does not have the same potential to be disastrous as it would in a high-stakes assessment structure.

It is also easier to fold ongoing competence frameworks into a portfolio, meaning that skills are not assessed on their own (e.g. in a drafting exam) but as part of other work, just like in practice. That means multiple opportunities to hone a skill over time, and it allows portfolio assessments to infuse skills with appropriate context.

Contextualization is an important factor when learning. I am sure we have all had the experience of IT training in one form or another. Usually, what this involves is going to a specific computer room and being shown how to use those computers in a series of simulated experiences before going back to your desk/office/home and completely forgetting everything you have just been told. There is a reason for 'just-in-time' learning via short videos being so popular: it is targeted precise learning that can take place exactly when the learner needs it. If you needed to change a light switch, for example, where you might have once attended an evening course or found a reference book on the subject you can now jump onto YouTube and find a video on the topic that lasts no more than a couple of minutes. The way that people are learning has evolved without formal education catching up.

With portfolios, skills and knowledge can be examined together, with a single skill assessed across multiple knowledge topics or vice versa. In addition, portfolios can be used in conjunction with actual real-world working. There is no better context for learning than the environment in which you are actually going to work. It is for this reason that on-the-job courses such as apprenticeships use portfolios extensively, as you can apply real-world working to the framework of skills and knowledge in the apprenticeship to show your progression. Even if they are not used in conjunction with real-world work, portfolios are still useful once the student reaches the workplace, as they are an effective mechanism for law firms and businesses to evaluate the learning status of their new joiners against a clear checklist of the skills they have acquired. The same portfolio can then be built up into the basis for lifelong learning, with individuals having a choice over whether to further specialize in a single skill or strengthen a weaker skill during their continued training and development in their professional career. Regulators around the world are still searching for the best way to monitor the ongoing skills and competences of lawyers, and a single portfolio that starts in education and is built over time is a good way to demonstrate that progression. With electronic portfolios, this evidence can stay with a person no matter where they work in the future.

With Law+ skills, the ideal portfolio assessment method would be to assess each of the quadrants in conjunction with the core and elective legal knowledge areas being assessed. This means that legal education needs to evolve in order to provide an appropriate environment for examining those skills.

CHAPTER 11

Building Law+ skills as a university

There is an understandable conflict in the way in which universities teach law, as they have to balance teaching the professional side of law with teaching law as an academic subject. In jurisdictions where lawyers are divided between those who provide advice outside of court (solicitors, in England and Wales) and those who represent their clients in court (barristers, in England and Wales), even those students who are sure they want to become lawyers are potentially travelling towards two different potential careers with entirely different qualification routes. And even where the divide is not so marked, it would be naive to think that every single student enrolled on a law course wants to end up practising as a lawyer, and that if they do, it will be as a corporate lawyer.

The elephant in the room is in deciding the point of university education. Is it supposed to prepare people for work? Is it to provide academic depth and understanding? Is it to teach you how to steal a traffic cone after a night out?* Whatever the purpose, universities can benefit from introducing elements of the Law+ model. Indeed, some are already doing so, with innovation courses, law and computer science labs, law and psychology courses, and more.

In jurisdictions such as the United States, the most common educational path is to take an undergraduate degree in a subject other

---

* As a lawyer, it would be remiss of me if I did not point out that stealing traffic cones is not something that I condone and is referenced here only for comedic purposes.

than law at university and then to study law for a longer period at law school (usually three years of study). The truth of the matter is that the US system is more inclined to produce Law+ lawyers than systems that allow law as an undergraduate degree. Why? Because having to complete an undergraduate course in a topic other than law before going to law school instils a more rounded set of skills. I have worked in the United States with a lawyer who had completed a degree in data science and another who had a degree in psychology. In both cases, the individual's understanding of another field bolstered their ability to stand out from the crowd and gave the advice they delivered another angle. Does that mean that, if you can, you should avoid law as an undergraduate topic and instead do something else for your degree and then convert? Perhaps be a business student and spend your last year collaborating on a project with law students before joining a law firm? The answer to that is a hard ... *maybe*. And yes, I know, that is a *very* lawyer answer.

Law degrees do still have their place in providing a solid foundation of legal knowledge for lawyers. In England and Wales, the conversion courses that give people the basics of law tend to run for around a year, and it is generally agreed that a lot needs to be fitted in during that time. Is all of what is taught in that conversion course needed for practising law? No. But just as there are plenty of lawyers who first did a History, English or Classics degree and found the transition to legal practice a relatively simple process, there are plenty of law students who did not end up in practice and still found value in their law degree. Not all degrees have a defined job at the end of them and it is not the aim of this book to argue that they should have; as I have said a number of times, we have to look at how things are done today and build from there.

One of the core tenets of the Law+ model is the recognition that the skills we have often bundled together with the tagline 'lawyer of the future' deserve to be split up and examined in full, permitting deep specialization among legal services professionals in skills not traditionally associated with the legal profession. With that in mind, my advice to universities is to offer choice between academic and professional routes. Of course, the existence of such a choice depends on how the university wishes to position itself, whether as a professional training provider, a traditional academic research centre, or both. All these positionings are valid, but this chapter is most relevant for those institutions that decide to introduce professional training elements to their degrees.

A strong foundation in law is important. I see myself as an innovator in this space – one who is looking to disrupt how legal services are delivered – but I still firmly believe that. That said, I do think we place a little too much emphasis on the level of black letter law required. It is likely that anyone who studied law in England and Wales will be able to reference a famous case involving a snail in a beer bottle, with the mere mention of *Donoghue v Stevenson* inciting a knowing smirk.[1] Readers from the United States might similarly crack a smile when recalling the 'haunted house' case of *Stambovsky v Ackley*, in which a buyer seeking to get out of a contract of sale due to the lack of a presence of ghosts on the property led to a court declaring a house legally haunted.[2] But these cases have little bearing on the world of corporate law, and studying them only serves to reinforce the idea of there being a legal clique, with lawyers somehow being set apart from others with whom they work and speaking their own secret language. I can honestly say that knowledge of cases such as these assisted me in no way, shape or form during my legal career, and they serve only to create a gulf between those with a legal education and those without one. This is hardly conducive to an environment in which legal teams are multidisciplinary.

To give you an example of this, I present an occasion on which I delivered training to a client. The audience was a mix of legal and business services professionals, so some lawyers and some not. The feedback I received was that my session was the first time a lawyer had delivered training that was accessible to those who were not lawyers. Attendees specifically referred to the fact that there were no instances of 'as you will remember from law school' or 'as Lord Denning might have said' or similar. If we recognize that understanding core concepts of law does not require an extensive deep dive into the historical context of that law, then we free up more time for students to learn about other areas of the profession.

A path that strikes a good balance between providing a legal foundation and allowing some element of Law+ to those who are only just embarking on their understanding of law is to provide a two-track option for final-year university students, with the tracks being Legal Theory and Legal Practice. Legal Theory is not something I am going to spend any further time considering, as its structure and delivery are envisaged as being similar to the way the majority of the academic studies in law degrees at universities proceed at present. As such, it is outside the scope of this book. Studying Legal Theory would be the recommended option for those who have an academic interest in law or who wish to pursue a path other than legal practice. It is with the Legal Practice year that we can start to bring some elements of the Law+ model into university.

STUDYING LEGAL PRACTICE AT UNIVERSITY

If you are reading this in a jurisdiction where a separate under-graduate degree is undertaken before a longer stint at law school, then I would advise you to treat the first two years of university education discussed here as your first year, with the 'final year' dis-cussed below serving as your second year. The next chapter can then be treated as your third and final year of law school.

Following an initial two years (or one year in US-style models) of legal foundation, the Legal Practice element of a degree should take one year. In some instances, there may be an additional year added to the degree, but this is reserved for 'sandwich' courses, with the additional year dedicated to a placement within a law firm or legal team.

The placement year

To those educational establishments considering introducing or lev-eraging a placement year in a Law+ model, and to those individuals wondering whether a placement year is right for them, I stress that placements are useful not only in granting additional experience to future legal professionals but also in providing ever-important contextualization to legal knowledge and skills. When I was a law lecturer it was very hard to convince students that the things that we were telling them were actually important to their careers. Despite organizing numerous conferences, events, talks and demos for students, across all aspects of legal technology and innovation, attendance remained low. Part of the reason for this was the students not being able to see a need for it. It was not examined, and therefore it was not important. We could tell the students that these things mattered until we were blue in the face, but unless we brought in a representative from a law firm these pleas fell on deaf ears. Being able to experience the legal industry and see how these things are used in the real world is vital if students are to realize that they are important.

A placement year helps with this issue, because it will mean law students seeing how Law+ skills assist in the day-to-day practice of law. At the same time, students will get experience of a working environment. How the placement functions needs to align with the way in which the legal team giving the placement works and with the assessment method of the university, but provided the student is given real-world work to do, their education will be enriched and their awareness will expand.

Case study. Reed Smith and Exeter University Innovation Placement LLB

Reed Smith and Exeter University announced in 2019 that they were to partner to launch an LLB with an innovation placement year in the firm's London office. By the time the first students enrolled in the 2020/21 academic year, the pandemic was disrupting the way in which people worked and studied. The placement was originally intended to involve students sitting in two different practice groups within the firm over the course of the year, but the pandemic reduced the amount of time available for the placement and it had to become virtual in nature.

Working within the confines of what was now a nine-month virtual placement, the Reed Smith and Exeter teams agreed a new structure in line with Exeter's assessment processes: students would spend three months sitting (virtually) with the innovation team before spending a six-month seat in one of the firm's practice groups. During their time with innovation, the students would not only learn about the innovative tools and methods available to them, but would also research the practice group that they were due to join in their second seat. By interviewing key stakeholders from the practice group, the students' assignment was to target a problem, process or project and to use their three-month innovation seat to develop/prototype a suitable solution that could enhance the way in which that problem, process or project was tackled. Following a presentation of their suggested solution at the end of their innovation seat, the students would then join their respective practice groups and work as a lawyer in that area. Now armed with information about how the practice group actually functions and with first-hand experience of what it is like to work there, the students would reflect on their suggested solution and consider what they would have done differently and/or what the next steps should be for implementation. The first group completed their placement in 2021, with great feedback from students, practice groups and the university. The same style of placement has since been rolled out in partnership between Reed Smith and Queen Mary University.

There are a range of potential options for placement years that may be purely legal or may involve students working in business services teams within law firms to learn more about how the law firm functions as a business. It is not just law firms, either. If in-house teams can be found who are willing to take students for placements, then not only will students be learning about a side of law they do not see much of during their degree but they will also be learning about their future workplace/clients from the inside. Students could also be offered placements with alternative legal service providers, perhaps sitting with lawtech companies or working with legal engineers, for example. More interaction with varying professions prior to joining the law can only be a good thing for future careers.

The final Legal Practice year

The initial two years of foundational law (one year in a US-style law school qualification system) should be enough to give students a solid base on which to build. Indeed, as mentioned above, for a long time in England and Wales it was determined that a one-year conversion course was all that was required to give a graduate from a subject other than law a suitable basis in legal education. This is what informs my belief that the same will work in jurisdictions where students have already completed an undergraduate degree before law. It is in their final Legal Practice year that students can start to learn more about the profession.

Students should be given an overview of some key features of working in legal services. This should include how a law firm functions as a business as well as a foundation level in each of the Law+ quadrants. In terms of teaching, these elements of the legal profession could be taught via a simulated scenario (not unlike the one I discussed in chapter 8) during which students can examine a single fact pattern through the various Law+ lenses. I would advise against too much specialization in a particular quadrant at this stage; it is important for students to build up that entry-level proficiency in all quadrants, and is too early for an individual to be making choices during their university degree course that are likely to narrow their options in their future career. When I was at university I did not even know if I wanted to practise law. The Legal Practice year should give each student an opportunity to gain an overview of what the four Law+ skills quadrants mean within the context of law – probably going no further than the entry level – so that they are equipped with enough information to choose which quadrant to specialize in later.

In terms of what that actually means for the teaching timetable, I foresee five modules along the lines described below.

Following the introduction to practice module, the modules dealing with each of the quadrants should cover two legal scenarios based on real-world fact patterns. The quadrants could be studied all at once, with the fact pattern presenting Law+People considerations on a Monday and then Law+Business on a Tuesday, for example. Alternatively, the quadrants could be taught one after the other, with the scenarios presenting issues requiring Law+People skills, then Law+Business, and so on. The scenarios should differ in some way, e.g. one could relate to a law firm while the other could involve an in-house team, or one could contain a primarily legal problem with the other requiring a technology solution to a legal problem.

- **Module 1. An introduction to practice.** This would involve introducing students to how the profession works, from in-house teams to law firms to ALSPs. Topics would include some of the elements from Law+Business, specifically focused on how legal teams themselves function as businesses. This stage is about providing information as context for the following modules.
- **Module 2. Law+People.** This module would focus on getting to know the people involved in a simulated scenario, and understanding the problem they are encountering. Some options for working in these elements are to require collaborative teams to work together, to use role play to ensure good communication, and to introduce unexpected scenarios to throw students off track and test their adaptability. For example, you could have the director who was pushing for a particular solution leave the business, or it could be discovered during due diligence that the company the client was due to buy had previously breached certain laws or regulations, meaning that options for how to proceed with the purchase while navigating the issues would have to be presented.
- **Module 3. Law+Business.** In this module students would be required to learn more about the structures, strategies and financial status of those in the scenario and how their advice fits within that context. It would also introduce elements of the strategy being pursued by the legal services provider for whom they are 'working', so that consideration can be given to how the scenario fits in with that strategy. There should be an introduction to financial statements here, with students required to interpret a profit and loss account and a balance sheet for the client. This should lead to a change in the advice being given.
- **Module 4. Law+Change.** It is here that students should be introduced to design thinking as a method for identifying and solving the legal problem. They could work on process maps in a collaborative manner in order to understand the current way that things are done and how they might be done in the future, and they can use the knowledge they have acquired during the Law+People module to build personas. Legal research could fit into this module as part of the comprehension area of Law+Change.

- **Module 5. Law+Technology.** In this final module the students can be introduced to technology in the legal profession, and they should be required to use technology to solve an element of the problem. With regard to the two scenarios, I would suggest that one requires the use of coretech (perhaps with some lengthy advice having to be turned into a short slideshow, compiled into a database, or manipulated in Microsoft Word) and one requires the use of lawtech (perhaps working with computer science students to build a technology product).

The assessment method for these modules would, unsurprisingly, be a portfolio. A suggestion I would offer here is to make the portfolio a reflective diary or a statement kept over the course of the simulated scenarios, preparing students for more complex portfolio assessments throughout their professional education and their working life. There may well be larger assessed elements that are produced, such as pieces of advice or other submissions that can be marked, but the emphasis should be on where the students have had the opportunity to build Law+ skills multiple times across the scenarios.

ALTERNATIVE OPTIONS

Every university functions differently, and each has its own existing structure for the delivery of legal education. It would not be very in keeping with the flexibility encouraged by Law+ to say that there is just one correct way of getting these skills into education. Here, then, are some other options for universities to consider in the final year. Some may align better with universities that have opted not to have a more traditional three-year undergraduate degree.

Clinics

A university might not have a relationship with a law firm or other legal team, making a placement year impossible. In such an instance, legal clinics can help to provide that on-the-job experience and an introduction to the practice of law with real people. Legal clinics are programmes that have been set up to provide hands-on legal advice, usually on a pro bono charitable basis. Examples of clinics include the provision of free legal advice to individuals faced with action following unpaid debt, advising refugees on immigration laws, reviewing people's leases, and even the provision of advice to start-ups. The exact format changes from clinic to clinic but each provides hands-on experience for the students involved, all while being supervised by a qualified lawyer.

While clinics do not mirror the exact environment in which corporate lawyers are likely to end up working, they do provide a vital insight into the importance of legal advice and they also promote thinking about the delivery of such advice. For example, when assisting refugees who do not have English as a first language, the question of how their legal position is communicated becomes very important, along with what they need to know and how much detail to provide and in what format. The more practical applications that students can engage with, the more prepared they will be to deliver legal services to a range of clients.

Apprenticeships

Apprenticeships involve working while learning.* People tend to think of trades and crafts when talking about apprenticeships, but the popularity of professional services apprenticeships is increasing, and the movement is to be lauded. In England and Wales, apprenticeships do not have to start after secondary school, as you might think; they can in fact start at the graduate or even post-graduate level. Lots of universities make such avenues available, and various professional apprenticeship companies specialize in delivering apprenticeships to those who are already working. This opens up the option to create master's-level apprenticeship courses that start later in a student's life, well into their career. For those individuals who need monetary assistance, the loans and support available apply equally to undergraduate and postgraduate apprenticeships.

---

* Rather confusingly for someone involved in the worlds of education and technology, apprenticeships are sometimes referred to in the educational sphere as 'apps'.

At first glance, it might not seem like apprenticeships are a good fit for law. The traditional apprentice operates on what is known as a 'day release' model, splitting their working week between the job and learning. Legal matters – particularly in the corporate world – do not always work to a set timetable that lends itself to such a structure. It can be difficult to find a consistent two days a week of free time in which to study when client matters do not follow a regular schedule. What you may not realize is that while it is true that apprenticeships require an 80/20 split between learning and work, apprenticeships can also be taught via a 'block teaching' model. This involves a blocked-out period of learning that may take place at the start of a period of combined work and study, e.g. spending a year learning before joining a workplace. In this way, an apprenticeship can act just like the current route to qualification, with a period of study followed by a period of training. The caveat to this is that apprenticeships are required to have a capstone assessment that must be completed at the end of the apprenticeship. This means that in a block teaching model the students should return to education for a short spell in the run-up to their assessment in order to prepare for it.

For those wondering if an apprenticeship is right for them, it is worth noting that students undertaking one should be working in a job reflecting the subject of the apprenticeship. This means that while you might be thinking that a good method for lawyers to diversify their skills is for them to undertake, say, an apprenticeship in data science, this is only a viable option if that lawyer is able to work in a data science role. You should therefore carefully consider whether the apprenticeship model is an appropriate one for you. I should stress, though, that there are many different types of apprenticeship available to the legal profession. As well as paralegal and solicitor apprenticeships, there are also apprenticeships that could be used for training business services professionals, and in the future I predict there will be ones covering hybrid roles such as lawtech.

One incentive for law firms and legal teams in England and Wales to engage with apprenticeships is the 'apprenticeship levy'. The levy is a pot of money that businesses can access in order to fund the study elements of apprenticeships. Companies over a certain size are required to pay into the apprenticeship levy pot, but it can be accessed by companies of pretty much any size. Where a company is not required to pay into the pot, this is potentially a pool of 'free' money, and where a company is required to pay the levy, there may be good business reasons for getting that money back via an application to fund apprenticeships. Just remember that apprentices are working for you, so they still need a salary!

Collaboration with other subject areas

Just as the Law+ model posits a world in which lawyers work with other business services professionals, law students are not the only ones who can benefit from Law+. While I have so far been looking at the application of Law+ skills to the law degree, collaborative final years that combine law students with other subjects are – in my opinion – the ideal state of affairs.

If we accept that it should not be solely lawyers that acquire Law+ skills and that those who already specialize in a Law+ quadrant should gain a foundation knowledge of the law, then the best way to achieve that is to have different subject areas working together. Not only does this give students an insight into another topic, it also emphasizes the advantages of working in a team with people who may not think like they do.

A good example of what we have to learn from those in other subjects is in Reed Smith's student innovation events. The firm hosted the same event for two different groups of students: once for law students and once for science, technology, engineering and mathematics (STEM) students. Guided by Alex Smith (at the time Reed Smith's Innovation Hub manager), the groups approached problem solving in markedly different ways, with the lawyers reverting to text and notes while the STEM students favoured diagrams and process maps. There is no one way of doing problem solving 'right', but the difference in approach shows that each group has something to gain from working with the other.

Some universities have already started to deliver collaborative courses (see the Northwestern Pritzker School of Law case study below), but there are still opportunities to give other Law+ skills a chance to shine. Business studies students could work with law students on a more holistic response to problems that are causing profits to fall, or psychology students could work with law students on understanding how teams can work effectively together. Ideally, there would be students from each of these areas all working on a large-scale problem together, but I have a feeling that this would be too difficult to timetable and schedule no matter how far into the future we look.

Case study. Northwestern Pritzker Innovation Lab
At the Northwestern Pritzker School of Law in Chicago, Illinois, law students are offered the opportunity to work with computer science students to partner on a real-world legal services delivery problem and produce a technology solution. Part of Northwestern's Innovation Lab, the interdisciplinary teams work with Professors Kris Hammond and Dan Linna and external partners to immerse themselves in the product development process, during which they will explore the problem, develop an understanding of stakeholders' needs, brainstorm, prototype, test ideas and iterate through the development of a technology-based solution.

The teams receive training in, and use, agile Scrum project management to self-organize, plan their work and communicate within the team and with their project partners and instructors. The teams also learn scientific thinking and use Toyota Kata as a framework for working together to improve, adapt and innovate while tackling difficult challenges and uncertainty.

Following completion of the development of a prototype, the teams demo their technology solutions to a panel of experts, who may ask follow-up questions to aid their assessment. For more information visit www.law.northwestern.edu/student-life/events/innovation-lab.

TEACHING METHODOLOGY

Just as the way in which legal advice is delivered can be as important as its content, so too can the delivery of education be as important as the topic that is being learned.

I should point out that I have deliberately avoiding calling this section 'Learning styles'. The school of thought that we all have a learning style to which our minds are attuned has been revealed to be largely false.[3] Although different types of input do engage with different parts of our brain, there is no proof that somebody is primarily a read/write learner who prefers lists and text, an auditory learner who prefers listening, a kinaesthetic learner who prefers role-play and movement, or a visual learner who prefers to learn via charts and images. While it is an appealing myth, especially to those lawyers who claim they are 'read/write' learners and cannot therefore turn their work into a process or flowchart, there is no evidence that delivering learning to someone in the style they believe most suits them gives any advantage to the learning, and at worst this sort of thinking can feed into a fixed mindset. Everyone learns best from a combination of all the styles, but trying to accommodate every learning style for every single activity, rather than simply picking the best style of delivery for the material, can in fact cause negative effects in the form of cognitive overload. Think of showing someone a slide with some words on it while also reading those words out: having to deal with both inputs at once is less effective than delivering just one or the other.

When looking at teaching methodologies, if we move away from considering learning styles and instead consider the structure of learning, then there are two methods of teaching that work particularly well for building these types of skill: problem-based learning and project-based learning.

Problem-based learning

True problem-based learning is rare. The idea behind it is to allow learners to solve complex problems by giving them real-world problems to solve. Problem-based learning starts with the identification of a problem (whether that originates from the teacher or the learners), and then the learners work collaboratively to plan out a solution to that problem before implementing it, testing it, gathering feedback and then reflecting on its success. In some ways this resembles the phases of design thinking. The reason it is difficult to implement is that the problems should be as realistic as possible rather than having simulated elements, and the solution the learners might come up with is therefore a complete unknown. Finding real business problems to work on can be a problem for universities and law schools that do not have ready access to those who work in practice. The unknown of the solution also makes these sorts of assignment more difficult to mark, especially when one is trying to have an established benchmark for performance.

This type of learning encourages critical thinking and collaboration. It starts to prepare learners to be flexible and adaptable and to engage with problem solving in a real-world way. It is also quite fun for the learners because they get to decide the direction that is taken. Even if you do not adopt problem-based learning wholesale, it can be useful for certain activities and assignments.

Project-based learning

In some ways, project-based learning is a 'lite' or 'diet' version of problem-based learning. Project-based learning is much more common in the world of legal education. Rather than starting with an open question about a real-world problem and involving the learners as part of the process throughout, project-based learning has a defined problem that is given to all learners and set parameters within which the solution is to be achieved.

For example, learners might be given access to a fictional data room full of the various documents that are relevant to an upcoming acquisition of a company by a client. That data room has specific problems and issues that have been planted there by the teacher, and the learners are expected to find and highlight them before coming up with a solution. Although the solutions they might come up with are theoretically infinite, the set parameters reduce the range of viable options, thereby making such activities easier to mark.

Although project-based learning might feel like the lesser cousin of problem-based learning, it still helps learners to develop critical thinking and to collaborate in solving a problem, and it is easier for universities to implement. While it is not as adaptable as problem-based learning, project-based learning still requires learners to think their way around a problem.

CHAPTER 12

Building Law+ skills as a law school

Law school is sometimes described as the first year of practice rather than the last year of education, and it is where academic legal knowledge is given practical application to the profession. For those in jurisdictions such as the United States, where law school takes place after a separate undergraduate degree, you should treat the suggestions in this chapter as being applicable to the final year of law school.

The difference with this stage of education is that we can now assume that you actually want to *practise* law rather than just pursuing the subject out of academic interest. As a result, it is vitally important that we start to build the skills that are relevant for such practice. But this cannot just be the skills that are required to practise law *right now*. By the time people have finished law school and are ready to join the profession, the world will have moved on. And if the purpose of law school is to provide a solid foundation for practice, then it needs to prepare students for their whole career, not just for the first year.

It is an unfortunate truth that right now there are still law firms and legal teams that do not value Law+ skills as highly as they might. There are also businesses that still see their legal department as a quasi-external entity in the business, only to be consulted in relation to specific legal matters rather than becoming part of the strategy of the business as a whole. There will probably always be those who feel like this. However, the number of law firms, legal teams and businesses looking for something different is increasing; I strongly believe that the future of law is dependent on multidisciplinary individuals working together to solve problems and that it would be remiss of us to prepare future lawyers only for the profession as it is now if we can also prepare them for the profession as it will be in the future.

THE ROLE OF LAW SCHOOLS

I believe that the purpose of law school is to give students a solid foundation for practice, and as a result the role of a law school is to provide a toolkit of skills and behaviours that the student can draw on throughout their career. Yes, knowledge must be provided as well as skills, but the real focus needs to be on the latter rather than on specific knowledge. Knowledge changes, and if all that students have achieved is to memorize a bunch of case names along with some laws and regulations, then they are going to struggle in the world of practice. If they have instead learned how to understand a client's problem, and how to properly research the correct answer or work with those who will do so, then that is how they will continue to excel at their job. I can assure you that nobody ever got a promotion in the legal profession because they remembered more case names than their peers. While laws change entirely, rendering older knowledge outdated, skills simply continue to evolve. You may have heard of Flash Player, for example. Flash was a piece of software that, among other things, allowed people to make and share animations. I took the time to learn how to code in Flash's ActionScript language, but Flash is now defunct and is no longer used, so the knowledge I gained about ActionScript is useless. The skill of understanding how the code had to be slotted together, on the other hand, along with the confidence I acquired to be able to work with code, have stuck with me and have been applied every time I have considered detailed Microsoft Excel formulae or tried to understand the basics of coding languages such as HTML, CSS or Python.

I have written about this topic previously and I still believe the fundamentals I discuss in the quote below remain true.[1]

> You would think it odd if students who were learning about contract law spent an entire module looking in detail at the relationship

between the law and sponsorship agreements. While some of the fundamentals of contract law could be picked up by looking at one type of agreement, it is too specialised a topic to teach the under-lying skills needed to draft and negotiate contracts in general. In addition, once in practice it hardly seems sensible that new entrants would not have experienced any other types of contracts and there-fore have no idea how to deal with – for example – an employment contract.

Instead, I am sure the profession would much prefer new entrants with the skills to adapt to the drafting and negotiating of any contract. That means giving students a toolkit of skills that assist when drafting and negotiating legal contracts, including legal writing, negotiation, drafting, etc.

In much the same way, teaching lawtech does not mean teach-ing blockchain. Nor does it mean teaching lawyers how to code. What people really want when they ask for lawyers who can code is lawyers who have a certain way of thinking. Yes, an awareness of current and future lawtech is important – lawyers need to know what they might encounter in practice and what is available to use, but that does not mean creating a course that isolates lawtech from the wider business world around it. That means embedding law-tech into practice-focused education that mirrors how students will work in the real world, with additional horizon-scanning to ensure students stay up-to-date.

While this quote specifically discusses contract law and lawtech/ legaltech, I hope it is easy to see how it applies to any set of laws.

If law school is to prepare students for practice, then as much time needs to be spent on skills as on knowledge. In fact, I would argue that *more* time should be spent on skills. The profession is changing fast, and our current focus is wrong. It is very rare nowadays that we would have to memorize any specific laws or regulations given the wealth of technology at our fingertips that can do the research for us, and even if we *had* memorized it, then it would still need backing up with evidence that would require research and comprehension. Having memorized the black letter law is not something that clients hold in particularly high regard when it comes to large-scale legal and business matters.

To fulfil their role of preparing lawyers for practice, law schools need to ensure that the necessary skills are embedded into their courses, that the assessment methods they use reflect practice, and that the profession for which they are preparing students has a say in how that course is delivered.

Case study. Reed Smith's 'Professional SQE'

The announcement of the Solicitors Qualifying Examination as the sole route for qualification for solicitors in England and Wales from September 2021 gave law firms an opportunity to analyse the way they were delivering training and education and how that offering might evolve in a world where there was no required course of study.

Reed Smith was one of the first firms to announce their new route, dubbed the Professional SQE. Taking place over the same year-long timeframe as the previous Legal Practice Course, the Professional SQE will provide students with (i) preparation for their SQE 1 and SQE 2 examinations, (ii) additional knowledge and skills relevant to practice, (iii) experience of working at a law firm in business services departments, and (iv) a master's qualification following the completion of a real-world reflective business intelligence project.

Delivered in partnership with BARBRI and the College of Legal Practice, the key differentiator of the Professional SQE course is that prior to starting any legal training course or period of qualifying work experience, students will study three days a week while working two days a week within a business services department (which may be in knowledge management, marketing, innovation, learning and development, client value, or pro bono) or on a client placement. This equips students with knowledge of the business of a law firm and how business services professionals can work with lawyers to solve client problems. Increased business knowledge and the opportunity for client placements also means that there is the potential for future lawyers to be better business partners for clients.

Outside of the regulated SQE examinations, students will be assessed in their additional knowledge and skills over the duration of the course via portfolio and oral assessments with their designated supervisor, akin to how appraisals will occur in practice.

Reed Smith states that this course will (i) ensure that new joiners will be better prepared for their legal career as they will already be familiar with the firm and those within it, (ii) provide new joiners with a more rounded skill set and knowledge of the business of law, and (iii) ensure that learning is delivered in a contextualized manner within the scope of real-world work.

EMBEDDING

I will start by saying that I am not a fan of optional 'bolt-on' courses that students are expected to complete in their own time if they have an interest in them. One of the failings of the LPC in its later years was that it was packed full of so much 'core' content that more extensive changes in the profession or in the skills and knowledge required of lawyers had to be reflected in various short-course add-ons, whether these were related to understanding the law firm as a business, to legal technology or to business strategy. Sandwiching Law+ skills in among everything else students have to do – such as passing their actual course – without making them mandatory or assessable means that they will understandably be perceived as less important.

Learning needs context. No matter how high quality an add-on course is, it is just that: an add-on. Unless these add-ons can be embedded and made part of the real work that the lawyers will be doing, then there is unlikely to be a lasting effect.

This does not mean that we need a timetable that has students doing 'law of property' in the morning and then 'business skills' in the afternoon. It means finding ways to weave Law+People, Law+Business, Law+Change and Law+Technology skills *into* that law of property course. I do not care whether you specifically refer to Law+, or to the names of each of the quadrants, when you are teaching (different law schools might want to use different nomenclature) so long as the substance of the skills is being taught.

If a client in a problem scenario needs advice on leases, for example, they will of course need to know the law. But the imagination does not need to be stretched very far to make that simulated client operate in a WeWork-style arrangement, say. Once you imagine that, then you can require students to consider this client needing not one lease but a series of shorter leases. This necessitates a different focus to the advice, as students should recognize that there is not a lot of time to negotiate such leases, so the process to sign leases may need to be changed, or the leases might need to be automated with technology.

Alternatively, perhaps the format of the advice needs to be considered, as the legal department of the client in the simulation states that they are having a meeting with the CEO of the company in the next week and they need something they can share with them. Students who provide a thirty-page dissertation on the minutiae of legal detail with a plethora of citations and references to black letter law may of course be right from a knowledge perspective, but the client's legal department would not be happy with that work output no matter how right the law was; it was not what they asked for, and additional work will now be needed to put the advice into a format suitable for their CEO.

If we are serious about teaching future lawyers new skills, we must be prepared to integrate those skills with the practice of law. Having separate courses for 'lawtech' or 'process mapping' will mean little if they are not considered part of the whole that is required to advise clients.

STRUCTURE

If we assume that the traditional period of law school to which this chapter applies is around a year, then there are two options available depending on the course structure. In the first, where there are three terms of study – as in England and Wales – I would envisage the first two terms covering the topics that traditionally make up a law school course, such as business law, property law, litigation and any additional elective knowledge that is required. During these subjects, students should have been given the chance to understand how to apply each quadrant of Law+ skills to a variety of practice areas, and they should therefore be starting their final term with the fundamentals of Law+ in place. While in a perfect world these fundamentals would be fully covered off at university, we cannot always assume this. In any event, it will do those who have learned about Law+ at university no harm to reapply the skills in new contexts. In jurisdictions such as the United States where the course structure comprises two semesters instead of three terms, most of these traditional topics would feature in the first semester. It may be that the elective knowledge is covered off in the first part of the second semester, depending on the hours available and the curriculum.

In the final term/semester – or the latter half of the final semester where some of that semester is taken up with elective knowledge – students can start to specialize in one area of Law+, just as they might specialize in an area of law. What this means is that after being introduced to Law+People, Law+Business, Law+Change and Law+Technology, students would select a specialist project in one of the four quadrants or they could choose a fifth option of undertaking a project in legal knowledge, specializing in a previously taught topic. I will not talk more about the fifth option here, but for ease of roll-out, management and marking for the university, I would recommend a single assessment structure across each of the four Law+ options. My recommendation for the assessment at this level would be to produce a single artefact in response to a real-world (or simulated real-world) scenario.

For Law+Technology, the artefact might be to develop a new software solution in response to a request from a business to find a more efficient method for providing initial legal advice to new clients. For those with coding skills, that could mean building a new software tool that actually works. Alternatively, it may simply be the development of wireframes: sketches that show what the solution would look like and how a user would interact with the solution. For Law+Change, the scenario could be a client who needs help managing a project and the artefact could be a Gantt chart for said project. Alternatively, it could be the analysis of an existing process in a law firm for running a conflicts check, say, with the artefact produced being a report identifying current wastes and recommendations for efficiency improvements. For Law+People, the project might be to design psychometric tools or exercises to improve employee selection

THE LEGAL TEAM OF THE FUTURE

for a legal department at the recruitment stage. Finally, Law+Business students could be required to interpret accounts to understand the legal implications for a client who is a shareholder in another company that is about to go bankrupt. While the artefacts will be different across all four areas, the bulk of the marks available will be attributed to the same factors: that is, the researching of the problem and the appropriateness of the solution to that problem in line with the requirements of the simulated client. For those law schools with clinics or links to law firms and businesses, the client need not be simulated and the problem could instead be a real-world one.

Accompanying the artefact would be an element that is identical across the four areas: a reflective portfolio that is maintained during the entire project, showcasing the student's research, their understanding of the client, their analysis of the problem, and the ways in which they might have done things differently. Reflection is notoriously difficult for all types of student – not just lawyers – and some training would therefore be required on how to reflect appropriately. The criteria for marking would be the same for Law+Business, Law+Technology, Law+Change and Law+People, meaning that educators would find it easier to mark and moderate this portion of the assessment. These assessments should ideally be collaborative in nature. I realize that collaborative assessments are a nightmare to mark, though, so while the project should involve people working together, and a single artefact should be produced by each team, the reflective portfolios – in which they discuss as part of their reflection how they worked with others – will be individual to each student. This can help to avoid some of the traditional pitfalls associated with team assessments where not every member pulls their weight or where there are other issues encountered while working as a team. Regardless, the act of having to work together is a Law+ skill in and of itself so it should be encouraged if at all possible.

ASSESSMENT

Students should be maintaining a portfolio throughout every term/semester of law school. While studying the traditional legal subjects, students should be given at least two attempts to complete any task, with a supervisor (in the form of a lecturer or professor) checking the work and giving feedback. By using a portfolio, students can be tracking their skills and knowledge in a framework of competencies, and educators can be assessing students against those competencies as they work through the course. This means looking at how a student deals with Law+Change in the context of business law one day, and then looking at it again in the context of property law the next – and likewise for each of the Law+ skills. The working world does not have a hard delineation between knowledge and skills, and nor should professional education.

The final assessment of competence in Law+ skills has already been discussed above, but when combined with the portfolio from the study of traditional legal topics it should be something that can be handed to a law firm or held on to by the individual that can then form the basis for their continuous training and development in practice.

INVOLVING LAW FIRMS AND LEGAL DEPARTMENTS

It can be difficult for educators to think up real-life scenarios when planning activities and assessments. Unless the teaching staff is made up of a large number of lawyers who are teaching part time while also practising, it can also unfortunately be the case that those scenarios can either be based on out-of-date information from when the educators used to work in the profession or they can be based on entirely incorrect information if the educators have never practised. For that reason, it is imperative that law firms and legal departments work with law schools to ensure that the projects they choose match the real world. This is a mutually beneficial arrangement: the law schools gain the benefit of real-world assessment scenarios, and the law firms and legal departments ensure that future lawyers coming through the education pipeline are properly equipped to deal with law as it is being practised.

It is also essential that both law firms *and* in-house legal departments provide input here. The way in which each practises law is quite different, as is their approach to solving problems and, indeed, the identity of their 'clients'. In England and Wales law firms recruit the most lawyers, and they therefore have exclusivity arrangements and a lot of sway with law schools. But if we follow the value chain, then *their* clients are in-house teams, and is it not simply good sense to talk to the customers of our customers? With that in mind, there should be a balanced approach to scenarios in law school: they need to deal with both law firm and in-house practice scenarios so that students can understand the realities of their future workplace.

CHAPTER 13

Building Law+ skills as a law firm or in-house team

The burden of creating the Law+ path does not fall solely on legal education. Legal education takes place in the early stages of a person's career and, as such, it can provide only the foundations. If we devote all of our time and effort to future lawyers while ignoring those already in practice, then any large-scale transformation is going to take at least a decade until those students have reached positions of seniority across the profession. I would argue that university and law school education should teach each of the model's quadrants to the entry-level stage – with maybe one or two quadrants to established proficiency – and feel satisfied that it has then done its job well. The continued specialization of an individual throughout their entire career is something that should become the norm, which means the burden falls as much on legal teams and individuals themselves as on universities and law schools to ensure that they engage with 'lifelong learning'.

There is a contradiction in professional services between the skills organizations say that they value and the activities that are incentivized within those organizations. We often hear that 'soft skills' are vitally important to the world of work, but evidence shows that the reward for 'hard skills' in terms of salary is around double the reward for soft ones.[1] With the world of work heading toward a shift as automation and new technologies take on a number of these hard skills, organizations in general – not just legal teams – need to find a way to incentivize soft skills so that they are fostered and supported over the coming decades.

For those hiring professionals in the legal services sector, it is worth noting just what is important to the younger generations. While salaries continue to rise year on year in the hope that the best people will continue to be attracted, those people are increasingly interested in other areas, with a recent poll finding that money was the least important of six factors when selecting a new job, with culture, status, making an impact, corporate purpose and (most importantly) personal and professional development all ranking higher.[2] If you accept that lawyers need more rounded skill sets, then the number one way to ensure that these new skills are learned is to incentivize lawyers to learn them.

THE BARRIERS TO LAW+

There is an argument that the best way to bring Law+ skills to the legal profession is to simply wait: that by changing the grass roots of the profession through introducing new ways of training at university and law school, Law+ skills will filter through the profession over time, eventually into senior roles. That is certainly one option, but those who choose it will be overtaken by others who choose to do things differently now. If you are entirely reliant on your new joiners to drive change, then by the time they are in a position to do so, there is a good chance that it will already be far too late to catch up with your competitors who refused to wait. It is also possible that the transformation that is being waited for might not happen exactly as expected and any resulting adjustments to the education path of future lawyers will then take *another* decade to come to fruition.

And even if you decide to simply wait, in the spirit of lifelong learning it is not enough to train in Law+ skills at university or law school and then just stop. There is a short-termism to this thinking that does no favours either to the lawyer or to the organization in which they work. Without continuous training, lawyers cannot and do not progress over time. While there is often plenty of support within organizations to continue to develop legal knowledge and skills, training for alternative Law+ skills is often scarce or non-existent. This lack of support for individual evolution is likely to cause those who studied Law+ in their university and law school years to feel demotivated and disenfranchized, meaning either that they will fail to do their best work or, ultimately, that they will leave the organization for another that better supports them. I believe that law firms need to be able to recognize and reward those who think differently to ensure that the profession continues to evolve.

There are barriers to building Law+ skills in law firms and in-house teams that I have already alluded to in this book: namely, the pyramid structure and the bonus schemes of law firms, and the perception of in-house teams within the wider business. Law firms have been structured in a very similar way for many years, and it is a model that has traditionally been successful. That structure is focused on producing lawyers who bill by the hour and whose expected job trajectory is to make partner. It is not one where finding efficiency is particularly rewarded; more hours worked mean more fees for the firm. Even in a fixed-fee or capped-fee arrangement that works to a set budget, the individual associates working on the matter often have internal hours targets that they have to meet in order to qualify for a bonus. Those targets mean that unless Law+ skills can count toward bonuses, any work done in upskilling a particular individual lawyer to learn more skills is not going to be recognized, meaning they will be less likely to do it in the first place.

While I do not intend to write an essay on why the billable hour is a problem, I cannot talk about how firms can encourage Law+ skills without also asking firms to consider alternative ways of incentivizing their lawyers. We should be encouraging lawyers to provide a better service, not just one that accumulates more hours. Over time, clients are going to encounter other legal services providers who are able to either provide more services for the same cost or are able to offer reduced fees. This is especially important in the world of metrics and evaluations; a legal team who can explain not only how long they spent on tasks but also how they made good use of that time is always going to get better feedback and repeat work.

One of the barriers to embracing the change that is necessary might be that we feel like our clients would not accept any other way of doing business – that law will always mean working long hours to meet deadlines. Of course, if the status quo were such a good thing, then clients would be really happy with things the way they are, right? Evidence shows that this assumption may be incorrect, however. The overwhelming feedback received by organizations such as the O Shaped Lawyer group is that clients want a good business partner who is able to interact with them in a human way and understand their business. Yes, they need to have their legal problems solved, but what if those problems could be solved faster and cheaper? They would then be first in line to sign up to new ways of doing things. At a time when organizations are increasingly reflecting on their purpose and the mental health and well-being of their employees, they expect their professional advisors to be doing the same. There will always be demanding clients, but the direction of travel is away from unpredictable long hours as much as possible. Besides, if we can find new ways of working that mean that tasks that currently take fourteen hours can be done in half that time, surely that is a good thing? The corollary of this does not have to be less revenue for a firm, as there are alternatives to pricing on an hourly basis that can be considered, and any extra time can be used to acquire new clients or create new products and services for clients.

For in-house teams, the main barrier to diversification into Law+ skills is that the legal team can often be seen as its organization's 'no' department. What do I mean by that? I mean that in many businesses the legal team is the last team to hear about any new undertaking and, as a result, they often have to explain all the reasons why a business cannot do what it wants. The issue is that bringing in lawyers at the end of the process means not only that they have not helped guide the direction of the undertaking from the start, but also that they are now usually under time pressure to provide advice so that the undertaking can proceed along the schedule the business has attached to it. This situation may be an issue caused by the legal team itself or by those in the wider business, but it builds the perception that the legal team is just there to say 'no' when asked if the business can do anything new. Just as with law firms, this barrier to the introduction of Law+ skills is largely a cultural one. Either those in the wider business do not believe that the legal team should be involved in strategic business decisions, or the legal team itself does not have the skills and/or inclination to be involved in such decisions. While not every organization functions in this way, the legal team are often the last to know about business decisions, and by the time they do hear about them it is usually much more difficult to slightly course-correct any decision, meaning that 'no' might be the only answer available. Even if there are other options, that legal team has been prohibited from exhibiting Law+ skills in helping guide the business along its future trajectory.

Despite the barriers in place for in-house teams, they are often in a better position than law firms to take advantage of Law+ skills, partially because many of the lawyers in these teams are already encouraged to be adaptable to new scenarios and to be generalists rather than specialists. It is also much less likely that there is a culture of billable hours, and there is a higher chance of interacting with business professionals on a daily business. An in-house team's client *is* the business, and the business itself is more likely to value rounded skill sets so that lawyers can solve legal problems within the context of their direction and strategy as opposed to in a vacuum. This is something that clients expect from their external advisors, but when the business is your only client, this need becomes paramount. Ironically, the biggest barrier for in-house teams may well be the former private practice lawyers who bring with them the mindset and culture from their previous firms.

There is a near-constant war for talent in the legal profession. Salaries are increasing while attrition rates are at an all-time high. According to the '2022 Report on the State of the Legal Market' from Thomson Reuters, despite rising salaries and the improved economic performance of law firms, we are in a situation where firms were 'edging dangerously close to ... losing one-quarter of their associates in 2021'.[3] Contributing to this is the fact that firms who have experienced the least attrition are those who generally had the lowest compensation growth among the firms in the market. Action clearly needs to be taken in order to make the profession one in which lawyers can not only work but thrive, and the answer does not seem to be money.

POTENTIAL SOLUTIONS

Lawyers are time-poor professionals who are valued for their legal knowledge and are not always incentivized to engage with anything beyond that narrow lens. There are, however, a number of ways in which lawyers and business services professionals can be encouraged to build Law+ skills.

Salary

Although the legal profession is ever more aware of the importance of factors that contribute to a better quality of working life, it would be impossible to argue that the amount someone is paid is not a factor when it comes to their motivation. There are two potential ways to introduce Law+ skills by using remuneration: one that seeks to entice professionals from other industries and one that looks to reward lawyers who wish to diversify.

In the first instance, as law firms and legal teams look to bolster their services with professionals who possess Law+ skills, they are encountering a problem: namely, that those same professionals are paid more in their own industries than if they took the leap to law. Data scientists, business analysts, process engineers and others can earn more in the IT industry or in accountancy or other professional services firms. This is partly down to the culture of exceptionalism we have in the legal services profession: there is a hesitation to stand other professionals on the same level as the lawyers. It is also down to the fact that the activity of the lawyers who are delivering advice to clients by recording their time in six-minute segments can be directly linked to revenue generation for the firm, which is easier to measure than the return-on-investment provided by business services professionals. It is true that those with legal knowledge and skills are the essential elements of a *legal* team, but I would advocate for some closer salary benchmarking between 'pure' lawyers and those with Law+ skills. If we do not get closer to parity, then we are going to be constantly attempting to have lawyers training other lawyers in new skills rather than learning from specialists in other professions. This parity is starting to happen in some teams, with the deregulation of legal services allowing those without legal degrees to hold 'partner' positions and with more senior business services positions among the C-suite (Chief Information Officers, Chief Knowledge Officers, Chief Innovation Officers) becoming available, but there is a lot more than can be done to recognize and reward increased diversity at mid-level positions.

In the same vein, lawyers who want to take a non-traditional career path at law firms are not currently incentivized to do so. There is a clear progression and, in many cases, a 'lock-step' in the form of a yearly fixed incremental increase in pay as someone advances through the traditional path to partnership, but the same level of thought has not been given to those who wish to diversify as legal engineers or legal technologists, for example. Not only are these people able to provide clients with legal advice, but they are also able to bring in other Law+ skills that are essential to future-proofing the organization. This fact needs to be recognized.

Splinter points

Linked to the above point is the issue of seniority. I have already mentioned that the number of firms who are looking to open up alternative career paths is on the increase, but the traditional path to promotion, with election to partnership as the prize, is still the most prevalent. The methods for progressing in an alternative fashion are haphazardly implemented, with different organizations having differing levels of consistency and clarity.

Law firms need to make the best possible use of their people. Rather than sticking with the usual process of making people partners (and therefore owners) of the firm based on their longevity and legal skill alone, firms should recognize that there are numerous ways in which those that work there can provide value. Those who are amazing at delivering advice but have no interest in owning and managing the firm should be allowed to get on with delivering advice without being penalized for not being on the 'partnership track'. Those who want to explore Law+ skills or be seconded into different teams should, similarly, be encouraged to do so. That the profession is not acting in this fashion is part of the reason for the high levels of attrition for lawyers, with those sitting at 3–5 years qualified most likely to move on, especially if they are not on the 'partnership track'. I certainly felt adrift when I was an associate who did not want to be a partner. It seemed there were literally no other options were I to stay in law, to the extent that I enlisted the services of an organization who specialized in 'life after law' while I tried to find my path. That such an organization even exists is telling, and I am not alone in having left. The top reasons for associates leaving law firms include searching for 'more interesting work', a 'better work/ life balance', 'clearer career progression' and the 'opportunity to move in-house'.[4] If legal teams were able to give people more options, they could stem the tide of attrition.

What is needed is for people to take the time to understand where the highest levels of attrition are within their own team. Is it at 3–5 years post-qualification, as I mention above as the norm? Or is it just before making partner? Perhaps it is shortly after qualification? Every point at which attrition increases can be categorized as a 'splinter point', where someone chooses to splinter off onto another path. Just as there are 'partnership tracks' with specified allocations of work and opportunities for progression, so there should be tracks for each of the Law+ skills at these splinter points. This means identifying the areas of interest or work with which people engage and then ushering them into the appropriate specialization path and supporting them on that journey. I can only imagine how my own career progression might have differed if someone had said something like 'You seem to enjoy and be skilled in training people, how would you like to start on our Law+People track?' or 'You are keen on finding new ways of doing things – we would like to place you on our Law+Change track.' My trajectory could have been very different.

To flesh out the details a little more, my vision for an ideal future path is that the year 3 post-qualification appraisal meeting should be an opportunity for an associate to identify a future path for themselves. The available paths should include the ability to further specialize in their chosen area of law or to engage with a Law+ track that supplements their legal knowledge and skills. The first step on a Law+ track could be a secondment into a business services team, or an investment in a training course that gives lawyers additional qualifications.

This would require law firms and in-house teams to consider how those who are on a Law+ track will progress through the firm in terms of seniority. Will they be considered for partnership? Should their bonus structures be different from those of colleagues who are solely providing legal advice? If they fail to put in place a structure around this sort of progression, law firms risk losing talent in what is a competitive market and they might also lower the morale of the workforce.

Take legal design training as an example. If this is given to all lawyers but they are never given the chance to use it, it is almost worse than if they had never had the training at all. All you have done in this instance is show your lawyers how practice could be different, only to then close that door. In much the same way, starting someone on a Law+ track without putting in place a structure for what happens next will lead to them being underutilized and undervalued. This is how you lose people. These tracks should be supported by additional training and opportunities for work in the chosen area, with a change in the way in which hours and rewards are calculated in order to recognize that this is a track that is separate from the traditional legal advice path. This 'alternative' path should be just as viable a proposition for making partner – or some other form of senior leadership – as keeping to pure legal advice.

For in-house teams, there may be opportunities to progress into other areas of the business, albeit that this is not always a decision that can be made within the legal team. Allowing specialization of multidisciplinary individuals would open up the legal profession to lots of new ways of working and to the improved provision of services to clients. There should be internal secondments that allow lawyers to transfer to other areas of the business and also allow those in other areas of the business to sit within the legal team in order to understand how they work. This will encourage not only networking but also familiarity with the how and, more importantly, the *why* of the ways in which the different teams work.

Junior legal operations and legal technology paths to working in law are opening up on a regular basis, but that does not solve the problem of those who are already 3+ years qualified and are looking to diversify their skill set. While some law firms have roles such as 'legal technologist', recognizing more senior individuals with Law+ skills is the best thing that firms can do here; it is what clients want and it is what will ensure that a law firm will continue to evolve its model so as to be relevant – and profitable – over the next decade. It is fundamental to the Law+ model that positions such as legal technologists and legal engineers are put on the same level of importance as lawyers so long as the same value is being provided. Letting existing lawyers enter those roles and incentivizing them appropriately will ensure not only that the firm can pivot with new developments in the profession in five to ten years but also that it can start to do so now.

Qualification path

I have talked about senior individuals and how legal teams might support their progression, but there are also opportunities right at the outset of qualification that can allow specialization and diversification. This means allowing people to qualify as, for example, legal technologists or innovation lawyers or legal engineers, allowing specialization in a Law+ quadrant from the moment of qualification. Introducing new qualification paths like this is a complicated process, and legal teams should think very carefully about the other issues raised in this section around promotion prospects, pay and recognition within the firm. An initiative that seems fantastic at year one also has to have a plan in place for years three, four, five and beyond, otherwise the individuals involved in that path are likely to feel underappreciated and directionless, just as is the case when more senior lawyers are shown an alternative way of practising only for that diversification to not be supported later.

These hybrid paths do already exist, with legal innovation qualification courses, apprenticeships and seats within business services teams all available, but until now most of the focus has been on technology when there are three other Law+ quadrants that serve as the foundation of that technology and are equally important. These hybrid paths are not for law firms alone; larger in-house teams will increasingly find a need for these people as they start to produce their own solutions rather than seek the assistance of external firms. In the same way, more opportunities to specialize at the outset can help to diversify and incentivize the team.

Hours targets and bonuses

Here we are back at billable hours. These targets mostly exist at law firms, where they are tied to bonuses. More hours equals more money.

Take, for example, the process of creating a transaction 'bible' or closing set that evidences all of the documents from a matter. This is a time-consuming administrative activity that is often undertaken by trainees or junior associates. Considering that the activity is solely administrative in nature, this work should really be outsourced or be done by those who charge for their time at a lower rate. However, even if such an outsourcing service is available, there is little incentive for the lawyers in the transaction to take advantage of it. If the transaction is not priced on a fixed-fee or capped-fee basis, then there is no pressing incentive to direct anyone to outsource or speed up work. And even if it is, the individual associate probably has billing targets (i.e. a minimum number of hours to work in order to obtain a bonus), which (depending on the firm) might not be affected even if those hours are written off in the client's fees. As a result, the outsourcing only happens when there is no other possible option due to time. This is not just a fictional example: I have watched this happen numerous times.

This obviously does not reward any sort of diversification of skill sets, and it is for this reason that some firms have started to change the way in which bonuses are calculated. For some firms, that means including 'innovation hours' or 'knowledge hours' as part of the billable total, just as many firms already do with pro bono hours. For others, it might mean looking at client feedback and other factors when establishing bonuses. For a rare few, these targets may include training time. The exact structure of the apportionment of billable hours is an important point to consider. Just providing hours for a variety of new activities without a structure around them can lead to a large number of conflicting ideas and solutions that do not tie back to the overall strategy of the firm or business. Innovation and progression require experimentation, but that experimentation should still be documented and learned from when undertaking similar activities in the future. Implementing this sort of recognition may add another wrinkle of difficulty if the firm is international, especially if the method for calculating bonuses differs between jurisdictions. The advantages of Law+ are by no means locked into a single jurisdiction, and firms should find a way to recognize new bonus structures on a global basis.

It is often said that lawyers do not have enough time to save time, and in many respects this is true. It takes time and effort to find new ways of working and implement them properly, and it is vital to reward those who seek out these new ways. There is a reason every single industry engages in research and development: if you do not evolve, you die. Updating the way people are rewarded for how they spend their work time is a key first step in engaging in research and development that can drive the evolution of your organization. This means introducing a more multifaceted approach to reviewing the work done by lawyers, including their willingness to engage with innovation, training and business development, and also including key performance indicators like client satisfaction ratings. Some law firms, such as Slaughter and May, Clifford Chance and Pinsent Masons, are spearheading these changes by experimenting with removing billable hours from bonus calculations altogether, or by making those hours much less important to the level of bonus, instead relying on other factors such as value-adding activities and innovation, or even by removing hours targets altogether. Other firms have abandoned the billable hour model or drastically changed it, replacing a 'one-size-fits-all' approach of a target such as, say, 1,800 hours, and instead customizing the target to the individual, for example by reducing that number proportionally based on holiday and sick leave.

It is worth taking the time to consider whether hours targets are the best way of fostering productivity in legal teams, or whether it might be better to use a different set of metrics: one linked to efficiency, relative profitability, client satisfaction, further work opportunities, profit from new services, engagement with training, etc. This could change the way in which lawyers work without reducing the level of service provided to clients. It can be difficult to track all of these things, of course, but given the abundance of technology that could be applied to gathering such metrics it is certainly not the impossible proposition it might once have been.

Seats and secondments

You do not know what you do not know. There could be – and there probably are – hundreds of lawyers sitting at their desks right now who would be amazing at Law+Technology or Law+People. There will be yet more people currently working in other professions who would thrive in the legal profession. But unless we introduce those people to these things, they will never know that they are missing out on that opportunity.

For law firms, this means encouraging secondments and seats within the business services teams of the firm and its clients, and for in-house teams it means seeking out those same opportunities within the wider business. While recognizing that the provision of secondments requires careful thought around resourcing for the team the secondee has temporarily left, not only can secondments strengthen links with clients, the business and the business services teams, but they will also introduce lawyers to new ways of tackling problems. It is in these secondments that they may find their passion. I knew nothing about legal innovation when I was in practice; it was only when I was introduced to the concept while working at a law school that I realized it was one I wanted to work with. How many people out there are in a role that is wrong for them, simply because they are not aware that there is another way? These seats and secondments do not have to happen only during the early-stage career of lawyers, either, although it does make a lot of sense to have these opportunities before people over-specialize. Secondments could also form part of the approach to the 'splinter points' discussed above.

It is not just internal and client seats and secondments that can be considered. Many law firms currently partner with technology providers or ALSPs. What if there were secondments set up between those organizations? The firm's lawyers could learn new skills in a new place of work or could familiarize individuals from the partner organizations with the practice of law. Imagine, say, a developer from a lawtech company seconded within the IT department of a law firm. Their greater knowledge of the requirements of law firms would assist with selling and implementing their tech in the future.

It does not have to be long placements either. The O Shaped Lawyer group recently hosted its first ever intern, who joined the group from Clifford Chance for a four-week period. It may not seem long but this sort of 'sampler' initiative all helps in giving lawyers a more holistic view of the profession and the skills required to thrive within it.

As already discussed, there may be opportunities for in-house teams to be seconded within the wider business, or possibly for seconding those from the wider business into the legal team. This could give a different perspective on the way in which work is done and how legal advice is needed in the context of the business, as well as strengthening the ties to the business so that the legal team can be more involved in the strategic direction of the organization.

Training in Law+

Linked to providing awareness and opportunities for specialization in seats and secondments is the provision of learning and training. Though they are sometimes overlooked, learning and development teams are absolutely vital to implementing new ways of working. The number one barrier I encountered to selling new solutions to clients is that the partners who should be selling those solutions either do not know enough about the solution itself or do not know enough about the quadrant of Law+ within which that solution sits. What is the point of developing all of these new ways of providing legal services if they never get the chance to be implemented because we neglected to train those that are selling them?

There are fantastic learning and development teams in firms who are well-equipped to support the development of Law+ skills, and there are external providers and consultants who are more than willing to help. In addition, the arrival of new educational technologies has meant that having personalized learning paths for each individual is a more viable prospect than it ever was before, with these tools predicting the future learning path someone should take through the available materials based on their previous work. You could source this technology yourself by investing in an AI-assisted educational software package such as Century Tech or by taking advantage of virtual learning environments or learning management systems that increasingly include some element of personalization of the learning path out of the box. Alternatively, there are many law schools that are exploring or using this technology and have training available for all levels of an organization, should you be seeking outside support.

Any available personalized path should reflect the specialization of individuals through Law+, providing training at every level, from entry level to expert, for each of the quadrants. If effort is put into using personalized learning paths and interrogating the data about who is doing what training to what level, this will also support the identification of those who should engage in Law+ splinter points. When searching for lawyers according to their experience, we tend to focus on the work they have done and ignore the training they have completed. While the work they have done might show their past, the training shows where they want to go next and is an important data point in supporting them in getting there.

It is obviously difficult to provide live training to lots of people at the same time now that the status quo involves a hybrid working environment, so different ways of providing training need to be investigated. Asynchronous (non-real-time) resources – such as video snippets, simple quick reference cards, and interactive online resources – can help in this regard, and the use of personalized learning (as discussed above) can give a much more tailored learning journey than is possible when just getting a huge number of people together in a room for a workshop.

Learning and development teams can help with the establishment of initiatives such as internal or client-facing learning academies focusing on Law+ skills, client-facing training programmes, on-the-job training, and centres of excellence that showcase best practice around Law+. Outside providers offer courses and degrees in Law+ skills, and you should consider sponsoring individuals to engage with these paths. Some organizations in England and Wales might, for example, like to make use of their apprenticeship levy to fund apprenticeships into areas other than law, as I have already mentioned. There are also plenty of free resources (such as Lawtech UK's learning hub: https://lawtechuk. io/) that individuals can choose to access that you may like to provide via the legal team intranet. It is worth reiterating that no amount of amazing learning resources is going to drive change in any organization without some sort of plan about how to incentivize people in using those resources. Just like students in education only engage with activities that are assessed, so too will those in practice focus on what elements of their work get measured and rewarded. There is a reason for the maxim 'What gets measured, gets managed'.

Mentoring

One of the best ways to acquire new skills in a professional setting is to learn from others who have experience. There is a model in the learning and development sector that states that 70% of learning comes from work-related experiences, 20% from interactions with others, and 10% from formal education. Mentoring can give a more personal and tailored approach to progression, and it can allow people to navigate their career and development while getting support and guidance from someone with more experience.

The links with Law+ here are clear: there are options to have professionals in Law+ areas mentor lawyers to diversify their skill sets, or to have lawyers as the mentors teaching others within their organization about the application of their Law+ skills to the legal profession. Being a mentee can also help people to increase their self-confidence, to network and to improve their communication and organizational skills. There are lots of specialist providers that can assist with the provision of mentoring, and the exact programme can usually be tailored to the needs of an individual organization. It is not just mentees who benefit from such an arrangement, either: mentors gain similar improvement to their communication while also building empathy and leadership skills. The best way to cement your own learning about something is to teach it to someone else.

Incubators and partnerships

An incubator is an organization or initiative that can help early-stage companies to develop their business by providing support. In law, we most often see lawtech incubators, where law firms play host to technology companies such as Allen & Overy's Fuse, Mishcon de Reya's MDR Lab or Slaughter and May's Collaborate. The tech companies in these incubators usually get free office space and direct access to legal teams with whom they can test their products, and in return the law firm gets early access to new technologies and a chance for those solutions to be tailored for their firm. If you are considering establishing an incubator of this type, some thought is needed around the cohort of companies to include in each year of the incubator, should you take on a rolling group as most do. Are you looking to solve a specific problem, as some firms have done? Are you going to ask your clients which technologies should be included? Are you seeking to host the most cutting-edge companies or get a larger variety of technologies across all aspects of lawtech? There is a range of options to pursue. For the firm and companies in these cohorts, the incubator can be the first step in a longer-term partnership, either through the law firm investing in the company, purchasing the company outright, or even just through getting a really good deal on a licence!

Incubators are not the only partnerships available, of course. Legal teams have partnered with legal engineering organizations and with flexible resourcing companies, for example. Other law firms have chosen to set up subsidiary companies or 'captive ALSPs' that have a specific focus, usually on Law+Change or Law+Technology, or have set up consultancy arms that engage in Law+People and Law+Business practices. One piece of feedback I have consistently received when interacting with clients is that they wished their external firms would simply offer to help more. It is not a good business relationship when one of you is just sitting there waiting for the other to come and complain (unless you are a complaints department). If a law firm employs and enlists only lawyers to help clients with problems that may run the whole gamut of the Law+People, Law+Business, Law+Change and Law+Technology quadrants, then they are not going to be able to assist with those problems as effectively as those with skills in those quadrants can. Clients want this sort of engagement from their firms; I have seen RFPs that are specifically requesting the help of firms with process mapping and the use of technology as opposed to just legal advice. Imagine how much more effective a law firm could be if it was *proactive* with this offer of help. The same applies to in-house teams and their business. Considering that legal teams have historically been viewed as the 'no' department, the best way to show value could be to get more involved in the business. Doing so is going to require the legal team to have skills that go beyond law or a willingness on the part of the lawyers to work with others from the business who possess such skills. Law+ skills can therefore improve client relationships.

Other types of partnership that are available to law firms are with organizations such as the Mindful Business Charter, which would showcase a commitment to mental health and well-being,[5] or with organizations that are dedicated to sustainable business practices or diversity and inclusion. These organizations are often not just for the legal services profession, and as a result they are ones with which a lot of clients are aligned.

Increased visibility

Feeling 'seen' within your organization is a powerful incentive; not only are those who are more visible within an organization more likely to be promoted, but they also feel more valued and have an increased sense of self and motivation. It is no secret that work allocation and the building of the right legal team are key areas of concern for the legal profession, not only to ensure that people are receiving the right amount of work but that such work is distributed fairly in line with equality and diversity principles. This is even more important in a hybrid working world, where people are no longer in the office as much and teams cannot be built by senior people walking the corridors and seeing who is around.

So how can you promote Law+ skills through the use of increased visibility? If those in legal teams accept the idea that any full-service Law+ team should include at least one person who is at expert level in each of the quadrants, then expertise and training in such areas should be reflected in the experience search so that a senior lawyer building a team knows to what extent the Law+ skills are covered. Imagine being able to search not only by practice area but also by Law+ quadrant specialization: it would certainly make building alternative teams for new projects much easier, and it would show the commitment the firm has to developing Law+ skills. With experience search being something that legal teams are keen on investing in so that they can better understand their workforce, now is the perfect time to fold Law+ skills into the parameters of such a search.

Why do people care about being visible, and why should you care whether those with Law+ skills are visible or not? Well, there can be value in having your name attached to a project and being seen to be involved. For example, there is a reason why it matters to clients whose name features on a prospectus – and why, on occasion, clients will send somebody along with a ruler to measure the size of their logo compared with those of their competitors who may be co-sponsoring a prospectus with them. As much as we can fight against it, the culture of law is still one that rewards individuals rather than teams, and in order to get to a Law+ future, legal teams have to recognize that helping those individuals build their profile can be important. This means considering how new projects and ways of working are communicated and how those party to these projects are rewarded. Do the individual partners who are involved get a share of the profit from any new solution? An equity stake in the subsidiary if one is established? Should more junior individuals be touted in newsletters and external articles, or put forward for awards? Part of the danger here is that creating solutions that perpetuate the focus on individuals encourages a culture in which everyone is creating their own solution to the same problem just so they can have the visibility and potential monetary reward that goes with doing so. That does not make good business sense, and some consideration must therefore be given to how collaboration can be rewarded so that this siloed approach to working can be avoided, while also encouraging people to act in their own best interests by having individual recognition.

There are already plenty of people within legal teams who exemplify Law+ skills. One of the issues for legal teams is to find these people and establish who can do what. Particularly in law firms as opposed to in-house teams, there is a sometimes-confusing architecture of knowledge, innovation, technology, consultancy, pricing, client value and all sorts of other teams who possess different skills and who specialize in different Law+ quadrants. Knowing who to speak to is half the battle. There are often entire PR departments dedicated to telling the outside world about new teams and solutions, with fewer resources made available to communicate the same message internally. For in-house teams, there may be potential future collaborators and supporters in the wider business who currently do not know the full suite of offerings that the legal team can provide. Appointing individuals responsible for internal communications and advertising the work of those with Law+ skills is a key part of incentivizing people to come forward.

Another communication option that improves visibility revolves around the concept of champions. These are people scattered around an organization who specialize in different Law+ skills or who are connected to – or supportive of – such specialists. Having champions can help Law+ skills to permeate into the organization almost as if by osmosis; Law+ can be driven from within the legal team by champions rather than being solely located in other teams, as they might be in law firms. This means that new ideas can be interpreted within the language of those who work regularly on the matters that those ideas affect, and it helps with selling existing solutions to teams by reinterpreting their application so that it is relevant to whichever team the champion sits in.

Awards

While awards are part of increasing visibility, they are also worth considering on their own. There are two main types of award that are most relevant here: external awards that are granted by third-party organizations and recognize the work of an entire team, and internal awards that may be granted to individuals or teams within the organization to which the legal team belongs. Projects that involve multidisciplinary teams working together to solve problems using Law+ skills should be celebrated, and making sure that teams can collect awards is a good way of incentivizing them to try new things. Having internal awards for those who put Law+ skills to good use is another way of showing that such skills are valued.

It seems like such a small thing, but everyone loves an award, whether it is a Most Innovative Company trophy or a childhood swimming certificate. Awards demonstrate recognition, and they increase the visibility of the individual or team who receive them. For those who think that awards are unimportant, I point you toward the influx of 'badging' that is available in training, where people receive mini virtual awards for progression. This is known as gamification, and it is a tried-and-tested method of advancing learning within certain parameters. For instance, a series of design thinking workshops my team created for lawyers and business services professionals was advertised as a contest, with the winners receiving a virtual reality headset. Framing the workshop as a contest with a prize increased attendance more than simply advertising a hands-on experience of design thinking in law. While having awards for those who think differently or who find new ways of working is unlikely, on its own, to do much to make people feel like Law+ skills are valued, including awards as part of a cultural shift can be part of a constructive – and fun – way of demonstrating that those skills are important.

Training in law

Law firms and legal teams tend to focus on training their lawyers to possess new skills. This is to be applauded, and it is certainly a large step towards recognizing and rewarding Law+ skills – and therefore towards improving the delivery of legal services. It is, however, only half of the story.

Let me pose a question. Would you let an experienced IT professional who had completed a weekend course in law advise your client? If the answer is no, then I would ask you whether it makes any more sense to let a lawyer who has completed a weekend coding course build a technology solution? That is not to say it is not worth that lawyer completing that coding course; doing so can bestow that lawyer with the necessary skills to engage with IT professionals and to have new solutions built in a multidisciplinary fashion so that they are more likely to be adopted and introduce real change. Even if the lawyer managed to get to the 'established' level of Law+Technology, though, a client would not necessarily feel comfortable with them doing the software development when their job should be to make sure that the legal advice that is being delivered is correct and in line with the context of the client's situation.

Consider, then, whether part of your strategy for adopting Law+ should involve training those in business services and external teams in law, so that you may better collaborate with them. As much as people external to law may claim that lawyers cannot communicate with other professions, communication is a two-way street, and the more we can do to facilitate that, the more chance we have of improving legal services delivery.

Culture

From a culture perspective, by encouraging people to be curious and to find new ways of doing things, you will find that they are more engaged with their day-to-day work. Feeling like they are being listened to and believing they can help to guide the direction of their firm or business is key to helping people feel as if they are making a difference.

The more you can excite people about being involved in multidisciplinary projects, the more you create 'fear of missing out' (FOMO) around what you are doing, which can lead to others getting involved. Changing culture may involve any and all of the incentives discussed so far, but it also means shouting from the rooftops about projects and making those who are part of a project feel like it is worth doing. That could mean engaging in co-creation with clients, creating new subsidiaries and spin-offs dedicated to Law+, working towards greater salary parity, or even just giving a Lego mini figure to all of those involved in a project as a memento of their efforts. The Lego thing may seem silly at first, but think about how creating an inclusive group can help to drive change; humans have tribalism programmed into them, and by creating a tribe around Law+ skills you can foster that feeling of exclusivity that drives new people to become involved. I can guarantee everyone I have given a Lego mini figure to has been excited about seeing themselves as a little yellow figurine. Another example is a legal innovation consultancy who used to invite people to their yearly conference via a golden ticket; this created a buzz for those who got a ticket and a desire from those who did not get one to get one next time.

Changing the culture of your organization to be more accepting of additional skill sets and mixing that with a willingness to experiment leads to a better environment in which to work – and this is something that can help legal teams win the talent war. Mental health is also improved when individuals are appreciated for their skills and their potential rather than having to fit into one narrow mould. Take the inclusion of training as part of the bonus or promotion criteria, for example. Moving in this direction delivers the message that you really care about the individual and their progression over time, and it allows individuals to take the time to engage with training as something that is advantageous to their career, rather than the way that training is often presented now as a minimum requirement for maintaining a practising certificate. Mental health can also be improved by making the changes to the billable hour model. Recognizing there is more to delivering legal services than just law can therefore improve talent retention.

Leadership

You can introduce all of the positive measures you like, but if you fail to get buy-in and endorsement from senior management, and recognition that your organization will benefit from Law+ skills, then those incentives are likely to produce only minimal change. For example, if you encourage people to spend a certain number of hours engaging in Law+ activities but their overall reward is still tied to how long they work and the manner in which they work, then Law+ is never going to take off as there are no personal incentives for those people to get involved. And even with all the incentives in the world, there will still be those who refuse to follow this path.

Take the example of outsourcing the process of creating a transaction closing set. As I have mentioned, the biggest problem I encountered in practice when trying to roll out such a solution was the lack of uptake. There was no incentive, from a personal point of view, to be more efficient. The one practice area in which it *was* successful was the one in which the practice group leader sent out an email to all the associates stating that the outsourcing process was the only way in which closing sets could be produced.

While incentives can help, they might not be enough on their own. As much as we would all love to live in a world in which people self-select for experimenting in new ways of working and adopting multidisciplinary teams because they can see an exciting future, there will always be those who are more wary of changing how they work. This reticence can be for a variety of reasons, and we must not rush to say that anyone who disagrees with us about innovation, change or Law+ skills is a 'colleague against virtually everything' (or a CAVE). Some will point to their previous successes as a reason not to change, while others may feel like they do not have the capacity to learn Law+ skills and are fearful of being left behind.

The legal profession is full of individuals who have alternative skills and new ideas, but if we are going to drive real change, we need strong leaders who are going to empower those people and to loudly proclaim them as the future.

CHAPTER 14

What next?

Whether you are a student, a lawyer, a lecturer or a business services professional within law, I hope this book contains the starting point on your journey towards recognizing that there is more to our profession than the delivery of legal advice. How you use this knowledge is up to you. It could feature in the strategic goals of your organization, it could provide the essentials of your training path, it could show you an aspect of the profession that you never knew existed, or it could help you recruit individuals in the future. I hope you continue to learn more about the skills and follow up on the resources I have highlighted throughout these pages. The next step for Law+ is wide open. One option is to create psychometric testing based on real-world scenarios that can show an individual their proficiency level in each of the quadrants. Another is to build university and law school courses around the model, developing skills frameworks that can be tested and built upon throughout a person's career. My hope is that law firms and legal teams will take on the Law+ language and model to build out new skillsets in their lawyers and to develop training paths and initiatives that reward new ways of working. If any of these paths ignite a spark of passion within you, then I encourage you to reach out. This book is by no means the end of the journey for Law+, and it is not a journey I can – or want to – take alone

I am genuinely excited by what our profession can achieve and, as far as I am concerned, the future of the law looks bright. I want as many of you as possible to imagine a world in which legal teams are human-centric, recognizing the breadth of skills possessed by the people who work there and the business context within which their clients sit – a world in which legal teams are not only aware of change but are actively driving it and are making the most of technology to fuel modern delivery methods for legal advice. Treat this book as your starting point for change. Ask questions. Be curious. Challenge the norm. Find new ways of working. Work with people you may never have previously thought of working with. Find other people who think differently and learn from them. We can make the delivery of legal services better if we work together. Join me.

Endnotes

PREFACE

1   Law Society. 2018. LawTech delivery panel. Guide, 1 October (see https://bit.ly/3P8bP4n).
2   P. Ertmer. 1999. Addressing first- and second-order barriers to change: strategies for technology integration. *Educational Technology Research and Development* 47(4), 47–61.
3   Legatics. 2021. Barriers to legal technology adoption. Report funded by Innovate UK (https://bit.ly/3ubYCzg).

PART I

1   Deloitte. 2017. The legal department of the future: how disruptive trends are creating a new business model for in-house legal.
2   KPMG. 2016. Through the looking glass: how corporate leaders view the general counsel of today and tomorrow. Report, September (https://bit.ly/3v05nor).
3   O Shaped Lawyer. 2020. O Shaped Lawyer GC report, February. Produced in association with Aspirant.

CHAPTER ONE

1   Pictures courtesy of AlternativelyLegal Pty Ltd, IE Law School, the O Shaped Lawyer Group, and Alyson Carrel (www.alysoncarrel.com).
2   R. Brook Lea, D. N. Rapp, A. Elfenbein, A. D. Mitchel and R. Swinburne Romine. 2008. Sweet silent thought: alliteration and resonance in poetry comprehension. *Physiological Science* 19(7), 709–716.
3   The book is *The Undomestic Goddess* by Sophie Kinsella (Black Swan, 2006).
4   STEM Future Lawyers: see https://stemfuturelawyers.co.uk/.
5   See, for example, 'Hacking diversity with inclusive decision making', a White Paper from Cloverpop (https://bit.ly/3QSg0mx); and 'Teams solve problems faster when they're more cognitively diverse' by Alison

Reynolds and David Lewis in *Harvard Business Review* in 2017 (https://bit.ly/3HYWHnv).

6   See 'Why diversity matters' from 2015 (https://mck.co/3u7K4k8); 'Delivering through diversity' from 2018 (https://mck.co/3noPi7t); and 'Diversity wins: how inclusion matters' from 2020 (https://mck.co/3nsyDQs).

7   Boston Consulting Group. 2017. BCG diversity and innovation survey 2017. For further information, see Lorenzo, R., Voigt, N., Tsusaka, M., Krentz, M., and Abouzahr, K. 2018. How diverse leadership teams boost innovation. Report, Boston Consulting Group, 23 January (https://on.bcg.com/3OYMIRx).

8   The data comes from a search of legal roles on indeed.com. In the United Kingdom, 233 out of 10,148 lawyer roles earned more than £100,000 per annum, while 78 out of 20,760 business services roles earned that much. In the United States, 5,110 of 24,789 lawyer roles earned more than $136,000 per annum (exchange rate calculated based on rates from xe.com and rounding down to the nearest thousand), while 233 of 10,148 business services roles earned the equivalent. Calculations correct as of time of writing.

9   Gartner. 2021. State of the Legal Function. Report, September.

10   Terry Pratchett. 2002. *Night Watch*. Doubleday.

CHAPTER TWO

1   Jemma Slingo. 2021. Financial results: big firms saw big gains despite pandemic – buy why? *Law Society Gazette*, 6 September (https://bit.ly/3nti2Mq).

2   David J. Parnell. 2014. Richard Susskind: Moses to the modern law firm. *Forbes*, 21 March (https://bit.ly/3xWltQg).

3   Polson. M. 2016. Ashurst news, deals & awards. Legal functions being squeezed as pressure to deliver more for less intensifies. Report, Ashurst Advance Director, 13 July.

4   Lucy Leach. 2021. Global trends in legal 2021: growth opportunities are there, but law firms will have to work for them. Reuters.

5   LawtechUK. 2021. Shaping the future of law. Report.

6   FTI Consulting and Relativity. 2022. General counsel report 2022.

7   Association of Corporate Counsel (ACC). 2021. 2021 legal technology report: for in-house counsel. Report, ACC.

8   KPMG. 2016. Through the looking glass: how corporate leaders view the general counsel of today and tomorrow. Report, September (https://bit.ly/3v05nor).

9 Deloitte Insights. 2020. The kinetic leader: boldly reinventing the enterprise. Findings from the 2020 Global Technology Leadership Study. Report, Deloitte.

10 Robert van Eerd and Jean Guo. 2020. Jobs will be very different in 10 years. Here's how to prepare. Report, World Economic Forum, 17 January.

11 Source: Saïd Business School and Meridian West. 2018. Strategic learning and development in professional services. Paper 3. Early career pathways. URL: www.meridianwest.co.uk/early-career -pathways-in-psfs/

CHAPTER FOUR

1 More than 80% of young lawyers in England and Wales have experience imposter syndrome. Source: Junior Lawyers Division Survey, 2019.

2 *R. (on the application of Mercury Tax Group Ltd) v Revenue and Customs Commissioners* [2008] EWHC 2721 (Admin) (13 November 2008).

3 Mind. 2020. The mental health emergency: how has the coronavirus pandemic impacted our mental health. Report, June (https://bit. ly/3a1zEf3).

4 McKinsey & Company. 2021. The great attrition: the power of adaptability. Blog post, 22 November (https://mck.co/3Nx90sj).

5 Cary Cherniss and Daniel Goleman. 2001. *The Emotionally Intelligent Workplace: How to Select For, Measure, and Improve Emotional Intelligence in Individuals, Groups, and Organizations.* Jossey-Bass.

6 Susan T. Fiske and Cydney Dupree. 2014. Gaining trust as well as respect in communicating to motivated audiences about science topics. *Proceedings of the National Academy of Sciences of the United States of America* 111 (Supplement_4) 13,593–13,597 (https://doi. org/10.1073/pnas.1317505111).

CHAPTER FIVE

1 Richard Susskind and Daniel Susskind. 2015. *The Future of the Professions: How Technology Will Transform the Work of Human Experts.* Oxford University Press.

CHAPTER SIX

1 Source: Google Data, Global, March 2016.

CHAPTER SEVEN

1   Thomas Alsop. 2022. Legal tech market revenue worldwide 2019–2025. Report, Stastista, 4 March.
2   Figure based on £11.4 billion of revenue generated from serving unmet demand, £8.6 billion of cost savings for SMEs, and £1.7 billion from productivity gains in legal businesses. Frontier Economics. 2021. Report on the economic contribution of lawtech. Lawtech UK.
3   Jonathan Ames. 2022. Firms 'must harness technology'. *The Times*, 14 July.
4   URL: www.legaltechnologyhub.com.
5   Legatics. 2021. Barriers to legal technology adoption. Report funded by Innovate UK (https://bit.ly/3ubYCzg).
6   Gartner. 2022. Gartner predicts that 'Human-in-the-Loop' solutions will comprise 30% of new legal tech automation offerings by 2025. Press Release, 15 February.
7   P. Kirschner and P. De Bruyckere. 2017. The myths of the digital native and the multitasker. *Teaching and Teacher Education* 67, 135–142.
8   Reuters. 2018. Amazon scraps secret AI recruiting tool that showed bias against women.

CHAPTER NINE

1   Coursera's website is at www.coursera.org/.
2   16Personalities provides free personality tests at https://bit.ly/3AhVCFl.
3   For more information visit lawcare.org.uk or call their helpline on 0800 2796888.
4   URL: https://profile.innovationbeehive.co.uk/.
5   Adapted from A. Osterwalder, Y. Pigneur and T. Clark. 2010. *Business Model Generation: A Handbook For Visionaries, Game Changers, and Challengers*. Wiley.
6   URL: https://bit.ly/3alVoCu.
7   Margaret is a lawyer and designer, and she is the director of Stanford University's Legal Design Lab. You can access her resources at https://lawbydesign.co.
8   URL: www.thisisservicedesigndoing.com.
9   Legaltech Hub's website is at https://legaltechnologyhub.com/.
10   LawtechUK's 'Explore and learn' resources can be found at https://lawtechuk.io/explore.

CHAPTER ELEVEN

1   *Donoghue v Stevenson* [1932] AC 562 (26 May 1932).
2   *Stambovsky v. Ackley*, 169 A.D.2d 254 (N.Y. App. Div. 1991).
3   For an overview of the proof, see 'Learning styles as a myth', an article on the website of the Yale Poorvu Center for Teaching and Learning.

CHAPTER TWELVE

1   Adam Curphey. 2018. Teaching legal tech? Forget the tech. Article, Artificial Lawyer, 25 May (https://bit.ly/3ytWIwr).

CHAPTER THIRTEEN

1   Julie Avrane-Chopard and Jaime Potter. 2019. Are hard and soft skills rewarded equally? Blog post, McKinsey & Company, 4 November (https://mck.co/3Aeg2za).
2   Poll conducted by Dan Kayne and Emma Lilley as part of 'The Legal Cheek Commercial Awareness Academy', which is run in partnership with the O Shaped Lawyer and BARBRI.
3   Source: Thomson Reuters. 2022. 2022 report on the state of the legal market. Report, 11 January (https://tmsnrt.rs/3PepEhu).
4   Antony Cooke. 2020. Why lawyers leave their firms. Chambers Associate, January (https://bit.ly/3uaZV1k).
5   The Mindful Business Charter website is at www.mindfulbusiness-charter.com/

Index